Science Fiction Serials

Science Fiction Serials

*A Critical Filmography of
the 31 Hard SF Cliffhangers;
With an Appendix of the 37
Serials with Slight SF Content*

by ROY KINNARD

McFarland & Company, Inc., Publishers
Jefferson, North Carolina, and London

Acknowledgments: The author wishes to thank the following individuals, who provided valuable material and information for this book: Kay Aldridge (deceased), Ed Bernds, Phyllis Coates, Buster Crabbe (deceased), Tony Crnkovich, Rosemary C. Haines (Library of Congress), Russell C. Maheras (m/sgt., USAF), Jerry Ohlinger, Shirley Patterson (deceased), Jean Rogers (deceased), Steve Sally, Dr. Christopher Shannon (George Eastman House), Jim Shoenberger, Veto Stasiunaitis, Maurice Terenzio, George Turner, Jerry Vermilye and Richard Vitone.

Author's note: Most of the commentary on *Flash Gordon* appeared — in slightly different form — as an article in the April 1988 issue of *Films in Review* magazine.

Frontispiece: *Flash Gordon*, 1936—Buster Crabbe, Jean Rogers

LIBRARY OF CONGRESS CATALOGUING-IN-PUBLICATION DATA

Kinnard, Roy, 1952–
    Science fiction serials : a critical filmography of the 31 hard SF
cliffhangers : with an appendix of the 37 serials with slight SF
content / by Roy Kinnard.
      p.   cm.
    Includes bibliographical references and index.

    ISBN 978-0-7864-3745-0
    softcover : 50# alkaline paper ∞

    1. Science fiction films — Catalogs.   2. Motion picture serials —
Catalogs. I. Title.
PN1995.9.S26K56   2008
016.79143'615 — dc21   98-38738

British Library cataloguing data are available

On the cover: Poster art for the 1949 serial *King of the Rocket Men*
(Republic Pictures/Photofest)

Manufactured in the United States of America

McFarland & Company, Inc., Publishers
  Box 611, Jefferson, North Carolina 28640
  www.mcfarlandpub.com

Contents

Acknowledgments   iv

Introduction   1

The Vanishing Shadow (1934)   11
The Lost City (1935)   14
The Phantom Empire (1935)   22
Flash Gordon (1936)   30
Undersea Kingdom (1936)   41
Dick Tracy (1937)   48
Flash Gordon's Trip to Mars (1938)   53
The Fighting Devil Dogs (1938)   61
Buck Rogers (1939)   69
The Phantom Creeps (1939)   77
Flash Gordon Conquers the Universe (1940)   84
Mysterious Dr. Satan (1940)   91
Dick Tracy vs. Crime, Inc. (1941)   98
Batman (1943)   103
Manhunt of Mystery Island (1945)   109
The Monster and the Ape (1945)   116
The Purple Monster Strikes (1945)   121

The Crimson Ghost (1946)   126

Brick Bradford (1947)   132

Superman (1948)   136

Batman and Robin (1949)   141

King of the Rocket Men (1949)   148

The Invisible Monster (1950)   152

Atom Man vs. Superman (1950)   156

Flying Disc Man from Mars (1951)   160

Mysterious Island (1951)   164

Captain Video (1951)   170

Radar Men from the Moon (1952)   175

Zombies of the Stratosphere (1952)   179

The Lost Planet (1953)   184

Panther Girl of the Kongo (1955)   189

Appendix: 37 Serials with Incidental Science Fiction Elements   197

Bibliography   205

Index   207

Introduction

Most published histories of science fiction movies cite producer George Pal's 1950 Technicolor epic *Destination Moon* as the first noteworthy genre film. Although there had been outstanding examples of screen science fiction before *Destination Moon* (for example, Alexander Korda's 1936 production of H.G. Wells' *Things to Come*, and director Fritz Lang's silent masterpiece *Metropolis* a decade before that), the George Pal space adventure usually gets the deferential nod as the first "serious" science fiction film. Certainly, *Destination Moon*, though it may seem dull and stodgy to modern viewers, was a critical and financial success in its day, inspiring a decade-long run of science fiction movies that included some of the best (as well as come of the worst) excursions into the imagination every committed to celluloid.

Usually ignored in histories of science fiction movies, or casually dismissed, are the serials, the "continued next week" chapterplays shown in weekly episodes (running 15 or 20 minutes each), somewhat derisively known as "cliffhangers" in reference to the hair-raising situations that left viewers dangling in suspense until the next week's installment. The reasons for neglecting serials are obvious and understandable. The chapterplays were low-budget productions exhibited at theaters as Saturday matinee fare and targeted almost exclusively at children. Lacking stars and top-notch writing or directing talent, the serials went largely unnoticed and unacknowledged by either critics or the film industry.

Yet serials were financially important to the Hollywood studios. Drawing their inspiration from fringe cultural sources like pulp magazines and comic books, they were often free — by their very lack of acclaim and respectability — to exploit subjects that the producers of more "distinguished" movies considered too outlandish and too much of a risk to bother with. At least as early as 1934, in Universal's *The Vanishing Shadow*, serials were adapting science fiction themes and

concepts on a regular basis. There had been a vogue for horror and fantasy movies in Hollywood originated by *Dracula* and *Frankenstein* (both 1931), but science fiction, although widely read in pulp magazines, had been all but ignored by mainstream Hollywood until serials like *The Phantom Empire* (1935) and *Flash Gordon* (1936) brought the genre to the screen for general audiences.

Serials were commonly regarded as a breed apart from features, yet there was a two-way cultural street connecting them. Although the chapterplays were often influenced by features, the lowly cliffhangers were sometimes the innovators, and this was certainly true in the case of movie science fiction, at least before 1950. Every familiar science fiction theme and cliché that would be exploited by Hollywood *after* 1950 — extra-terrestrials, interplanetary travel, robots, ray guns, time travel — had been introduced to film by the movie serials in previous decades. Taking this into account, it only seems reasonable to conclude that if low-budget science fiction features like director Roger Corman's *It Conquered the World* (1956) are worthy of discussion, then low-budget serials like *King of the Rocket Men* (1949) deserve at least an appreciative nod in passing. The cheap serials and features were, after all, shown together on the same theater programs, and auteurist debates aside, they should certainly be considered "equals."

The American movie serial was a staple of film programs from 1913 until 1956. The very first serial, *What Happened to Mary?* (1913), starring Mary Fuller, was produced by famed inventor Thomas A. Edison during his pre–World War I stint as a pioneering filmmaker, and had been conceived as a merchandising tie-in with the magazine *McClure's Ladies' World*. The story was first serialized in the magazine, and after each published installment a corresponding film episode would be released to theaters. *What Happened to Mary?* was not the fast-paced, action-oriented story that later serials would be, and it did not imperil its leading character in a "cliffhanger" situation at the end of each chapter, as would later be the norm; but this was the film that established the basic "continued next week" serial format that would endure for over four decades.

The silent chapterplays quickly became popular screen attractions with filmgoers, and (unlike their descendants in the sound era) the silent serials were somewhat respectable as well. Some of the performers in them, like Pearl White in *The Perils of Pauline* (1914), became front-rank stars as a result of their exposure in serials. By the mid–1920s, though, the serials began to wane in popularity as an increasingly urbane and sophisticated audience, now exposed to the mass medium of radio, started to lose interest. Unfortunately, few of the silent serials are still extant today. Of the more than 250 silent serials produced, only a handful survive in the form of either partial or complete prints. As an example, only nine of the original 20 episodes of *The Perils of Pauline* — the most famous silent serial — exist for reappraisal.

By the arrival of sound in 1928, serials had fallen into disrepute with both

Opposite: King of the Rocket Men poster.

Henry MacRae (center, foreground), producer of *Flash Gordon*.

audiences and critics, and might have vanished entirely in the early sound era if it hadn't been for the efforts of one man: Henry MacRae. MacRae, a producer and director at Carl Laemmle's Universal Pictures since the early silent era, supervised the company's short subject division, and in 1930 he directed the 12-chapter serial *The Indians Are Coming*. A standard cowboys-and-Indians shoot-'em-up that was nothing special in terms of subject, *The Indians Are Coming* was nevertheless outstanding at the time, since it was the first sound (meaning optical sound-on-film, instead of a synchronized disc) serial of any quality. *The Indians Are Coming* was a big hit with the public, and MacRae, almost singlehandedly with this one film, had rescued the serial from oblivion and popularized the format with a new (although now largely juvenile) audience. Even though adult filmgoers would generally ignore serials in the sound era, MacRae had breathed fresh commercial life into the chapterplays, and would increase their popularity even more when he produced the hugely successful *Flash Gordon* for Universal in 1936.

Although silent serials had been enjoyed by a wide spectrum of the filmgoing public, including adults, the sound serials, as previously noted, were mainly

The Perils of Pauline— the classic silent serial.

Saturday matinee fodder aimed squarely at children. Also unlike their silent ancestors, sound serials were almost never shown at first-run theaters, being relegated to the smaller neighborhood movie houses in the cities and rural theaters in less populated areas of the country. There were only a few exceptions to this rule. Universal's three *Flash Gordon* serials starring Buster Crabbe and the two *Superman* serials from Columbia were given wider releases due to the overwhelming popularity of their comic-strip sources with a pre-sold audience.

There were 231 sound serials, and most of them were produced by only three studios: Republic, Universal and Columbia. Independent producers, forced out of the market by the big three, ceased production of serials in 1937, while the majors, MGM, Paramount, Warner Bros. and 20th Century–Fox, considered the format beneath them. For instance, RKO-Radio produced only one serial, a bad one, *The Last Frontier* (1932).

Republic had the justifiable distinction of producing the finest all-round serial product, featuring top-of-the-line cinematography, music scores, stunt work and special effects. Universal made some excellent chapterplays, including Buster Crabbe's three Flash Gordon epics, but Universal's serials were, at times, marred by crude special effects, an over-reliance on newsreel stock footage, and unnecessarily dense plotting that tended to hamper the action with an abundance of dialogue.

Columbia had the dubious "honor" of producing the worst serials. Although some of Columbia's earlier chapterplays like *The Spider's Web* (1938) and *Batman* (1943) were very enjoyable, the studio's cliffhangers were for the most part a hokey and sometimes even deliberately campy lot. The situation at Columbia worsened when Sam Katzman — surely one of the crassest producers in Hollywood history — was assigned control of the studio's chapterplays after 1945. To Katzman's credit, he did produce two of the most financially successful serials of the sound era, namely *Superman* (1948) and *Atom Man vs. Superman* (1950). Katzman's other serials at Columbia, however, were mediocre at best and most of them were so disappointing that the artwork on the posters used to advertise them was often more dynamic and entertaining than the serials themselves.

Their lowly position in Hollywood notwithstanding, movie serials were vitally important to the pre–1945 film industry. The average serial was produced for $100,000 to $150,000 (the *total* budget for *all* of the episodes), and a total of four to five hours of release footage was shot on a hectic four- to six-week production schedule. Serials were filmed more quickly and cheaply than features were, and a young serial fan attending every weekly installment of, for example, the 15-chapter *Flash Gordon's Trip to Mars* (1938) was in effect paying to see the same movie fifteen times.

Despite the fact that the serials were lucrative ventures for the film industry, not much care was taken in their production. Republic's serials were technically excellent, but at Republic, as well as at Universal and Columbia, unimaginative scripting and flat, pedestrian direction was commonplace. All of the 231 sound serials were scripted by the same group of 20 or so studio-contracted writers (working in various combinations), and the directors — with the outstanding exception of William Witney at Republic — were competent but uninspired craftsmen.

Eventually, the very predictability of serials began to work against them, even with their juvenile audience. After World War II even that formerly loyal core audience began to dissipate, lured away by similar fare shown for free on the new medium of television. Universal stopped producing serials in 1946, falling back on rereleases of their older titles to exploit what the studio correctly saw as a fading market. Republic made its final serial, *King of the Carnival*, in 1955. Columbia hung on until the bitter end, releasing the very last serial, *Blazing the Overland Trail*, in 1956.

After its demise in 1956, the serial became an all-but-forgotten motion picture format, its memory kept alive only by constant television airings of the three *Flash Gordon* serials, always popular in TV syndication, and the efforts of a few dedicated fans. With the advent of the home video market, though, most of the sound serials, many of them unseen since their original theatrical runs, were once again available. Of the 231 sound serials made, over 200 are now available on videocassette in either officially licensed or bootleg versions.

As an important and frequently overlooked facet of the science fiction film genre, the science fiction serials should be accessible for consideration in any serious discussion. Now, after years of obscurity, most of them are. Many of the serials included occasional science fiction devices and gadgets used in one or two chapters as an audience-grabbing ploy (for instance, the briefly glimpsed futuristic machinery used to destroy airplanes by remote control in Universal's otherwise routine *Ace Drummond* [1936]). Television, then a proven but still-experimental technology unavailable to the public, and still considered science fiction by the average person, was a common serial gadget, with scores of cliffhanger villains callously disregarding the privacy of heroes by spying on their unsuspecting victims in Orwellian fashion with ubiquitous TV screens. Of the 231 sound serials, 31 can be designated as clearly defined science fiction movies — that is, serials that have stories driven by science fiction themes and concepts and not just futuristic paraphernalia.

These 31 science fiction serials are discussed in this book, with cast and credit information as well as plot descriptions and historical commentary. Although the distributors of officially available VHS releases are indicated, specific video availability should be verified by the reader for the simple reason that such information is quickly dated. As an example, the Republic serials have, since the inception of the home video market, been distributed by three different officially licensed companies, with the public domain (copyright expired) Republic titles being offered by several more companies. *All* of the films covered in this book, with the exception of *The Vanishing Shadow* (apparently lost), are available on VHS cassettes in varying degrees of quality, and can be found with minimal effort through specialty publications like *The Big Reel* and *Movie Collector's World*. If a specific video distributor is not indicated, this means that the serial is only available in the form of unofficial, bootleg tape copies, or that no officially available tape cassette version is recommended. Also, the serials were frequently reedited into feature-length movies, and some of these condensed versions are also available on video. These pretend-features are usually callously edited and are an inaccurate representation of their source materials. They are not recommended; however, they have been noted and discussed where appropriate.

In recent years, a "sophisticated" elite has wasted far too much effort in the belittlement of low-budget movies, including serials, as campy relics good only for derision. Although gone from theaters for over four decades, the serial has influenced such recent blockbuster films as producer-director George Lucas' *Star Wars* Trilogy and *Indiana Jones* adventures, patterned on the *Flash Gordon* and Republic Picture serials respectively. As pop culture artifact, and as an important part of film history, the movie serial should not be allowed to fade into oblivion, and the better serials, at least, should be preserved for posterity. It is from this historical perspective that these serials are discussed in this book, with the hope that the open-minded reader will be inspired to view the films in a more informed, more appreciative light.

The Serials

The Vanishing Shadow

(Universal, 1934)

Associate producer: Henry MacRae. Director: Louis Friedlander (a.k.a. Lew Landers). Story and dialogue: Ella O'Neill. Continuity: Het Mannheim, Basil Dickey, George Morgan. Photography: Richard Fryer, A.S.C. Film editors: Edward Todd, Alvin Todd. Art direction: Thomas F. O'Neill. Electrical effects: Kenneth Strickfaden, Raymond A. Lindsay, Elmer A. Johnson

Cast: Onslow Stevens (Stanley Stanfield), Ada Ince (Gloria Grant), Walter Miller (Ward Bernett), James Durkin (Prof. Carl Van Dorn), William Desmond (MacDonald), Richard Cramer (Dorgan), Sidney Bracy (Denny), Eddie Cobb (Kent), Philo McCullough (smuggler chief), Don Brodie (pilot), Al Ferguson. Monte Montague. (henchmen), Tom London. William Steele.

Chapter Titles

(1) Accused of Murder. (2) The Destroying Ray. (3) The Avalanche. (4) Trapped. (5) Hurled from the Sky. (6) Chair Lightning. (7) The Tragic Crash. (8) The Shadow of Death. (9) Blazing Bulkheads. (10) The Iron Death. (11) The Juggernaut. (12) Retribution.

Story

Stanley Stanfield, young scientific genius and the son of a newspaper publisher, seeks vengeance against a cabal of dishonest politicians who persecuted his father and caused his death. Stanfield has invented a device capable of making him invisible, and he hopes that Carl Van Dorn, a respected authority on electrical energy, will help him perfect it. Van Dorn agrees to assist him in the completion of the invisibility device; when the matter of funding arises, Stanfield tells Van Dorn that he plans to sell valuable newspaper bonds in order to back the project.

Leaving Van Dorn's office, Stanfield rescues Gloria Grant, a newspaper reporter, just as she is about to be struck by a fire truck, only to find that she is the daughter of his chief enemy, Wade Barnett, leader of the crooked politicians. Gloria tells Stanfield that she is opposed to her father's activities and disapproves of his methods, and that she has adopted an alias while working for the Tribune as a reporter.

When Stanfield visits his attorney to sell the newspaper bonds, he finds Wade Barnett there. A violent argument ensues and Barnett pulls a gun. A struggle breaks out, Stanfield's attorney is accidentally shot and Stanfield wrenches the gun away from Barnett. When Barnett's henchmen arrive in the office, they find Stanfield holding the gun, and Barnett frames Stanfield for the lawyer's death. Realizing that he appears to be

The Vanishing Shadow: Eddie Cobb, Ada Ince, Onslow Stevens.

guilty, Stanfield bursts out of the office and hurries back to Van Dorn, chased by Barnett's lackeys. Aided by the "invisibility ray," Stanfield escapes capture, but he is pursued by his enemies after he leaves the building. He drives away and attempts to cross railroad tracks in front of a speeding train; his car is demolished, but he survives the accident.

With Van Dorn's assistance, Stanfield employs a vast array of super-scientific devices (including a "destroying ray" and a robot) in his struggle against Barnett and his cronies. Stanfield eventually succeeds in his crusade to prove his innocence when Barnett is killed while trying to escape from the police. With Barnett's criminal activities revealed, Stanfield's name is cleared and he is free to pursue romance with Gloria Grant.

Comments

Apparently similar in its "vengeful scientist" plot to Universal's later Bela Lugosi serial *The Phantom Creeps* (q.v.), *The Vanishing Shadow* is difficult to assess today, since it seems to have lived up to its title and literally vanished. No print of the film appears to have survived; a 35mm nitrate preview trailer running three minutes, currently held by the George Eastman House archive in Rochester, New York, may well be the last extant footage. Unfortunately, even this brief trailer is unavailable for screening, as it has not yet been recopied onto safety film stock. A handful of surviving stills showing an impressive laboratory set and well-designed robot only add to the frustration of *The Vanishing Shadow*'s unavailability.

The serial starred Onslow Stevens, best remembered today for his role as a vampiric mad scientist in Universal's 1945 horror feature *House of Dracula*. An interview with Stevens, published in Universal's *Vanishing Shadow* pressbook, claimed that Stevens performed his own stunt work. "Why should I allow some other fellow to take a chance?" Stevens asked. "I never have been a coward. I fully believe it is the star's place to do whatever the script calls for, and not sit back watching another do his acting for

him. It takes all the thrill out of working in a picture to have another fellow do my part. I recall as a kid, how excited I would get watching episode after episode of some thrilling serial, and often wished the day would come when I could be playing the leading role in one. Today that wish has materialized. With all the hard knocks I received during the weeks of filming *The Vanishing Shadow*, I would not hesitate to accept the same role again. I thoroughly enjoyed every moment of the time, there was something doing every second of the day. Excitement is a thing I like, and I surely received plenty in the making of this truly thrilling screenplay."

Like most pressbook stories and star interviews released by studios for publicity purposes, this interview was probably a fabrication. According to an actress who worked at Universal, Stevens was a serious stage actor from Pasadena Playhouse, and was in fact very displeased that Universal had cast him in serials under his contractual obligation to the studio.

As usual with Universal serials, *The Vanishing Shadow* made liberal use of newsreel stock footage showing fires, train wrecks and exploding ships. One spectacular scene in Chapters 5 and 6 involved a full-scale old-fashioned Jenny airplane crashing into the sea (the plane exploded in the air close to the water, flipped over and fell into the sea). Onslow Stevens and Ada Ince (who had bailed out of the plane earlier in the scene) are rescued from the sea by a gang of toughs led by Philo McCullough, who explains that he and his gang are involved in rum-running and would be in trouble if this were known. "I've forgotten it already!" Stevens replies.

The special effects, in expected serial

fashion, were done quickly and inexpensively. For the most part, the invisibility effects were accomplished with wires simply manipulating doors and various objects, employing none of the time-consuming (and more convincing) techniques used in features like Universal's *The Invisible Man* (1933). Invisibility as a plot device was not new in movies, but a unique gimmick in the serial had Stevens' shadow remain visible even though *he* himself was unseen — hence the title.

Many of the props used in *The Vanishing Shadow* later saw service in other serials. A control belt worn by James Durkin was later used in Republic's 1936 cliffhanger *Undersea Kingdom* (q.v.), and a ray gun with an egg beater-shaped muzzle turns up in Mascot's 1935 *The Phantom Empire* (q.v.). Another device, a ray gun that looks like a 1930s fold-out Kodak 120 camera, was later used as the "paralyzer ray" in Universal's 1938 *Flash Gordon's Trip to Mars* (q.v.). Laboratory machinery seen in Universal's *Frankenstein* (1931) is also used in *The Vanishing Shadow*. Although publicity photos exist showing starlet Lois January posing with the *Vanishing Shadow* robot, her name does not appear in any official cast listing, and she probably did not have a role in the serial. This fascinating robot costume, which would have been a natural for the studio's later *Flash Gordon* and *Buck Rogers* serials, was never used in another cliffhanger.

The Lost City

Krellberg/Regal Pictures/ Super-Serial Productions, Inc./ Principal Distributing Corp., 1935

Producer: Sherman S. Krellberg. Director: Harry Revier. Screenplay: Perley Poore Sheehan, Eddy Graneman, Leon D'Usseau. Story: Zelma Carroll, George M. Merrick, Robert Dillon. Photography: Edward Linden, Roland Price. Special effects: Norman Dawn. Art director: Ralph Berger. Electrical effects: Kenneth Strickfaden. Film editor: Holbrook Todd. Music: Lee Zahler. Sound: Cliff Ruberg. General production manager: George M. Merrick. Technician: James Altweiss. Dialogue director: Zelma Carroll. Assistant directors: William Nolte, Richard L'Estrange. Feature versions: *The Lost City* and *City*

Opposite: The Lost City poster.

The Lost City—William Bletcher, Joseph Swickard, Claudia Dell.

of *Lost Men*, both for theatrical release.

Cast: William (Stage) Boyd (Zolok), Kane Richmond (Bruce Gordon), Claudia Dell (Natcha Manyus), Josef Swickard (Dr. Manyus), George F. Hayes (Butterfield), Ralph Lewis (Reynolds), William Bletcher (Gorzo), Eddie Fetherstone (Jerry), Milburn Moranti (Andrews), Margot D'Use (Queen Rama), Jerry Frank (Appolyn), William Millman (Colton), Gino Carrado (Ben Ali), Sam Baker (Hugo), Everett Brown (giant), Henry Hall (officer), Curley Dresden (Arab).

Chapter Titles

(1) *Living Dead Men.* (2) *Tunnel of Death.* (3) *Dagger Rock.* (4) *Doomed.* (5) *Tiger Prey.* (6) *Human Beasts.* (7) *Spider Men.* (8) *Human Targets.* (9) *Jungle Vengeance.* (10) *The Lion Pit.* (11) *The Death Ray.* (12) *The Mad Scientist.*

Story

The entire world is plagued by incessant atmospheric storms. Bruce Gordon, an intrepid young electrical engineer using a "magnetic detector" that he has invented, traces the source of the disturbances to an unexplored region of central Africa. With the financial backing of the government, Bruce travels there with his friend Jerry and two associates, Colton and Reynolds.

In Africa, Bruce meets Butterfield, a grizzled, unscrupulous trader, and with

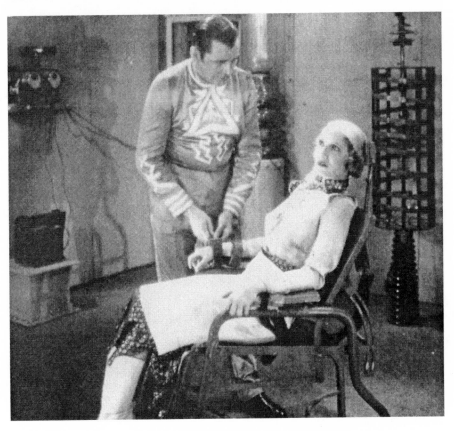

The Lost City— William (Stage) Boyd, Claudia Dell.

his magnetic detector learns that the violent storms emanate from nearby "Magnetic Mountain." Within Magnetic Mountain lies "The Lost City," a super-scientific metropolis ruled by Zolok, a maniacal, strangely garbed technical wizard. Zolok's assistants include Gorzo, a malignant, hunchbacked dwarf, and Appolyn, an obedient muscle-bound henchman. It is Zolok who has caused the disasters plaguing mankind with the intention of conquering the world, but Zolok's scientific marvels are really the creation of Dr. Manyus. Manyus, held captive by Zolok, is an elderly, benevolent genius,

forced to comply with Zolok because Manyus' beautiful daughter Natcha is also imprisoned by the madman.

Zolok tricks Bruce Gordon's expedition into entering the Lost City, forcing Natcha to scream over a loudspeaker as a lure. Within the bizarre futuristic city, Bruce and Jerry discover the extent of Zolok's ruthlessness when they learn that he commands an army of lobotomized African giants, created in his laboratory by physically enlarging and transforming the local inhabitants.

Meeting Zolok in his lair, Bruce is informed that he will either assist Zolok or be transformed into a lobotomized

The Lost City—Claudia Dell, Sam Baker, Kane Richmond.

zombie. Colton and Reynolds, also captured by Zolok, have managed to leave the Lost City with Dr. Manyus in a plot to steal his technological secrets and double-cross Bruce Gordon. Learning this, Natcha informs Bruce and Jerry, leading them out of the Lost City and into the surrounding jungle in an effort to rescue her father.

Colton and Reynolds are eventually killed and the amoral Butterfield winds up forming an alliance with Bruce and his friends. After a harrowing series of misadventures involving Arab slave traders, marauding giant zombies, a tribe of pygmy "spider-men" and a beautiful, love-starved jungle queen, Bruce, Jerry, Natcha and Dr. Manyus are recaptured and taken back to the Lost City, where an enraged Zolok tries to kill Bruce with a laser-like death ray. Aided by rebelling tribesmen, Butterfield invades the Lost City to rescue his newfound friends, and they escape.

Zolok, now totally insane and cackling wildly, attempts to destroy the entire world with his laboratory devices, but the powerful machines backfire and

The Lost City— **Milburn Moranti, Claudia Dell.**

Zolok only succeeds in blowing up himself, the Lost City and most of Magnetic Mountain. With the threat to civilization ended, Bruce and Natcha, now romantically involved, prepare to leave Africa and return home.

Comments

The Lost City was produced by Sherman S. Krellberg, a New York theater owner and independent producer whose company was known at various times as Regal, Super-Serial Productions, Goodwill and Filmcraft. The first full-blown science fiction serial, released in January 1935, *The Lost City* looks like a 1930s science fiction pulp magazine cover come to life. The costumes, dialogue and props are obviously influenced by the pulp literature of the time, and for a low-budget production the film's physical attributes are impressive. Aware that Mascot was in production with *The Phantom Empire*, producer Krellberg assigned three units to handle the direction simultaneously in a (successful) attempt to cut the shooting schedule from 35 to 21 days to beat the rival

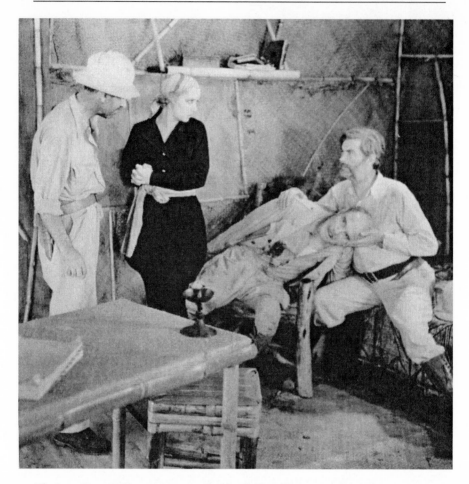

The Lost City— **Milburn Moranti, Claudia Dell, William Reynolds, George F. Hayes.**

Mascot production into theaters. Harry Revier and Ben Cohen directed sound units, with Robert Dillon directing a silent unit. Harry Revier received sole directorial credit for the serial.

Revier, a long-time associate of Krellberg's (he was married to glamorous 1930s actress Dorothy Revier), was an old hand at low-budget film production, shooting many cheap Westerns and action pictures over the course of several decades. Known as "three finger Harry" because he had lost a couple of fingers from his right hand, Revier was one of the first producer-directors working in California (possibly *the* first). *The Squaw Man* (1914), directed by Cecil B. DeMille, is often incorrectly identified as the first feature made in California, but the barn that DeMille rented to film *The Squaw Man* was the Harry Revier studio. Revier had established himself in southern California before DeMille, but has been generally forgotten, lost in the shadow of his more illustrious successor.

Revier manages to generate considerable power in some scenes in *The Lost City*, and his handling of the few action scenes is competent. The actors, however, are directed to perform in a wild-eyed, over-the-top manner that would have embarrassed the worst silent movie ham. The fact that Revier learned his craft in low-budget silents seems to be the main problem. His handling of the performers exhibits insensitivity to dialogue, and as a result the movie frequently collapses into giggly camp; although it may be enjoyable on that level, this certainly wasn't the original intention. Revier's direction isn't the only flaw. The screenplay is old-fashioned and sloppily constructed, with the entire middle of the serial bogging down into slow-paced jungle tedium.

There are a few pleasant surprises in the technical department. The electrical machinery was supplied by Kenneth Strickfaden, who contributed the same effects to Universal's *Frankenstein* (1931) and many other 1930s and '40s horror-fantasy movies, including *Flash Gordon* (q.v.). The effective art direction was by Ralph Berger, who also designed the Bela Lugosi thriller *White Zombie* (1932) and *Flash Gordon*. *The Lost City* was photographed by Edward Linden, who shot *King Kong* (1933), with Roland Price, an experienced documentary cinematographer, assisting.

The cast of *The Lost City*, although ill-served by the direction and screenplay, is solid and capable. William (Stage) Boyd (so-named in order to differentiate him from another actor, future *Hopalong Cassidy* star William Boyd) is top-billed as the maniacal Zolok. Boyd interprets what would have otherwise been a stock "mad scientist" role as an aggressive, loud-mouthed urban gangster type, constantly barking orders at his subordinates. The actor goes way over the top in the last chapter, as Zolok collapses into total insanity and threatens to destroy the world, but overall he makes an impressive villain. Boyd died soon after the serial was released.

Kane Richmond, cast as Bruce Gordon, was an excellent leading man and a good actor, as he would prove in Republic's superlative wartime serial *Spy Smasher* (1942), but he never rose above B-movies and serials; by 1947 he was still at it, playing the lead in Columbia's serial *Brick Bradford* (q.v.). Claudia Dell, a pretty 25-year-old blonde, had been under contract to Warner Brothers a few years earlier, but soon wound up appearing in low-budget fare. She is decorative in *The Lost City* but, like the rest of the performers, is directed in a shrill, melodramatic style. Dell's career faded soon after *The Lost City*, and one of her films, a 1936 drama called *Speed Limited*, went unreleased until 1940.

George F. Hayes, who would soon be known as "Gabby" Hayes opposite Roy Rogers in B-Westerns, seems in retrospect an odd choice for a semi-villainous role like Butterfield, but Hayes is convincing and demonstrates that he was capable of handling a wider range of roles beyond the benevolent Western sidekick types he usually played. William Bletcher, cast as Zolok's assistant Gorzo, had a booming, imposing voice that belied his diminutive physical stature, and probably had his greatest role as the voice of the Big Bad Wolf in Walt Disney's cartoon *The Three Little Pigs*. Bletcher also supplied the voice of the villainous Don-Del-Oro in Republic's 1939 serial *Zorro's Fighting Legion*. Other noteworthy performers in *The Lost City* include Margot D'Use as Queen Raman the jungle monarch and Gino Corrado as Arab chieftain Ben Ali.

One troubling aspect of *The Lost City*, and a factor that prevents the serial from being as enjoyable as it should be, is the film's blatantly racist attitude toward its black characters. The tribesmen captured by Zolok and subjected to laboratory experimentation are directed to emote in an eye-bulging manner, speaking only in growls and monosyllabic grunts. Granted, these characters are supposed to be mindless zombies, but the normal tribesmen inhabiting the jungle outside Zolok's city fare little better, and the occasional racial slurs peppered throughout the dialogue imply that the black characters are cowards at best and something less than

human in general. These attitudes were way out of line even in 1935; when a New York TV station broadcast *The Lost City* in the 1950s, the serial was considered so offensive and protests against it were so vocal that it was pulled in mid-run.

Its many flaws aside, *The Lost City* is historically important as one of the earliest sound science fiction movies, and as one of the first science fiction serials. The Five-Star Library issued a novelization of the serial in 1935, and in the 1940s the film was adapted as a comic book series. For years, *The Lost City* was commonly available only in the form of a re-edited feature version, but in the 1980s the complete serial (as well as two different feature versions) were made available on videocassette.

Video availability: Sinister Cinema.

The Phantom Empire

(Mascot, 1935)

Producer: Nat Levine. Directors: Otto Brower, B. Reeves "Breezy" Eason. Supervisor: Armand Shaeffer. Story: Wallace McDonald, Gerald Gerahty, Harry Friedman. Continuity: John Rathmell, Armand Shaeffer. Photography: Ernest Miller, William Nobles. Special effects: Ellis "Bud" Thackery. Special props: Howard Lydecker,

Theodore Lydecker, Billy Gilbert. Sets: Mack D'Agostino, Jack Cole, Ralph M. DeLacy. Film editors: Earl Turner, Walter Thompson. Sound: Terry Kellum. International Sound Recording Co. Costumes: Iris Burns. Assistant director: William Witney. Camera operator: William Bradford. Songs ("In My Vine-Covered Cottage," "Just Come On In,"

Opposite: The Phantom Empire poster.

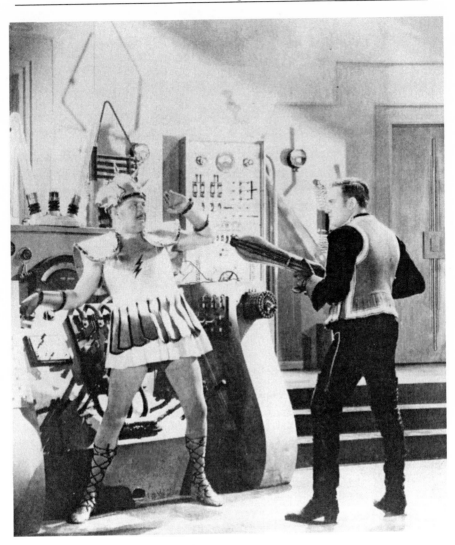

The Phantom Empire—Stanley G. Blystone, Gene Autry.

"Uncle Noah's Ark," "I'm Oscar," "Moon-Eyed View of the World," "No Need to Worry") by Gene Autry and Smiley Burnette. Feature version: *Radio Ranch* (71 minutes), released theatrically in 1940.

    Cast: Gene Autry (himself), Frankie Darro (Frankie Baxter), Betsy King Ross (Betsy Baxter), Dorothy Christie (Queen Tika), Wheeler Oakman (Argo), Charles K. Franch (Mal), Warner Richmond (Rab), Frank Glendon (Prof. Beetson), Lester [Smiley] Burnette (Oscar), William Moore

Opposite: The Phantom Empire poster.

(Pete), Edward Piel, Sr. (Dr. Cooper), Jack Carlyle (Saunders), Frankie Marvin (Frankie), Wally Wales. Fred Burns. Jay Wilsey. Stanley G. Blystone. Richard Talmadge. Frank Ellis. Henry Hall. Jim Corey (Muranians).

Chapter Titles

(1) *The Singing Cowboy.* (2) *The Thunder Riders.* (3) *The Lightning Chamber.* (4) *The Phantom Broadcast.* (5) *Beneath the Earth.* (6) *Disaster From the Skies.* (7) *From Death to Life.* (8) *Jaws of Jeopardy.* (9) *Prisoners of the Ray.* (10) *The Rebellion.* (11) *A Queen in Chains.* (12) *The End of Murania.*

Story

A gang of crooks led by the nefarious Prof. Beetson seeks a valuable radium deposit located beneath Radio Ranch, managed by popular country–western radio star Gene Autry. Autry must broadcast his radio program once a day to fulfill a clause in his lease and maintain control of Radio Ranch. Realizing that Autry's popularity draws a crowd to the ranch, Beetson attempts to eliminate Autry by murdering the singer's business partner (the father of Autry's two young friends Frankie and Betsy Baxter) and framing Autry for the killing.

Autry escapes custody in an effort to prove his innocence. Frankie and Betsy, loyal to Gene and knowing that he did not kill their father, aid him in his quest, along with a group of their friends who have formed a children's club called the Thunder Riders, patterned after a mysterious group of masked horsemen (called the Thunder Riders) periodically seen in the area.

Eventually, both Autry and Beetson discover that the real Thunder Riders come from an advanced, forgotten civilization called Murania, located 25,000 feet below Radio Ranch.

Autry is eventually imprisoned in the subterranean city, ruled by the haughty Tika. Young Frankie and Betsy, along with Autry's dim-witted buddies Pete and Oscar, are also captured when they follow Gene into Murania. Although Gene manages to escape Queen Tika's clutches repeatedly so that he can return home and deliver his mandatory radio broadcasts, he and his friends are constantly threatened by Queen Tika and the Muranians until Argo, a treacherous underling of the monarch's stages an armed revolt and overthrows her.

Gene and his friends escape from Murania just as a powerful death ray goes out of control, disintegrating the entire city and all its inhabitants. Safely returning to the surface, Gene, Frankie, Betsy and the sheriff contrive to eavesdrop on Beetson as he discusses murdering Frankie and Betsy's dad. With this evidence, Gene is finally able to prove his innocence and clear his name, with Beetson punished for his misdeeds.

Comments

A bizarre mixture of science fiction themes, country–western music and B-Western clichés, *The Phantom Empire* is easy to dismiss as campy nonsense. But when viewed with an open mind, the film is an impressive (if undeniably juvenile) production, and in terms of subject matter it was certainly one of the most influential serials ever made.

Opposite: **A view of Queen Tika's impressive throne room.**

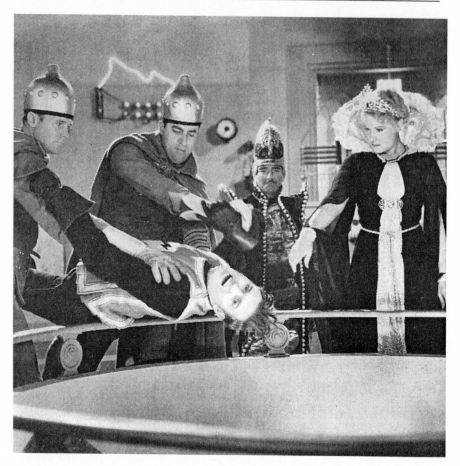

The Phantom Empire— Gene Autry learns the hard way that the boundaries of imagination extend beyond Radio Ranch. Wheeler Oakman and Dorothy Christie are at right.

Released in early 1935 right after independent producer Sherman S. Krellberg's *The Lost City* (q.v.), *The Phantom Empire* popularized science fiction in movie serials, and its considerable financial success paved the way for Universal's *Flash Gordon* (q.v.) the following year.

Cowboy star Ken Maynard had originally been cast as the lead in *The Phantom Empire*, but after difficulties with Maynard arose, producer Nat Levine re-cast the serial with newcomer Gene Autry in the lead. Autry had already played supporting roles for Levine in the Ken Maynard serial *Mystery Mountain* (1934) and the Maynard feature *In Old Santa Fe* (1934). Levine placed Autry under contract for $100 per week; despite Autry's stated misgivings about his own acting ability, he handled his "singing cowboy" assignment well, eventually gaining Western superstardom as a result of his successful role in this serial. Although Autry was not an impressive actor, he projected a bland, infectious sincerity that was appreciated by moviegoers and led to his enduring stardom as a Western movie icon.

Produced for a mere $70,000, with exteriors shot on the Mack Sennett lot and in Bronson Canyon, *The Phantom Empire* manages to present impressive special effects that belie the film's low budget. The underground city of Murania was constructed in miniature, with the model shots sometimes used as rear-projection footage behind the actors. Economical shortcuts were used wherever possible to stretch the tight budget. Queen Tika's massive throne room was not a constructed set, but was filmed in a solar observatory then under construction. The far shots of the throne room were augmented with a glass painting showing the Muranian skyline outside a large window. Other special effects in *The Phantom Empire* were not as successful, with the robot costumes in particular inviting laughter even in 1935. Still, there are enough eye-popping views of Murania and crackling *Frankenstein*-style machinery to compensate for any minor technical shortcomings. The visuals gain even more raw power from the musical score, which includes energetic chase music by Henry Hadley, a "Murania Theme" by Hugo Riesenfeld, and a classical piece (Herold's "Zampa" overture). Some of the editing, particularly in Chapter 1, is ambitious for a serial.

The Phantom Empire is rural in its appeal, with the film's Western aspects and cowboy characters directed at the traditional horse opera audience, but the science fiction angle is cunningly used to attract younger comic strip and pulp magazine fans. Like most serials, *The Phantom Empire* is aimed squarely at juveniles, with a promotional trailer at the end of Chapter 1 speaking directly to the "boys and girls" in the audience. Although publicity claimed that one of the film's writers "imagined" the story while under medication in a dentist's chair, the film is a well-calculated attempt to exploit two seemingly unrelated pop culture genres, and it succeeds very well. The serial was promoted with a series of newspaper comic strips also titled *The Phantom Empire*. A theatrical feature version, *Radio Ranch*, was released in 1940, and was later re-released under the title *Men With Steel Faces*.

In addition to Gene Autry's easygoing charm in the lead, Dorothy Christie makes a strong impression as the regal Queen Tika. Silent movie and B-Western veteran Wheeler Oakman plays her treacherous lieutenant in a performance similar to his later role in *Flash Gordon's Trip to Mars* (q.v.). Frankie Darro and Betsy King Ross are likable as Autry's two juvenile friends, undoubtedly intended as screen extensions of the target audience.

The Phantom Empire is no classic, but it is that rare type of film in which even preposterously bad dialogue and acting are tempered with innocence, resulting in a movie with genuine charm.

Video availability: VCI.

Flash Gordon

(Universal, 1936)

Producer: Henry MacRae. Directors: Frederick Stephani, Ray Taylor (uncredited). Screenplay: Frederick Stephani, George Plympton, Basil Dickey, Ella O'Neill. Photography: Jerry Ash, A.S.C., Richard Fryer, A.S.C. Art director: Ralph Berger. Film editors: Saul A. Goodkind, Edward Todd, Alvin Todd, Louis Sackin. Special properties: Elmer A. Johnson. Electrical effects: Norman Dewes. Electrical properties: Kenneth Strickfaden, Raymond Lindsay. Sound: RCA. Original music: Clifford Vaughan, David Claxton. Music supervision: Jacques Aubran. Feature versions: *Rocket Ship* (68 minutes), released theatrically, and *Spaceship to the Unknown* (97 minutes), for television distribution.

Cast: Larry [Buster] Crabbe (Flash Gordon), Jean Rogers (Dale Arden), Charles Middleton (Emperor Ming), Priscilla Lawson (Princess Aura), Frank Shannon (Dr. Zarkov), Richard Alexander (Prince Barin), John Lipson (King Vultan), Theodore Lorch/Lon Poff (High Priest), Richard Tucker (Prof. Gordon), George Cleveland (Professor Hensley), James Pierce (Prince Thun), Duke York, Jr. (King Kala), Muriel Goodspeed (Zona), Earl Askam (Officer Torch), House Peters, Jr. (shark man), Bull Montana, Constantine Romanoff (ape men), Sana Raya (Tigron's mistress), Ray "Crash" Corrigan (orangopoid), Lane Chandler, Fred Kohler, Jr., Al Ferguson (soldiers), Glenn Strange (fire monster/soldier), Carroll Borland (woman in Ming's palace), Lynton Brent, Don Brodie, Jim Corey, Charles Whitaker, Bunny Waters, Fred Sommers, Monte Montague, Howard Christie.

Chapter Titles

(1) *Planet of Peril.* (2) *The Tunnel of Terror.* (3) *Captured by Shark Men.* (4) *Battling the Sea Beast.* (5) *The Destroying Ray.* (6) *Flaming Torture.* (7) *Shattering Doom.* (8) *Tournament of Death.* (9) *Fighting the Fire Dragon.* (10) *The Unseen Peril.* (11) *In the Claws of the Tigron.* (12) *Trapped in the Turret.* (13) *Rocketing to Earth.*

Story

A mysterious planet approaches Earth on an apparent collision course, threatening to destroy the world with its disruptive gravitational influence. As violent storms and meteor showers sweep the globe, Flash Gordon, a young athlete, travels aboard a passenger plane in an effort to reach his father, an astronomer, before the end of the world. Also aboard the plane is beautiful young Dale Arden. When the plane spins out of control in the turbulent winds, Flash bails out with Dale and the other passengers just before the plane is destroyed by a meteor.

Flash and Dale land safely in a remote area, and they are startled to see a futuristic rocketship nearby. Suddenly, a

Flash Gordon poster.

bearded, wild-eyed man appears from the bushes, aiming a gun at Flash and Dale, and announces that he is Dr. Zarkov. Zarkov, a brilliant scientist, claims that he can reach the rogue planet in his rocketship and possibly stop it from colliding with Earth, if Flash will help him. Flash boards the rocketship with Dale and Zarkov.

Zarkov blasts off and, after a swift journey through outer space, the rocketship lands on the mysterious planet. Emerging from the rocket, Flash, Dale and Zarkov are nearly killed by giant reptiles when another rocketship appears in the sky and destroys the monsters with a ray blast. The ship lands and an armored soldier, Officer Torch, accompanied by two armed guards, approaches and announces that they are prisoners of Emperor Ming. Flown to a city in the distance, they are escorted into a massive palace throne room and taken before Ming, the cruel tyrant who rules the planet (called Mongo). Ming, impressed by Zarkov's scientific knowledge, promptly imprisons him in a laboratory and then becomes infatuated with Dale. When Flash objects, he is thrown into the arena on Ming's orders and forced to battle three ape-men as a horrified Dale and Ming's beautiful daughter Aura, interested in the heroic Earthman, watch the fight.

Flash overcomes his bestial opponents, and Aura rushes into the arena to protect Flash from Ming's guards when they attack him. Aura shoots one of Ming's soldiers with a ray gun, and the dying man falls against a switch that opens a trap door beneath Flash and Aura. They plummet down a shaft, but are saved when Ming throws a switch that opens a safety net beneath them. Escaping from the shaft through a secret

door, Aura leads Flash through a subterranean cave to a rocketship at the cavern opening. Meanwhile, Zarkov is being forced to work on various devices that will aid Ming in his planned conquest of the universe. Ming's handmaidens for marriage are preparing Dale to wed the emperor; when she resists, Ming's high priest hypnotizes her with a machine called the "dehumanizer."

The lion men, led by Prince Thun, a race in rebellion against Ming's tyranny, attack his palace from the air in whirling gyro ships. Flash, concerned about his friends' safety, blasts off in the rocketship and engages the gyros in an aerial dogfight. Flash's rocketship crashes into Thun's gyro as they maneuver across the sky, and they both plunge into a barren valley below. Emerging from the wreckage unharmed, the two men begin fighting, then realize that they are allies against Ming and become friends. Stealthily gaining access to Ming's palace, Flash and Thun visit Zarkov in the laboratory, and are told that the hypnotized Dale is being married to Ming. Hurrying to stop the ceremony, Flash rushes into a cavern and is attacked by a giant, lobster-clawed reptile that tries to crush him in its grasp.

Thun arrives just in time and kills the monster with a ray gun. Flash continues on, disrupting Ming's wedding ceremony and escaping with the hypnotized Dale as Ming and his astonished retinue watch. Through a viewing lens, Ming sees Flash and Dale escaping and operates a control that opens a trap door beneath them. Flash and Dale fall into a pool of water and are attacked by shark men who force them to board an underwater ship called a hydrocycle. Dale (now recovered from her hypnosis) and Flash are taken to the underwater shark city, where they are confronted by King Kala, the ruler. When Kala orders Dale returned to Ming, Flash ridicules Kala's authority, denouncing him as a puppet of Ming's. An angry Kala challenges Flash to a fight. When Kala loses, he promises the victorious Flash that he and Dale will be freed. Instead, Kala tricks Flash into entering a locked aquarium chamber that quickly fills with water. A tentacled octosac is then released through a water chute and it attacks Flash as Kala forces Dale to watch through a porthole.

Thun and Aura gain entry into the shark city, and they force Kala to drain the water from the tank and save Flash. The deceitful Aura, trying to separate Flash and Dale, releases Flash from the tank and convinces him that he should destroy the master control board in Kala's engine room. Flash overpowers the guard and Aura destroys the control board with a ray gun. As the magnetic energy powering the shark city stops, the air dissipates and the city's walls buckle, allowing the sea to rush in.

Watching a spaceograph viewer, Ming sees the destruction of the shark city and quickly activates a powerful machine that magnetically elevates Kala's palace above sea level, saving the occupants. Escaping from the shark city, Dale and Thun are kidnapped by winged hawkmen and flown to their ruler King Vultan in a city that floats in the sky. Meanwhile, as Flash battles more hawkmen, Zarkov forms an alliance with an enemy of Ming's, Prince Barin, who promises to help him rescue Flash and Dale. Zarkov and Barin land in a rocketship just as Flash overpowers the remaining hawkmen and Aura arrives on the scene. Zarkov introduces Barin as their friend, and they board the

rocketship with Aura, heading for Vultan's sky city.

Within the sky city, held aloft by anti-gravity beams, the boisterous Vultan, lusting after Dale, terrorizes her. When a guard informs him that Barin's rocketship is approaching, Vultan orders it destroyed with a melting ray. A hawkman turns the powerful ray on the ship and it is blasted out of the sky, but it is held aloft by the city's nearby anti-gravity beams, and Flash, Zarkov, Barin and Aura are made prisoners. Taken before Vultan, Zarkov is ordered to work in the laboratory while Flash and Barin are condemned to hard labor shoveling radium ore into furnaces which supply the power needed to keep the city aloft. Flippantly dismissing the petulant Aura, Vultan continues to harass Dale.

Ming, accompanied by his fleet of rocketships, arrives in the sky city to reclaim Dale and assert his authority over King Vultan. Flash, Barin and Thun escape from the furnace room when Flash hurls an electrically charged shovel, secretly rigged by Zarkov, into the radium furnace, exploding the furnace room. As the anti-gravity beams fade and Vultan's city tips dangerously, Flash, Barin and Thun rush into Vultan's throne room. They are captured by Vultan's men but Vultan, resentful of Ming's tyrannical rule, allies himself with the Earth people. Ming, however, stipulates his right to call a Tournament of Death and orders Flash to enter it, forcing him to combat a horned, ape-like orangopoid. Flash kills the monster when Aura gives him a spear. As victor of the tournament, he earns his freedom.

Barin confesses to Flash that he loves Aura. When Ming offers to allow the

Jean Rogers as Dale Arden in *Flash Gordon*.

Earth people, Barin and Vultan to visit his city in peace, they accept, although Thun refuses and returns to the lion men. The vengeful Aura, jealous of Flash and Dale's love for each other, conspires with Ming's wily high priest to drug Flash with "drops of forgetful- ness," robbing him of his memory. Unable to remember Dale, Flash is taken away by Aura, but they are nearly killed in the catacombs below Ming's palace when a huge fire dragon attacks them. Zarkov arrives and destroys the monster with a grenade, restoring Flash's

Flash Gordon—Jean Rogers, Buster Crabbe, John Lipson, Charles Middleton.

memory after they return to the laboratory. Ming's soldiers, led by Officer Torch, arrive in the laboratory, acting on Ming's orders to execute Flash, but Zarkov makes Flash invisible with a machine he has secretly invented. The astonished soldiers, believing this to be magic, flee in terror..

An invisible Flash then defies Ming with impunity. After Zarkov restores Flash to visibility, the angry Ming orders Zarkov's machine destroyed. After Barin discovers a secret microphone planted in the laboratory by Aura, he hides Dale in the caverns beneath Ming's palace, fearing for her safety. Aura tracks Dale with a ferocious tiger-like beast called a tigron, which attacks Dale, but Flash suddenly arrives and kills the animal with his bare hands. Barin, reprimanding Aura, admits his love for her and convinces her to renounce her duplicity and befriend the Earth people. She agrees, and they all return to the laboratory so the Earth people can plan their return trip home.

Ming continues to plot against the Earth people, but when the lion men, led by Thun, attack Ming's palace, Ming's forces are overwhelmed and the defeated tyrant commits suicide by walking into a flaming corridor below his palace. With Barin and Aura now installed as the rulers of Mongo, Flash, Dale and Zarkov bid their friends farewell and embark on their return voyage home in Zarkov's rocketship.

They are nearly killed en route by a time bomb that Ming's fanatical high priest concealed aboard their ship; Flash, discovering the hidden bomb, throws it out of the ship just before it explodes. With Ming destroyed and the threat to Earth averted, Flash, Dale and Zarkov return home and are welcomed as heroes.

Comments

Created by artist Alex Raymond, the *Flash Gordon* newspaper strip, distributed by King Features Syndicate, premiered as a Sunday color page on January 4, 1934, with a daily strip beginning on May 27, 1940. Don Moore wrote most of the strips after the early installments; other artists over the decades have included Austin Briggs,

Mac Raboy, Dan Barry and Ric Estrada. Raymond had worked on a number of successful newspaper strips (including *Tillie the Toiler* and *Tim Tyler's Luck*) when, in 1934, King Features went shopping for a "high concept" fantasy-adventure strip to compete with the rival *Buck Rogers*. More than any other factor, Raymond's stylish artwork and precise delineation insured the wide popularity of the *Flash Gordon* strip, influencing a generation of artists in the process.

In 1934, Universal Pictures acquired the film rights to several King Features newspaper strips (including *Secret Agent X-9*, *Ace Drummond*, *Jungle Jim* and *Flash Gordon*), speculating that the established popularity of these strips would virtually guarantee profitable serial adaptations. The possibilities of *Flash Gordon*, with its ray guns, rocketships and interplanetary derring-do, were obvious, and Universal took a chance on the property by investing considerably more money than usual in the project. Producer Henry MacRae's serial department budgeted the chapter-play at a reported $350,000, over three times the average serial budget at the time.

Despite this comparatively lavish funding, some economizing was still necessary. The large budget allowed for a couple of spacious (if somewhat empty) sets, such as Emperor Ming's throne room, but many of the serial's sets and props were borrowed from other Universal productions of the time. The huge laboratory tower set from *Bride of Frankenstein* appears in Chapters 2 and 3, and the crypt from the same film, without the dust and cobwebs, is also used. The interior of the Transylvanian castle from *Dracula's*

Daughter, redecorated with electrical "mad scientist" equipment, became Ming's laboratory. The huge Egyptian idol seen in *The Mummy* represented the planet Mongo's "great god Tao" in a couple of scenes, and even Dr. Zarkov's rocketship was a second-hand prop, a miniature borrowed from the 1930 Fox feature *Just Imagine* (a bizarre science fiction-musical which also yielded some impressive footage of a huge, leering idol worshipped by an energetic chorus line of scantily clad dancing girls). Most of these scenes were not actual clips from *Just Imagine*, but were unused negative footage from the same scenes, including the shot of Dr. Zarkov's rocketship blasting off from Earth (which had been used as a rear-projection plate in *Just Imagine*). A scene of rioting savages used briefly at the end of Chapter 3, as Ming's soldiers watch a televisor screen, was also lifted from *Just Imagine*. A clip from the 1927 Universal feature *The Midnight Sun*, showing a dance number, was intercut with a *Flash Gordon* banquet scene in King Vultan's sky city. *The Midnight Sun* is now a lost film, and the clips seen in *Flash Gordon* represent the only surviving footage from the movie.

While the relatively large budget required to depict these outer space adventures permitted many luxuries usually denied serials, such as glass paintings and a few stationary matte and split-screen shots, there are still plenty of "rough edges" which, it should be noted, do not detract from the picture's entertainment value. There is a lot of clumsy vocal overdubbing on the soundtrack, done to cover inconsistencies in the dialogue as originally written. Unfortunately, the same easily recognized baritone voice is used to dub every

line, regardless of which character is speaking. The musical score for *Flash Gordon* is mostly a hodgepodge of compositions from other Universal movies, including W. Franke Harling's score for *The Invisible Man*, Heinz Roemheld's score for *The Black Cat* and Karl Hajos' score for *Werewolf of London*. The music for the main and end titles of each chapter, as well as the theme heard during the recap at the beginning of each chapter, was composed for the serial by Clifford Vaughan. Despite this patchwork scoring, the music is very effective at times, even improving scenes that are otherwise weak in style and content. In Chapter 1, Richard Wagner's *Good Friday* prelude to the opera *Parsifal* is used to impressive effect during the initial rocketship voyage from Earth to Mongo.

The serial's art director was Ralph Berger, who also designed the Bela Lugosi thriller *White Zombie* and the 1935 serial *The Lost City* (q.v.). (A vastly inferior production, *Lost City* has many visual similarities to *Flash Gordon*.) The costumes worn by the actors in *Flash Gordon*, especially the Roman armor sported by Ming's guards, may appear incongruous, but they are in fact perfectly in tune with Alex Raymond's original comic strip drawings, and a few of them, especially the costumes worn by Flash, Ming, Prince Barin and Officer Torch, are exact reproductions of Raymond's designs. These costumes were very expensive, perhaps unnecessarily so. Actress Jean Rogers told the author that the costumes were made in color, instead of the monochrome shades of gray and brown common to black-and-white film production, with Ming's robe made of red velvet.

In recent times, the *Flash Gordon*

serials have been unfairly criticized for their cheap special effects. The special effects in *Flash Gordon* are undeniably cut-rate compared to the technical work in other features of the era like *King Kong* and *Things to Come*, but this is due to the fact that the technicians shooting these effects were operating on a rushed schedule, not to any lack of expertise on their part. Although the budget was relatively high, *Flash Gordon* was, after all, still only a serial, and the entire production (with a total running time of four hours) was hurriedly shot on a schedule of only six weeks. Denied access to Universal's excellent miniature department (then under the supervision of special effects technician John P. Fulton), *Flash Gordon* cameraman Jerry Ash shot the serial's miniatures quickly, using an empty barn on the studio lot as a shooting stage. The miniatures in *Flash Gordon* involved small-scale models of the various rocketships, each about two feet in length; at least nine were constructed in addition to the one model inherited from *Just Imagine.* These were manipulated by wires or suspended in front of a moving background representing passing clouds. Actor Buster Crabbe, who saw these miniature shots being filmed, told the author that some of the miniature rocketships were suspended from microphone booms when they were required to fly toward the camera. These memorable rocketship models were fashioned out of wood (with metal fins and detailing) by prop man Elmer A. Johnson. Because of the restrictive time factors, such badly needed luxuries as traveling mattes, rear-screen projection and stop-motion animation were unthinkable. Simple split-screen photography was used in a brief scene in Chapter 1 (Flash

and his friends are attacked by huge dragons, which are really photographically enlarged lizards). Almost all of the shots were achieved cheaply, quickly and in the camera, without expensive and time-consuming lab work. Taking into account the conditions they were required to work under, Jerry Ash and the other technicians involved did a commendable job. While the special effects are by no means convincing in a realistic sense, they do work within the self-contained comic strip world of the serial, bringing an appropriately dream-like fantasy atmosphere to the picture.

Many of the serial's good points can be attributed to director Frederick Stephani, who also co-wrote the script. Veteran serial director Ray Taylor, uncredited, also contributed to the direction, supervising, as Jean Rogers told the author, "extra scenes that weren't important." After directing *Flash Gordon*, which was his first directorial assignment, Stephani left Universal to produce films like *Tarzan's New York Adventure* at MGM, and did not return to direction until the 1950s TV series *Waterfront*, starring Preston Foster.

Compared to other serials, *Flash Gordon* is remarkable because it combines plot and characterization into a solid whole. Much of the serial's enduring charm is due to the chemistry of the leading actors, Buster Crabbe (Flash Gordon), Jean Rogers (Dale Arden), Charles Middleton (Emperor Ming), Priscilla Lawson (Princess Aura) and Frank Shannon (Dr. Zarkov). Crabbe, always underrated and probably the most dramatically capable athlete turned actor in film history, was perfect as Flash, having won the role over Jon Hall, who also auditioned. Crabbe told the author: "They started shooting *Flash*

Flash Gordon— Buster Crabbe in a typical predicament.

Gordon in October of 1935, and to bring it in on the six-week schedule, we had to average 85 set-ups a day. That means moving and rearranging the heavy equipment we had, the arc lights and everything, 85 times a day. We had to be in makeup every morning at seven, and on the set at eight ready to go. They'd always knock off for lunch, and then we always worked after dinner. They'd give us a break of a half-hour or 45 minutes and then we'd go back on the set and work until ten-thirty every night. It wasn't fun, it was a lot of *work!*"

Beautiful young actresses Jean Rogers and Priscilla Lawson, both under 20 at the time, were ideal as the "good" and "bad" girls, respectively. Lawson's notable physical assets were responsible for incurring the wrath of censors. Jean

Rogers informed the author that when scenes filmed for Chapter 1 revealed too much of Miss Lawson's ample bosom, the censors ordered them reshot, with the actress wearing slightly less revealing garb. Charles Middleton, whose delightfully theatrical villainy enlivened several Laurel and Hardy shorts and many B-Westerns, found the role he was born to play in Emperor Ming, and the actor clearly relished the character. Jean Rogers recalled of Middleton: "When he was in his cloak, and made up like Ming, he strutted around like Ming — he really did strut! He was a very nice guy, but he had to stay in character. The minute he put on his street clothes, he was a different person ... it was really quite amusing!"

On its release, *Flash Gordon* was so

successful that it played evening performances at first-run theaters (serials were normally shown only at matinees). *Variety* called the 13-chapter epic "an unusually ambitious effort ... with feature production standards that have been maintained as to cast, direction and background." The serial proved to be Universal's second biggest-grossing film for that year, surpassed only by the Deanna Durbin vehicle *Three Smart Girls*.

Since *Flash Gordon* was first theatrically released, it and the two sequels, *Flash Gordon's Trip to Mars* (q.v.) and *Flash Gordon Conquers the Universe* (q.v.), have been distributed in a confusing array of re-edited feature versions and retitled prints. At the time of its original production, *Flash Gordon* was re-edited into a 68-minute feature of the same title, with a re-mixed soundtrack using different music and sound effects. The sequel serial *Flash Gordon's Trip to Mars* was also re-edited into a 68-minute feature entitled *Rocket Ship*. The *Flash Gordon's Trip to Mars* serial was released in the early spring of 1938, and when Orson Welles' famous *War of the Worlds* radio broadcast caused a national sensation on Halloween of that year, Universal hastily gave *Rocket Ship* the new title *Mars Attacks the World*, rushing the feature into theaters by November to exploit the publicity generated by Welles' broadcast. The title *Rocket Ship* was then transferred to the *Flash Gordon* featurization, resulting in a lot of confusion through the years, since publicity materials from *Rocket Ship* use photos from *Flash Gordon's Trip to Mars*. Even the American Film Institute Catalog is understandably confused on the subject, relying on Universal's legal files, which were apparently never corrected to reflect the *Rocket*

Ship title change. Both *Rocket Ship* and *Mars Attacks the World* were later distributed by Sherman S. Krellberg's Filmcraft company, playing continuously as a re-release double bill in the 1940s.

All three *Flash Gordon* serials were released to television in the 1950s, distributed by Motion Pictures for Television. These prints were retitled, presumably for legal reasons pertaining to the original newspaper strip copyright, and were called *Space Soldiers* (originally *Flash Gordon*), *Space Soldiers' Trip to Mars* (originally *Flash Gordon's Trip to Mars*) and *Space Soldiers Conquer the Universe* (originally *Flash Gordon Conquers the Universe*). Aside from these title changes, the serials were otherwise unaltered. In the late 1960s, ABC Films, Inc., picked up television distribution rights to all three *Flash Gordon* serials as well as the *Buck Rogers* (q.v.) serial, replacing the main and end title cards, and adding voice-over narration to the printed recap titles on each chapter spoken by announcer Jack Narz. New feature versions, running longer than the original theatrical featurizations, were also prepared, with two features edited from *Flash Gordon Conquers the Universe* (which had never spawned a theatrical feature) covering virtually the entire serial.

Until recently, the home video release of the *Flash Gordon* serials have been dominated by a variety of inferior prints and choppy feature versions. Even versions with altered music and sound effects have been offered, although these bogus "revised" editions have been withdrawn. All three serials, though, have been shown intact on the AMC cable television network and have recently been issued on laserdisc in a boxed set from Hearst Entertainment.

Video availability: NPS.

Undersea Kingdom

(Republic, 1936)

Producer: Nat Levine. Directors: B. Reeves Eason, Joseph Kane. Supervisor: Barney Sarecky. Original story: Tracy Knight, John Rathmell. Screenplay: John Rathmell, Maurice Geraghty, Oliver Drake. Photography: William Nobles, Edgar Lyons. Special effects: Ellis Thackery, Howard Lydecker, Theodore Lydecker. Supervising film editor: Joseph H. Lewis. Film editors: Dick Fantl, Helene Turner. Music supervision: Harry Grey. Music score: Arthur Kay, Jacques Aubran. Sound: Terry Kellum. RCA Sound System. Feature version: *Sharad of Atlantis* (100 minutes), for television distribution.

Cast

Ray (Crash) Corrigan (Crash Corrigan), Lois Wilde (Diana Compton), Monte Blue (Unga Khan), William Farnum (Sharad), Boothe Howard (Ditmar) Raymond Hatton (Gasspom), C. Montague Shaw (Prof. Norton), Lee Van Atta (Billy), Smiley Burnette (Briny), Frankie Marvin (Salty), Lon Chaney, Jr. (Hakur), Lane Chandler (Darius), Jack Mulhall (Andrews), John Bradford (Joe), Malcolm McGregor (Zogg), Ralph Holmes (Martos), John Merton (Moloch), Ernie Smith (Gourck), Lloyd Whitlock (Clinton), Everett Gibbons (Antony), Kenneth Lawton (Doctor), Bill Yrigoyen. Eddie Parker. George DeNormand. Alan Curtis. Tom Steele. Wes Warner. Don Rowan. Rube Schaeffer. David Horsley. Jack Ingram. Tracy Lane. Millard McGowan. William Stahl. Al Seymour.

Chapter Titles

(1) *Beneath the Ocean Floor.* (2) *The Undersea City.* (3) *Arena of Death.* (4) *Revenge of the Volkites.* (5) *Prisoners of Atlantis.* (6) *The Juggernaut Strikes.* (7) *The Submarine Trap.* (8) *Into the Metal Tower.* (9) *Death in the Air.* (10) *Atlantis Destroyed.* (11) *Flaming Death.* (12) *Ascent to the Upper World.*

Story

Newspaper reporter Diana Compton and Navy lieutenant Crash Corrigan learn from Prof. Norton that a series of destructive earthquakes originate from the submerged kingdom of Atlantis on the ocean floor. Boarding his futuristic rocket submarine, Prof. Norton journeys beneath the sea to Atlantis with Diana, Crash, Norton's young son Billy and three sailors, Joe, Salty and Briny. Joe, panicking as the rocket sub dives far below the waves, attempts to scuttle the expedition, but Crash prevents this disaster.

Ten thousand feet below the ocean's surface, the explorers emerge in lost Atlantis, which is protected from the waters above by a huge dome that encloses the fabled land. They discover that Atlantis is in a state of perpetual civil war as two political factions (one ruled by relatively benevolent monarch Sharad, the other controlled by the cruel tyrant Unga Khan) battle for supremacy. When the explorers are accosted by Unga Khan's men, Joe panics and is killed by Volkite robots using ray guns. Crash and Billy manage to escape, but Diana and Prof. Norton are captured and taken before Unga Khan. In his scientifically advanced headquarters, located in a metal tower, Unga Khan reveals that he plans to raise the tower above the waves using rocket engines for propulsion, and then conquer the surface world. The ruthless tyrant mesmerizes Prof. Norton, dominating his mind and forcing him to work toward this end.

Meanwhile, Crash has been taken prisoner by Sharad's forces. Sharad, believing that Crash is a Khan agent, sentences him to death in the combat arena. Crash emerges victorious, but refuses to kill his opponent. When Sharad is kidnapped by two of Khan's men who speed away with him in a chariot, Crash pursues and overtakes them, rescuing the monarch. A grateful Sharad rewards Crash by making him commander of the army.

Prof. Norton, his mind under Khan's control, continues to assist the tyrant in constructing rocket motors that will propel Khan's tower to the ocean's surface. After several narrow escapes in their struggle against Unga Khan, Crash enters the tower headquarters and manages to rescue his friends and restore

Norton's memory. But Norton has completed his work on the rocket engines; Khan ignites the engines, lifting the tower through the protective dome covering Atlantis. The sea rushes in, drowning the remaining inhabitants, but Crash's friends escape in the rocket sub, following the tower to the surface.

Remaining in the tower, Crash broadcasts a warning to the United States Navy that the tower is rising to the surface and poses a threat to humanity. Crash then escapes to the rocket sub with Prof. Norton, rejoining Diana, Billy and his other friends just before a U.S. Navy battleship blasts Unga Khan and his tower into oblivion.

Comments

Aware that Universal had started filming on their first *Flash Gordon* (q.v.) serial, Republic Pictures noted the popularity of the newspaper comic strip and, sensing a hit in the making, rushed *Undersea Kingdom* into production, using similar material of their own creation. Filmed at the same time as *Flash Gordon*, *Undersea Kingdom* was completed in only 25 days at a cost of $99,000 for the entire serial, less than a third of the $350,000 *Flash Gordon* budget. *Undersea Kingdom* compares favorably to its more expensive competitor, and was released the month after *Flash Gordon*. *Undersea Kingdom* is well directed by action specialist B. Reeves "Breezy" Eason and Joseph Kane. (The siege of an Atlantean city in Chapter 4 is handled with characteristic economy. A small group of bit players is expanded into a surging mob through meticulous camera angles and precise editing. The same sequence, printed dark to

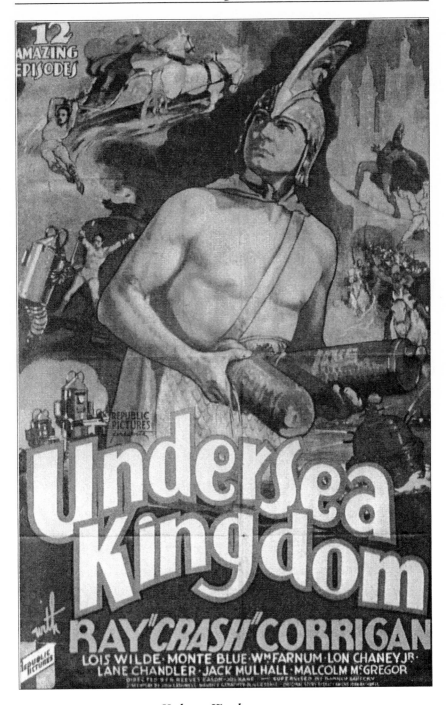

Undersea Kingdom poster.

Undersea Kingdom poster.

Undersea Kingdom poster.

Undersea Kingdom—Top: C. Montague Shaw, Ray "Crash" Corrigan, Lon Chaney, Jr. *Bottom:* Ray "Crash" Corrigan, C. Montague Shaw.

represent a night scene, is later re-used in Chapter 10.)

Undersea Kingdom is a well-calculated attempt to duplicate the basic elements of *Flash Gordon*, but despite its crass origins it succeeds on a creative and technical level. The basic plot is almost as colorful as that of *Flash Gordon*, and the miniature work is actually superior to the special effects in Universal's serial. But *Undersea Kingdom* falls short in its casting: Ray "Crash" Corrigan, a B-Western cowboy who also played gorillas in various features and serials, was a sincere if limited actor with a likable personality, and does well as the heroic lead, but he fails to make the enduring impression that Buster Crabbe did in *Flash Gordon*. Corrigan's contract with Republic allowed him to work as a gorilla in other studios' films provided he appeared unbilled; ironically, he played the ape-like "orangopoid" in *Flash Gordon*. Corrigan died in 1976 at age 72. The rest of the *Undersea Kingdom* cast is competent but generally unimpressive. Monte Blue's villainous Unga Khan, although a threatening figure, is an Oriental despot in the Charles Middleton mold, and a blatant rip-off of Emperor Ming. Another noteworthy cast member is Lon Chaney, Jr., then at the beginning of his film career and cast as one of Unga Khan's henchmen. At this point, Chaney, Jr., was still a few years away from his breakthrough role as Lenny in the Hal Roach production of John Steinbeck's novel *Of Mice and Men*. Chaney, Jr., is included here as a muscular counterpart to the athletic Corrigan, and makes a definite impression, although there is little hint of the talent he would exhibit in *Of Mice and Men*.

Like many Republic serials, *Undersea Kingdom* suffers from a dearth of imagination and atmosphere, despite the fantastic subject matter. The submerged kingdom of Atlantis, the various science fiction gadgets and paraphernalia, even Unga Khan's lumbering "Volkite" robots, are all presented in a straightforward, pedestrian manner that tends to weaken the film. A little more of *Flash Gordon*'s energy and poetry would have benefited *Undersea Kingdom*; much of the effectiveness that individual scenes do have can be attributed to the music score arranged by Jacques Aubran, featuring compositions by Arthur Kay, Leon Rosebrook, Meredith Willson, Rex Bassett, Charles Dunworth and Joseph Carl Breil. This powerful music supplies much of the emotional quality that the technically precise but sometimes insensitive direction fails to provide.

The menacing Volkite robots seen in *Undersea Kingdom* are memorable creations and were a great improvement over the ludicrous automatons seen the previous year in Mascot's *The Phantom Empire* (q.v.). The basic design was later stripped down, reduced in size and simplified, and the Republic robot became a familiar and welcome prop in later cliffhangers filmed by the studio.

Video availability: Republic Home Video.

Dick Tracy

(Republic, 1937)

Producer: Nat Levine. Associate producer: J. Laurence Wickland. Directors: Ray Taylor, Alan James. Screenplay: Barry Shipman, Winston Miller. Original story: Morgan Cox, George Morgan. Photography: William Nobles, Edgar Lyons. Supervising editor: Murray Seldeen. Film editors: Helene Turner, Edward Todd, Bill Witney. Sound: Terry Kellum RCA Sound. Music supervision: Harry Grey. Original music: Alberto Columbo. Special effects: Howard Lydecker. Feature version: *Dick Tracy*, released to home video.

Cast: Ralph Byrd (Dick Tracy), Kay Hughes (Gwen Andrews), Smiley Burnette (Mike McGurk), Lee Van Atta (Junior), John Piccori (Moloch), Carleton Young (Gordon Tracy, after operation), Fred Hamilton (Steve Lockwood), Francis X. Bushman (Clive Anderson), John Dilson (Ellery Brewster), Richard Beach (Gordon Tracy, before operation), Wedgewood Nowell (H.T. Clayton), Theodore Lorch (Paterno), Edwin Stanley (Odette), Harrison Greene (Cloggerstein/Durston), Herbert Weber (Martino), Buddy Roosevelt (Burke/Whitney/henchman), George DeNormand (Flynn/Max/Destino), Byron K. Foulger (Korvitch), Ed Platt (Oscar), Lou Fulton (Elmer), Milburn Moranti (Death Valley Johnny), Bruce Mitchell (Brandon), Sam Flint (Brock), John Holland (Carter), Monte Montague (Clancy), Forbes Murray (Coulter), Kit Guard (Farley), Edward Le Saint (Governor), I. Stanford Jolley (Intern), Harry Strang (Moffett), Al Ferguson (Henderson), Brooks Benedict (pilot), Roy Barcroft (henchman), Burr Caruth (Wickland), Walter Long (Whitney), Loren Raker (Tony), Wilfred Lucas (Vance), Alice Fleming (teacher), Jack Ingram, Donald Kerr, Charley Phillips (reporters), Andre Cheron (Renee), Roscoe Gerall (watchman), Bob Reeves (officer), Kernan Cripps (announcer), Harry Hall (Pete), Louis Morrell (Potter), Ann Ainslie (Betty Clayton), Mary Kelly (Georgetta), Hal Price (Crane), Al Taylor (Costain), Henry Sylvester (commander), Loren Riebe (Peters/henchman/riveter), Leander de Cordova (Stevens/dock official), John Ward (Fox), Wally West (Kraft/Harry), Jane Keckley (Mrs. Henkin), John Bradford (Joe), William Humphrey (James), Jack Cheatham (Morris), Jack Gardner (Mills), John Butler (Noble), Jack Stewart (cop), Eva Mackenzie (teacher), John Mills, Harold De Garro. Edgar Allan. Buddy Williams, Philip Mason. Henry Guttman.

Opposite: Dick Tracy poster.

Dick Tracy— Ralph Byrd.

Chapter Titles

(1) *The Spider Strikes.* (2) *The Bridge of Terror.* (3) *The Fur Pirates.* (4) *Death Rides the Sky.* (5) *Brother Against Brother.* (6) *Dangerous Waters.* (7) *The Ghost Town Mystery.* (8) *Battle in the Clouds.* (9) *The Stratosphere Adventure.* (10) *The Gold Ship.* (11) *Harbor Pursuits.* (12) *The Trail of the Spider.* (13) *The Fire Trap.* (14) *The Devil in White.* (15) *Brothers United.*

Story

A master criminal known only as the Lame One meets with five of his underlings aboard a speeding passenger train. When Korvitch, one of the five men, rebels against the Lame One's authority, he is later found shot to death. Six other criminals are murdered after Korvitch, each victim bearing a mark in the shape of a spider. West Coast FBI agent Dick Tracy investigates the killings, aided by his partners Steve Lockwood and Mike McGurk, along with his secretary Gwen Andrews and Tracy's young ward Junior. Tracy's brother Gordon is kidnapped by The Lame One's "Spider Gang," and Moloch, a crazed doctor and an underling of the Lame One, performs a brain operation that distorts Gordon's features and alters his mind. The transformed Gordon Tracy, now unable to distinguish right from wrong, joins the Spider Gang as a criminal.

The governor of California informs Dick Tracy that the Lame One has threatened to destroy the Bay Bridge unless Martino, a member of the Spider Gang captured by Tracy, is released from jail. Piloting a huge, futuristic aircraft called the Wing toward the Bay Bridge, the Lame One and his gang attempt to wreck the structure by projecting high-frequency sonic vibrations at it. Tracy foils the plan by driving a fleet of trucks onto the bridge and thereby changing the frequency needed to destroy it.

Dick Tracy opposes the Spider Gang

at every turn as they attempt, at various times, to steal millions of dollars worth of furs and sell the formula for a secret element called "nickolanium" to a foreign government. The Lame One then tries to steal gold from an old prospector named Death Valley Johnny, but Tracy prevents the theft after trailing the gang to a ghost town, and later stops the gang from stealing a million dollars worth of gold from a steamship. Tracy eventually tracks the Lame One down, and as they struggle, Tracy discovers that the Lame One's face is actually a mask hiding the features of Odette, a well-known philanthropist. Odette escapes from Tracy, ordering the still-lobotomized Gordon to drive the getaway car. The car veer off the road when Gordon spots Gwen Andrews and Junior in the auto's path and swerves to avoid hitting them, killing both himself and Odette in the crash. Before he dies, Gordon regains his sanity and expresses remorse for his misdeeds.

Comments

The *Dick Tracy* newspaper comic strip, distributed by the *Chicago Tribune-New York Times* syndicate, premiered as a Sunday color page on October 4, 1931, with the debut of the daily strip following on November 12, 1931. For over 30 years afterward, the strip was written and drawn, with various assistants, by creator Chester Gould. Over the decades, Tracy has proven to be a merchandising gold mine for his creator and distributor, inspiring myriad toys, comic books, movies and TV shows, including four Republic serials (more serials than any other comic book character), a series of 1940s B-movie features and a recent big-budget film adaptation starring Warren Beatty and Madonna. In the 1960s, the traditionally conservative law-and-order strip veered onto a bizarre science fiction tangent, with Tracy fighting crime on the Moon. Strangely enough, a science fiction angle had been present before in two of Republic's four *Dick Tracy* serials.

The first Republic serial based on the strip, entitled simply *Dick Tracy*, was filmed in 1937 on a 25-day shooting schedule for a total cost of $127,640 with $10,000 of the budget going to the *Chicago Tribune* syndicate for the screen rights to the character. In an offbeat casting decision, Republic had originally planned to sign famed FBI agent Melvin Purvis for the title role, but after negotiations with Purvis fell through, bit player Ralph Byrd was cast as Tracy and placed under contract for $150 per week. Byrd had a narrow acting range, but he brought a great deal of sincerity and conviction to the role, and continued on as Tracy in three more serials, two 1940s B-features and an early 1950s TV series filmed just before his death in 1952.

The first *Dick Tracy* serial, made before Republic had acquired its trademarked, fast-paced gloss, was producer Nat Levine's final serial, and seems very atypical today in comparison to Republic's other serials, including the three subsequent Tracys. Nevertheless, *Dick Tracy* has a weighty mood and atmosphere that the slicker follow-ups lacked; a great deal of its effectiveness is due to the powerful musical score, containing original compositions by Alberto Columbo, augmented with previously published music by Karl Hajos, Arthur Kay, Hugo Reisenfeld, William Frederick Peters and Jean Beghon.

The general plot of *Dick Tracy*, with

its masked super-scientific antagonist, proved to be influential, and prefigures the super-villains of the much later James Bond features. The science fiction angle is introduced via "The Wing," an immense, sleekly designed futuristic aircraft that is amazingly similar to contemporary Stealth Bomber planes designed by the United States Air Force. The miniature work on the Wing is very impressive. Republic's special effects department, under the supervision of Howard and Theodore Lydecker, was among the industry's best, with the studio's finely crafted miniatures shot at low angles, in sunlight, for maximum believability. The Lydeckers' inspiration for the Wing was possibly a similar futuristic aircraft seen in the British feature *Things to Come*, based on an H.G.

Wells novel and released the year before *Dick Tracy*.

Despite the flamboyant plot concocted for *Dick Tracy*, Republic attempted to make the proceedings more "realistic" by eliminating the familiar "cartoonish" aspects of Chester Gould's strip, such as character names like Tess Trueheart. Republic would generally follow this restrained approach in their next three Tracy serials, *Dick Tracy Returns* (1938), *Dick Tracy's G-Men* 1939) and *Dick Tracy vs. Crime, Inc.* 1941). *Dick Tracy Returns* and *Dick Tracy's G-Men* would follow more traditional criminal-on-the-loose plotlines, with the final entry, *Dick Tracy vs. Crime, Inc.* (q.v.) once again injecting science fiction elements into the storyline.

Video availability: VCI.

Flash Gordon's Trip to Mars

(Universal, 1938)

Associate producer: Barney Sarecky. Directors: Ford Beebe, Robert F. Hill. Screenplay: Wyndham Gittens, Norman S. Hall, Ray Trampe, Herbert Dalmus. Photography: Jerome Ashe, A.S.C. Art director: Ralph DeLacy. Supervising film editor: Saul A. Good-kind. Film editors: Saul A. Goodkind, Alvin Todd, Louis Sackin, Joe Gluck. Electrical properties: Kenneth Strickfaden. Mechanical effects: Eddie Keys. Dialogue director: Sara C. Haney. Sound: Western Electric. Feature versions: *Mars Attacks the World* (68

*Opposite: Dick Tracy—*Howard and Theodore Lydecker, Republic's special effects experts, with a miniature of the Flying Wing.

minutes), released for theatrical distribution in 1938, and *The Deadly Ray from Mars* (99 minutes), released for television distribution.

Cast: Larry [Buster] Crabbe (Flash Gordon), Jean Rogers (Dale Arden), Charles Middleton (Ming the Merciless), Beatrice Roberts (Azura, Queen of Magic), Frank Shannon (Dr. Zarkov), Donald Kerr ("Happy" Hapgood), Richard Alexander (Prince Barin), C. Montague Shaw (Clay King), Wheeler Oakman (Tarnak), Kane Richmond (stratosled captain), Kenneth Duncan (airdrome captain), Warner Richmond (Zandar), Jack Mulhall (flight commander), Lane Chandler (soldier), Anthony Warde (Mighty Toran), Ben Lewis (pilot), Stanley Price. Earl Douglas, Charles "Bud" Wolfe. Edwin Stanley. Lou Merrill. James C. Eagels. Hooper Atchley. James G. Blaine. Wheaton Chambers. Ray Turner. Edwin Parker. Jerry Frank. Herb Holcombe. Reed Howes. Jerry Gardner. Tom Steele.

Chapter Titles

(1) *New Worlds to Conquer.* (2) *The Living Dead.* (3) *Queen of Magic.* (4) *Ancient Enemies.* (5) *The Boomerang.* (6) *Tree Men of Mars.* (7) *The Prisoner of Mongo.* (8) *The Black Sapphire of Kalu.* (9) *Symbol of Death.* (10) *Incense of Forgetfulness.* (11) *Human Bait.* (12) *Ming the Merciless.* (13) *The Miracle of Magic.* (14) *A Beast at Bay.* (15) *An Eye for an Eye.*

Story

Returning to Earth from their previous adventures on the planet Mongo,

Flash Gordon, Dale Arden and Dr. Zarkov learn that a series of global weather disasters are being caused by a powerful beam of light aimed at the Earth from a "nitron lamp" in outer space. Analyzing photographic images of the beam, Zarkov determines that it emanates from the planet Mongo, and immediately journeys there in his rocketship with Flash and Dale. En route, they discover that a bumbling but persistent newspaper reporter, "Happy" Hapgood, has stowed away in their ship, and they are forced to take him along.

As the rocketship approaches Mongo, Zarkov discovers that his original calculations had been in error and that the destructive beam of light is really being projected from Mars. They change course, and Zarkov's rocketship, disabled by the Martian ray, crashes in a barren valley on the planet. The Earth people soon learn that Ming the Merciless is still alive and on Mars, where he has established an alliance with Azura, Queen of Magic, who has the ability to appear and disappear at will and cast spells on her enemies.

Fleeing approaching Martian soldiers under the command of Ming and Azura, the Earth people leave their wrecked ship and hide in a nearby cave, where they are overpowered by the Clay People, a strange tribe of hideous, gnome-like outcasts who dwell in the subterranean caverns and who have the ability to physically vanish into the solid cave walls. The Clay King tells the Earth people that his race has been cursed by Queen Azura, who draws her power from a magic white sapphire in her

Opposite: Flash Gordon's Trip to Mars— C. Montague Shaw, Buster Crabbe, Frank Shannon, Jean Rogers, Donald Kerr.

Flash Gordon's Trip to Mars — Facing: Donald Kerr, Buster Crabbe, Frank Shannon, Jean Rogers. Above: Richard Alexander, Jean Rogers, Frank Shannon, Donald Kerr, Beatrice Roberts and assorted clay men.

Flash Gordon's Trip to Mars— **Charles Middleton.**

possession, and that when this mystic jewel is destroyed, along with a black sapphire guarded by the forest-dwelling tree people, Azura's curse will be lifted and the Clay People returned to normalcy. With Dale and "Happy" held by the Clay People in order to guarantee Flash's cooperation, Flash and Zarkov are dispatched to recover the magic sapphires; they manage to acquire the black sapphire after numerous encounters with the forest people and Martian soldiers directed by Ming. Discovering that their old friend from Mongo, Prince Barin, is also on Mars, the Earth people team up with him in their struggle against Ming and Azura.

Ming double-crosses Azura and arranges to have her killed in a Martian bombing raid directed at the Clay People; Azura, in atonement for her misdeeds, gives the precious white sapphire to Flash before she dies. The jewel is destroyed in an electrical chamber along with the black sapphire previously acquired by the Earthmen; the process transforms the Clay People, restoring their normal bodies.

When Ming contrives to have himself proclaimed monarch of Mars, Flash confronts the assembled Martian nobles and informs them of Ming's complicity in Azura's death. His secret revealed, Ming retreats to his laboratory and intensifies his assault on the Earth with the nitron lamp. But the lamp is

Flash Gordon's Trip to Mars poster.

destroyed when Prince Barin drops a well-aimed bomb from a stratosled airship.

Tarnak, Ming's aide, finally turns on his master and forces him into a disintegration chamber, switches on the powerful ray and destroys the maniacal tyrant. With the Earth saved from destruction and their mission accomplished, Flash, Dale, Zarkov and "Happy" return home, leaving their friend Barin to rule the forest people on Mars.

Comments

The sequel to *Flash Gordon* (q.v.), *Flash Gordon's Trip to Mars* was filmed at a cost of $175,000, half the first serial's budget, but it was still an expensive production by serial standards. In many ways *Flash Gordon's Trip to Mars* is even more entertaining than its predecessor, introducing the eerie Clay People, but the sequel is marred by choppiness, lacking the overall narrative smoothness of the original. This is compensated for to a degree by its faster editorial pace.

The cast, with the principals from the first serial reprising their roles, is in good form. Charles Middleton, whose flamboyant portrayal of Ming contributed so much to *Flash Gordon*, is practically reduced to a supporting character in *Flash Gordon's Trip to Mars* in deference to the distaff villainy of Beatrice Roberts as the supernatural Azura, Queen of Magic. Roberts, although a less exotic type than one would expect in the role, is very good, appearing and disappearing in a puff of smoke (much like Barbara Eden in *I Dream of Jeannie*) and transforming her victims into Clay People with imperious gestures. Although his screen time is lessened, Middleton

(here referred to as "Ming the Merciless") makes a strong impression, and his makeup, accented by a dark skullcap, is even more satanic than in the first serial. When Ming goes totally insane in the last chapter like a deranged Mephistopheles, it's an over-the-top performance that has to be seen to be believed. The inclusion of comic relief Donald Kerr as bumbling reporter "Happy" Hapgood may be an irritation to some, but Kerr is undeniably amusing in many scenes, and was popular with young viewers when the serial was originally released.

Flash Gordon's Trip to Mars contains many of the characters and gimmicks that most filmgoers remember from the *Flash Gordon* serials. The Clay People (accompanied by an eerie musical theme lifted from *Bride of Frankenstein*) ooze in and out of cavern walls at will, a simple but powerful effect accomplished by a slow dissolve photographed in the camera. A "light bridge" in Queen Azura's Martian city is also memorable, with the characters seemingly walking high above the city across a beam of light superimposed on the scene. These are rudimentary special effects, but they are used in an inventive, playful manner that is entertaining. Most of the other special effects, including the wobbly rocketship and Martian "stratosled" miniatures, are even cheaper than the similar shots in the first serial, although a few matte and rear projection shots (absent from *Flash Gordon*) are used in *Flash Gordon's Trip to Mars*. Several alien creatures with large, bald heads, similar to the extra-terrestrials in recent science fiction movies, are in a couple of scenes but, strangely, they are not exploited and are used only as background figures. Infra-red photography, which alters the contrast of the costumes and makeup, is also used in some scenes to accentuate the alien location, but the process is used haphazardly and inconsistently.

A notable attempt is made to preserve storyline continuity from *Flash Gordon* to the sequel, with Flash, Dale and Dr. Zarkov returning to Earth in Chapter 1 dressed in the same costumes they wore in the last chapter of *Flash Gordon*. (The formerly blonde Jean Rogers is now a brunette, and the interior of Zarkov's rocketship has been redesigned.) Incongruously, *Flash Gordon's Trip to Mars* is both slick in presentation and editorially choppy, with frequent dependence on stock footage flashbacks to events in the original serial. Perhaps because of *Flash Gordon's Trip to Mars'* technical and narrative shortcomings, Universal employed the gimmick of enhancing the original release prints, tinting them a vibrant green by striking them on color film stock. Studio executives apparently liked the effect, using it again for the national double-bill re-release of *Dracula* and *Frankenstein* later the same year.

The original theatrical feature version of *Flash Gordon's Trip to Mars, Mars Attacks the World*, is worth noting since it contains upgraded special effects footage not used in the serial, including a couple of impressive rear projection shots depicting Zarkov's rocketship flying over a city as it blasts off from Earth. The film editors working on *Mars Attacks the World* also attempted to improve other *Flash Gordon's Trip to Mars* special effects footage by "cutting around" some of the cruder movements of the flying rocketship miniatures.

The Fighting Devil Dogs

(Republic, 1938)

Associate producer: Robert Beche. Directors: William Witney, John English. Screenplay: Barry Shipman, Franklyn Adreon, Ronald Davison, Sol Shor. Photography: William Nobles. Production manager: Al Wilson. Unit manager: Mack D'Agnostino. Film editors: Helene Turner, Edward Todd. Musical direction: Alberto Columbo. Sound: RCA. Feature version: *The Tor-* *pedo of Doom* (100 minutes), for television distribution.

Cast: Lee Powell (Lt. Tom Grayson), Herman Brix (Lt. Frank Corby), Eleanor Stewart (Janet), Montagu Love (Gen. White), Hugh Sothern (Warfield), Sam Flint (Col. Grayson), Perry Ivins (Crenshaw), Forrest Taylor (Benson), John Picorri (Gould), Carleton Young (Johnson), John Davidson (Lin

Wing), Henry Otho (Sam Hedges), Reed Howes (Parker), Tom London (Wilson), Edmund Cobb (Ellis), Alan Gregg (Macro), Allan Mathews (Todd).

Chapter Titles

(1) *The Lightning Strikes.* (2) *The Mill of Disaster.* (3) *The Silenced Witness.* (4) *Cargo of Mystery.* (5) *Undersea Bandits.* (6) *The Torpedo of Doom.* (7) *The Phantom Killer.* (8) *Tides of Trickery.* (9) *Attack from the Skies.* (10) *In the Camp of the Enemy.* (11) *The Baited Trap.* (12) *Killer at Bay.*

Story

Nineteen-thirty-eight, during the hostilities between China and Japan: In Linchuria near Shanghai, United States Marine lieutenants Tom Grayson and Frank Corby lead their platoon to a remote fort, only to discover that the occupants have all been killed by some unknown means — without any sign of violence. While they investigate the eerie mystery, an electrical torpedo hurtles through the air and strikes the fort, killing all of the men except Grayson and Corby, who have wandered outside the compound.

Lt. Grayson is summoned back to America to answer charges as an official inquiry is formed to investigate the tragedy; it is Grayson's contention that the dead men were victims of an advanced weapon, a sort of artificial electrical thunderbolt guided by remote control. Eventually, it is revealed that a masked super-criminal known as the Lightning is behind the mass murder, and Grayson and Corby are assigned to the case. A group of scientists (including Tom Grayson's father Col. Grayson; Crenshaw, an electrical inventor; and Warfield, a respected industrialist) unite

in a determined effort to apprehend the Lightning, but before they can even begin, their laboratory is destroyed and Col. Grayson is killed.

After examining a fragment of the torpedo that killed Col. Grayson, Grayson and Corby determine that the shell casing was molded from a rare alloy manufactured by the Atlas Steel Company. Grayson and Corby leave for the plant in an effort to trace the Lightning through the shell casing. But the Lightning, aware of this, radios ahead and instructs his gang at the plant to destroy the torpedo casings on hand. As Grayson and Corby drive to the Atlas plant, they are attacked by more of the Lightning's henchmen, who try to kill them with hand grenades. The thugs are blown up by their own bombs.

Grayson and Corby arrive at the Atlas Steel Company, but are attacked by the Lightning's men in Warehouse #5. After a terrific fight, the Lightning's men nearly kill Corby with an acetylene torch, but Grayson saves him. As the fight continues, the discarded acetylene torch burns through a rope suspending a heavy steel construction beam, and the beam falls, nearly killing Grayson, who saves himself by rolling aside just in time. The Lightning's henchmen escape, but Grayson and Corby recover one of the torpedo casings and take it to Warfield's laboratory for analysis.

The Lightning learns of this and orders his men to stop Grayson and Corby as the Marines drive back to Warfield's lab with the torpedo casing. Grayson and Corby are attacked by the Lightning's men when the hoods stage a phony roadside accident, but they emerge victorious. Back at Warfield's, one of the Lightning's captured henchmen, Jacobs, is questioned under the

Fighting Devil Dogs poster.

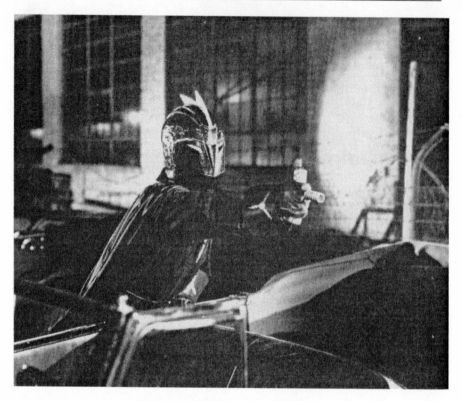

Fighting Devil Dogs— The Lightning.

influence of a truth serum, "Scopola-mine," but before Jacobs can reveal any-thing, the lights in the room go out and Jacobs is murdered with a projected electrical charge activated by the Light-ning.

Grayson receives a phone call from Mr. Brown, owner of the Atlas Steel Company, informing him that the pur-chase records in his office files may con-tain information leading to the person who ordered the torpedo casings. Gray-son leaves by motorcycle to pick up the forms, but the Lightning, aware of this, sends his men to stop Grayson. The Lightning's men arrive at the steel plant ahead of Grayson and murder Brown, stealing the purchase records. Arriving

just in time to see the Lightning's hoods leave in their car, Grayson finds Brown dead and immediately chases the killers on his motorcycle.

When the Lightning's gang shoots at Grayson during the high-speed chase, he drops back and detours along a side road, jumping his bike across a chasm and pulling ahead of the gang. Aban-doning his motorcycle, Grayson makes a daring leap off a nearby cliff and lands in the car driven by the Light-ning's gang. During the intense fight that follows, the hood driving the car is shot by accident, and the car spins out of control, smashing through a fence and hurtling off the road over a cliff. Grayson grabs the purchase records and jumps free of the car at the last moment.

Grayson and Corby discover through the purchase records that the torpedo casings had been shipped aboard the schooner *Aurora* to Gehorda Island. In an effort to track down the Lightning through the torpedo casings, Grayson and Corby leave for the island by seaplane. The Lightning, knowing this, boards his giant superplane the Flying Wing with his gang and heads for Gehorda, planning to stop Grayson and Corby. Grayson and Corby arrive at Gehorda first and find the *Aurora* docked there. While the *Aurora*'s crew watches a colorful native ceremony on the island, Grayson and Corby board the deserted ship to investigate.

Arriving on Gehorda in the Flying Wing, the Lightning and his men disembark and go to a hidden cave where a cache of the torpedo casings is stored. Through subordinates, the Lightning orders the *Aurora*'s crewmen to return to the ship and burn it, thus obliterating all evidence of the torpedo casings. The Lightning then boards a submarine waiting in the cave grotto, intending to pick up the crewmen after they have set the *Aurora* afire.

Meanwhile, Grayson and Corby have boarded the *Aurora* and, after overpowering a lone crewman on guard duty, discover one of the Lightning's torpedoes with a gyroscopic guidance device attached. As they examine the torpedo, the *Aurora*'s crewmen arrive and douse the ship with gasoline. When they discover Grayson and Corby aboard, a violent fight erupts and the ship bursts into flame. A burning mast collapses and falls to the deck, nearly killing Grayson, who saves himself by leaping off the burning ship with Corby. The Lightning's

submarine is waiting nearby; the *Aurora*'s crewmen, having escaped the fire in a lifeboat, board the sub. Leaving the sub, the Lightning flies back to the mainland in the Flying Wing.

Grayson and Corby, remaining on Gehorda, decide to use diving gear to search for the torpedo gyroscope still aboard the sunken *Aurora*. The Lightning, having learned of the salvage attempt, orders his submarine crew to stop Grayson and Corby. The Lightning's henchmen ambush Grayson and Corby in a dock warehouse, but are beaten off by the hard-fighting marines. Obtaining a diving suit, Grayson investigates the sunken *Aurora* while Corby operates an air pump in a boat above. The Lightning's submarine arrives during the salvage attempt and, exiting through a torpedo tube, one of the Lightning's henchmen attacks the submerged Grayson, cutting his airhose with a knife.

Grayson begins to suffocate as Corby, in a rescue attempt, dives off the boat. As he swims, Corby is attacked by a shark just as his boat is obliterated by gunfire from the Lightning's sub. Corby manages to kill the shark and swims to the island, while Grayson, in a last desperate effort, walks along the ocean bottom to shore, sustained by the air remaining in his diving suit. Grayson has also recovered the gyroscope they were seeking.

Grayson and Corby plan to ship the gyroscope to Warfield's lab via the Trans-Pacific Dirigible. As Grayson and Corby fly to meet the dirigible in their seaplane, two of the Lightning's henchmen attack the Marines, but fail to stop them. One of the men, Ellis, is captured after the other man falls out of the plane to his death. Mooring their seaplane to

Fighting Devil Dogs— Herman Brix, Lee Powell.

the dirigible, Grayson and Corby board with the prisoner. Learning the Lightning's radio frequency from Ellis, they are able to determine the exact position of the Flying Wing; returning to their seaplane, they depart to join an armada of fighter planes in pursuit of the Lightning's giant aircraft. In revenge, the Lightning fires an aerial torpedo to deflect it and save the dirigible. Grayson and Corby aim their seaplane at the torpedo to deflect it and save the dirigible, bailing out of the seaplane by parachute before the collision. They land in the ocean and are picked up when the dirigible descends and lowers a ladder. Now a captive, Ellis offers to tell what he knows about the Lightning, but he is suddenly electrocuted by the Lightning before he can reveal the madman's true identity.

Warfield learns through a note left at his laboratory that the Lightning has kidnapped his daughter Janet. Through a radio message, the Lightning tells Warfield that Janet will be released only if the captured gyroscope is surrendered. Janet speaks to her father by radio, and manages to blurt out the location of the deserted ship where she is being held. Grayson battles one of the Lightning's henchmen in a desperate attempt to rescue her, but another man escapes with Janet in a speedboat. Grayson pursues them in another boat, but as the chase moves through the harbor and between two docked ships, the huge ships drift together and crush Grayson's boat.

Grayson manages to save himself by diving overboard and swimming clear of the ships underwater. Although the gyroscope has been turned over to the Lightning as demanded, Janet is still a prisoner. Grayson and Corby depart in their seaplane, planning to use a radio to detect electrical disturbances in the atmosphere on Gehorda Island and locate the Lightning's secret headquarters. The submarine base is located, and Grayson battles the Lightning's henchmen in an attempt to save Janet, who is being held prisoner in a cave.

Grayson is overpowered in a fight. The Lightning's men tie him up, light a dynamite fuse to destroy the cave and take Janet with them when they leave in the Flying Wing. Corby arrives with a company of Marines and saves Grayson by extinguishing the fuse. Grayson and Corby return to America, and Janet is eventually rescued from the Lightning's men. Grayson and Corby intensify their efforts to track down the Lightning.

Grayson has long suspected that the Lightning is in reality one of the scientists associated with his late father. Finally, he and Corby succeed in exposing the Lightning as Warfield (who is really Janet's *stepfather*). His secret exposed, the desperate industrialist attempts to escape justice in the Flying Wing, but is blasted out of the air with a powerful death ray invented by Crenshaw.

Comments

Republic's *The Fighting Devil Dogs* presented one of the studio's most effective masked serial villains, the Lightning, obliterating his victims by remote control with electrified flying torpedoes. The science fiction angle is introduced by the Lightning's electrical torpedo gun and his futuristic superplane the Flying Wing, re-used from Republic's *Dick Tracy* (q.v.). The masked, black-clad Lightning looks like an ancestor of Darth Vader as he wields his deadly ray gun, and his deranged, hunchbacked assistant (John Piccori) seems to have wandered over from the set of a Universal horror movie.

Backed by a powerful Alberto Columbo musical score, *The Fighting Devil Dogs* opens with U.S. Marines Herman Brix and Lee Powell rescuing children from bombing raids in China (the two leads are unconvincingly intercut with pre-existing newsreel footage). The scene in which Brix and Powell discover a fort in Linchuria containing dead soldiers — with even the flies inside dead — is uncommonly atmospheric for a Republic serial; the men walk from room to room only to discover numerous corpses seated in chairs and at desks. The exterior of the fort — a well-crafted miniature — is promptly destroyed in a shower of crackling sparks by one of the Lightning's electrical torpedoes. Brix and Powell are then warned by a confederate of the Lightning: "The fiend is behind a monstrous plot to control whole nations! What happened in Linchuria is but a small demonstration of his powers!" Needless to say, the Lightning's disloyal assistant is immediately eliminated as the super-villain appears and fires an electrical ray gun, with the cartoon-animated lightning bolt aimed directly at the cameras.

It doesn't take long for Marine Lee Powell to deduce the Lightning's *modus operandi* in a discussion with his superiors: "It is my belief, sir, that a method has been found to charge an aerial torpedo with an immense amount of electricity, which upon striking at its target is immediately released." A few scenes later, a gold-laden steamship, the S.S. *Rockingham* (another excellent miniature), is destroyed by one of the Lightning's electrical torpedoes. "There's a monster to be tracked down!" Powell declares to respected industrialist Warfield (Hugh Sothern), unaware that the man he is speaking to is secretly the Lightning. "A fiend who can menace the entire world with his diabolical machine!" Powell continues. "Take it easy, Tom," Warfield replies soothingly,

"You'll need *clues.*" It's a rare moment of sophisticated humor in a Republic serial, apparent only when the Lightning is finally unmasked as Warfield.

Powell is very good in *The Fighting Devil Dogs*, and so is Herman Brix, who had played Tarzan in the independently produced 1936 serial *The New Adventures of Tarzan*. Brix was one of the very few serial actors who was able to successfully leave the cliffhangers behind and (under the new name Bruce Bennett) go on to appear in prestigious features, such as *The Treasure of the Sierra Madre* with Humphrey Bogart and *Mildred Pierce* with Joan Crawford. Eleanor Stewart is an attractive leading lady. The flying electrical torpedo sequences are well done, with the approaching bombs heralded by a screaming electronic whine and optically superimposed lightning bolts enhancing exploding miniatures.

One of Republic's best William Witney-John English directorial efforts, *The Fighting Devil Dogs* benefits from glistening photography by William Nobles and from Alberto Columbo's virile musical score. Witney and English were the best directorial team to ever work in serials, but (like all serial directors) even these skilled craftsmen were hampered by tight shooting schedules, and the music was sometimes vital in papering over unavoidable gaps in mood and atmosphere. Columbo, whose scores and arrangements contributed so much to the earlier Republic serials, was an invaluable asset to the studio.

Video availability: Republic Home Video.

Buck Rogers

(Universal, 1939)

Associate producer: Barney A. Sarecky. Directors: Ford Beebe, Saul A. Goodkind. Screenplay: Norman S. Hall, Ray Trampe. Photography: Jerome Ash, A.S.C. Art directors: Jack Otterson, Ralph DeLacy. Film editors: Alvin Todd, Louis Sackin, Joseph Gluck. Sound: Bernard B. Brown. Western Electric Sound. Music: Charles Previn. Feature versions: *Planet Outlaws*, edited for theatrical distribution, and *Destination Saturn* (91 minutes) for television distribution.

Cast: Larry [Buster] Crabbe (Buck Rogers), Constance Moore (Wilma Deering), Jackie Moran (Buddy Wade), Jack Mulhall (Capt. Rankin), Anthony Warde (Killer Kane), Philson Ahn (Prince Tallen), C. Montague Shaw (Dr. Huer), Guy Usher (Aldar), William Gould (Marshall Kragg), Henry Brandon (Capt. Lasca), Wheeler Oakman (Patten), Kenneth Duncan (Lt. Lacy), Carleton Young (Scott), Reed Howes (Roberts), Karl Hackett. Stanley Price. David Sharpe.

Chapter Titles

(1) *Tomorrow's World.* (2) *Tragedy on Saturn.* (3) *The Enemy's Stronghold.* (4) *The Sky Patrol.* (5) *The Phantom Plane.* (6) *The Unknown Command.* (7) *The Primitive Urge.* (8) *Revolt of the Zuggs.* (9) *Bodies Without Minds.* (10) *Broken Barriers.* (11) *A Prince in Bondage.* (12) *War of the Planets.*

Story

A huge dirigible piloted by Buck Rogers and his young assistant Buddy Wade is trapped in a polar ice storm and crashes on a frozen mountain peak in the Arctic. An experimental container of "nirvano gas" leaks after the crash and preserves Buck and Buddy in a state of suspended animation. Discovered and revived 500 years later by soldiers of the future, they learn that the entire world has been conquered by a super-scientific gangster named Killer Kane and his gang of ruthless cohorts. Transported by their rescuers to the Hidden City, concealed by huge stone gates opening into a remote mountain, they meet the brilliant Dr. Huer and his pretty assistant Wilma Deering. Learning that Dr. Huer, Wilma and the other inhabitants of Hidden City are dedicated rebels opposed to Killer Kane's tyranny, Buck and Buddy agree to help them in their war against Kane.

Dr. Huer has invented interplanetary spaceships, de-gravity belts, invisibility rays, disintegrator guns and many other strange and wondrous gadgets in defense of the Hidden City rebels, but more help is needed; Buck, Buddy and Wilma fly to the planet Saturn to enlist Saturnian aid in their struggle. Just as they reach the distant planet, though, they are bombed by one of Kane's pursuing spaceships. Buck, Buddy and Wilma save themselves by escaping to the surface of Saturn with their de-gravity belts.

Kane's men, led by the ruthless Capt. Lasca, follow them. After a desperate fight, Buck and his friends are over-powered by their attackers. Both groups are then captured by Saturnians and taken before the Council of the Wise for questioning. The devious Lasca con-vinces the council members that Killer Kane is a benevolent ruler and that Buck and his friends are troublesome revolu-tionaries. Buck, Buddy and Wilma, see-ing that they are about to be jailed, break free and return to Earth using one of Lasca's spaceships. As they try to pilot the craft through the huge stone gates of the Hidden City, Buck and his friends are nearly killed when the gates suddenly close and crush the ship, but they escape with their de-gravity belts after Buck uses a ray gun to blast a hole in the floor.

A Saturnian, Prince Tallen, arrives on Earth to sign a peace treaty with Killer Kane. Buck and Buddy, learning of this, invade Kane's heavily guarded palace in an attempt to prevent the alliance. Con-fronting Kane, Buck convinces Prince Tallen that Kane is a despot. Using their de-gravity belts, Buck and Buddy exit through a nearby window with Prince Tallen; they float to ground level, where Kane's guards overpower them with a paralyzer ray.

Buddy manages to destroy the para-lyzer ray machine with his disintegrator gun, saving Buck and Prince Tallen. Stealing one of Kane's spaceships, they head back to the Hidden City, but Wilma, piloting a spaceship and un-aware that her friends are in the Kane ship, bombs it and forces it down into the mountainous terrain below. As Buck, Buddy and Prince Tallen try to

reach safety, they are trapped in an explosion caused by a pursuing Killer Kane ship.

Realizing that Buck, Buddy and Prince Tallen are being threatened by Kane's men, Wilma abruptly changes course and drives the Kane soldiers away with her spaceship. She then picks up her friends and they return to the Hid-den City, where Tallen signs the agree-ment officially pledging Saturn's help in the rebels' war against Kane. Unable to communicate this news to Saturn because of radio interference, Buck, Wilma and Prince Tallen journey to Sat-urn in a spaceship to consolidate the treaty. Finding an empty Kane ship when they land, they enter it and try to wreck the controls. Lasca and his sol-diers, hidden nearby, ambush them and inject gas into the ship, knocking them out.

Buck, Wilma and Prince Tallen are re-moved from the gas-filled ship by Lasca's men and taken before the Saturnian Council of the Wise. Lasca's men outfit Tallen with a mind-destroying filament concealed inside his helmet. A puzzled Buck and Wilma hear Tallen denounce them and order their imprisonment, unaware that his will is under the dom-ination of Lasca's men. Grabbing Lasca's ray gun, Buck and Wilma use Tallen as a shield, escaping in a subterranean tunnel car. Attempting to prevent their escape, Lasca throws a lever closing the massive steel tunnel doors, and the speeding car crashes into the barrier.

Buck, Wilma and Tallen survive the crash, and Buck—finally realizing how Tallen has lost his will— removes the controlling filament from Tallen's hel-met. His mind now restored, Tallen rec-ognizes Buck and Wilma as his friends and they all return to the Council of

***Buck Rogers*— Philson Ahn, Buster Crabbe, Jackie Moran.**

the Wise, where they rectify the situation.

Lasca has discovered that an outcast race of hideous Saturnian primitives, the Zuggs, worship a robotized victim of Lasca's as a god, and that the Zuggs are planning a revolt. Using the human robot to control a Zugg mob, Lasca and his men lead an uprising. The enraged Zuggs charge Buck, and he is overwhelmed by the savage mob.

Escaping through a secret door, Buck rallies the Saturnian guards, overpowering Lasca and his human robot as they are inciting the Zuggs to further violence. Removing the mind-controlling filament from the human robot's helmet, Buck restores the man, a former Kane soldier, to normalcy. In gratitude, he tells the Zuggs, who still worship and obey him, to lay down their arms.

Grateful to Buck for his suppression of the Zugg revolt, the Saturnian Council of the Wise agrees to an alliance with the rebels of the Hidden City against Killer Kane. Returning to Earth with Wilma, Buck is attacked by Kane's forces and plunges toward Earth when his spaceship collides head-on with another. Buck manages to regain control of his ship and make a safe landing, but he and Wilma are captured by Kane's men and taken to Kane's palace, where Wilma is imprisoned and Buck is

Buck Rogers— Jackie Moran, Buster Crabbe, Anthony Warde.

outfitted with a mind-control helmet. Dr. Huer and the rulers of the Hidden City believe that Buck and Wilma have been killed, but Buddy, confident they are still alive, risks his life to invade Kane's stronghold and rescue them. Finding Kane's council room empty, Buddy activates the tele-eye viewing device and finds Buck in Kane's dynamo room, where Buck wears a mind-control helmet and has been transformed into a human robot. Just as Buddy leaves the council room, he is shot by a Kane guard and falls out of a window.

Buddy, only stunned by the shot, manages to find Wilma. Freeing Buck from the mind-control helmet, they escape in one of Kane's spaceships and return to the Hidden City, unaware that a Kane spy is hiding in the ship. In the Hidden City, the spy calls Kane's headquarters, reveals the location of the rebel stronghold and opens the city gates from the control room. As Kane's squadron bombs the Hidden City, Buck overpowers the Kane spy and hurriedly closes the City gates, barring entrance to all but the first of Kane's raiders. Buck

Buck Rogers—Stock footage of this scene from the 1930 Fox musical *Just Imagine* was used to represent Killer Kane's super-city.

and Buddy travel to Saturn to rally Saturnian aid in the battle, only to find that Prince Tallen is being held captive by Lasca, who has demanded that the Saturnians capitulate to Kane's domination. Buck urges the Saturnian rulers to refuse. As Kane's spaceships bomb the city, Buck and Buddy try to escape in the underground tunnel car. A Kane bomb caves in the chamber roof, pinning Buck under fallen debris.

Buck frees himself from the rubble

with his disintegrator gun and, with Prince Tallen, Buck and Buddy capture Lasca and his soldiers. With the Saturnians pledging their help in the war against Kane, Buck and Buddy return to Earth, and in a massive air battle, Kane's forces are defeated. As a reward for his courageous efforts, Buck is promoted in rank by his Hidden City superiors. With the peace of the world secure, his thoughts turn to romance with Wilma.

Comments

The *Buck Rogers* newspaper comic strip, distributed by the John F. Dille Syndicate, was written by Philip Nowlan (based on his novel *Armageddon 2419 A.D.*) and drawn by Dick Calkins. The daily newspaper strip premiered on January 1, 1929, and ran until 1967. The color Sunday strip first appeared on March 30, 1930, and ended in 1965. Other artists on the strip included Murphy Anderson, Rick Yager, George Tuska and Russell Keaton. *Buck Rogers* comic books published in the 1930s included a Kellogg's Corn Flakes premium give-away issue, used to promote a *Buck Rogers* radio show, and newspaper strip reprints published by *Famous Funnies* from 1934 through 1955.

Seeking a follow-up to their popular *Flash Gordon* serials, Universal adapted *Buck Rogers* as a chapterplay in 1939. It was one of the most opulent serials ever made; Universal went all-out with the film. In terms of set design, *Buck Rogers* has more physical detail, and looks far more substantial and believable, than any of the three *Flash Gordon* serials. *Buck Rogers* shared the same art director (Ralph DeLacy) with the previous year's *Flash Gordon's Trip to Mars*, and the interior sets are very similar in basic design to those in *Mars*, but are such an improvement that the deficiencies of the *Flash Gordon* sequel are thrown into even sharper relief. Even though many props from the *Flash Gordon* serials reappear here, Universal made a commendable effort to avoid further similarities to the *Flash Gordon* serials wherever possible, designing square-ish, angular spaceships that look nothing like the rocketships in *Flash Gordon*. More (previously unused) stock footage from Fox's *Just Imagine* turns up, with the vast futuristic cityscapes from the earlier film representing Killer Kane's super-city in *Buck Rogers*. Like *Trip to Mars*, *Buck Rogers* features a music score that is mostly borrowed from *Bride of Frankenstein* (but re-orchestrated here). Explanatory recap titles at the head of every chapter slant backwards and scroll off into infinity in a style that was adapted by George Lucas for the opening titles in *Star Wars*.

As Buck, Buster Crabbe (with his natural dark hair) turns in his usual competent performance. His casting draws inevitable comparisons between *Buck Rogers* and *Flash Gordon*. In fact, Mexican posters are in existence proving that, south of the border, *Buck Rogers* was re-titled and marketed as a *Flash Gordon* serial. As Wilma Deering, Constance Moore is a perfect choice, pretty but not overly glamorous, and believable in her role. Jackie Moran, as Buddy Wade, plays the sort of extraneous but popular juvenile sidekick character found in serials and comic books of the period, and C. Montague Shaw is properly benign and authoritative as Dr. Huer.

The one casting flaw in *Buck Rogers* is Anthony Warde's performance as the

Buck Rogers—Jackie Moran, Buster Crabbe, Constance Moore.

ruthless futuristic villain Killer Kane. Previously and subsequently a minor supporting villain in serials, Warde's acting is acceptable, and he does present a threatening figure, but he lacks the power needed to lend total conviction to the role. Henry Brandon, an excellent character actor who played the title role in Republic's 1940 serial *Drums of Fu Manchu*, is cast in a supporting role as Kane's chief henchman Capt. Lasca, and would have been impressive as Kane. The serial would have been improved to a degree if Warde and Brandon had been switched in their roles. One drawback that *Buck Rogers* shares with *Flash Gordon's Tip to Mars* is the

obvious stunt doubling in fight scenes, although this is not as sloppily done in *Buck* as in *Mars*.

Buck Rogers, released as a 12-chapter serial, was originally planned as a 13-chapter production. An extra episode, consisting mainly of re-cap footage from previous chapters, was prepared, and was originally intended to be Chapter 7. The storyline of this 22-minute chapter, of which bootleg 16mm prints have circulated, is as follows:

Dr. Huer (C. Montague Shaw) and Marshall Kragg (William Gould) receive a radio report from Buck Rogers on the planet Saturn, informing them that an alliance with the rulers of Saturn has been confirmed. Dr. Huer and Marshall Kragg then discuss what a godsend Rogers has been to their struggle against Kane. The narrative then repeats Buck's first appearance before the Saturnian Council of the Wise when Lasca turns the Saturnian rulers against Buck and Wilma. Then Lasca and Prince Tallen are shown visiting Killer Kane on Earth as Buck exposes Kane's tyranny to Tallen. Buck, Buddy and Tallen escape, Buddy is injured in the escape, and Tallen is captured by Lasca and robotized, betraying Buck. Tallen is kidnapped by Lasca, and Lasca uses another robotized victim to control the Zuggs. The chapter ends with the Zuggs overthrowing their Saturnian masters, and then continues into Chapter 8.

Except for the framing dialogue between Huer and Kragg, lasting only a couple of minutes, the entire chapter was cobbled together from previously seen footage, and was probably dropped by Universal because it was such an obvious "cheat." Nevertheless, the extra chapter was made available to theaters caring to exhibit it and expand the serial's run by an extra week.

Universal prepared a re-edited feature version of *Buck Rogers* for theatrical release. Entitled *Planet Outlaws*, this feature was later acquired, along with the *Buck Rogers* serial, the *Flash Gordon* serials and several other Universal serials (as well as their feature versions) by New York theater owner and independent producer Sherman S. Krellberg, producer of *The Lost City* (q.v.). Krellberg re-released these films profitably in the late 1940s and early '50s under his Goodwill and Filmcraft distribution logos. Krellberg altered *Planet Outlaws* somewhat from its original form, adding new footage with a narrator. The posters

and pressbook materials for Krellberg's Goodwill version of *Planet Outlaws* indicate that the additional footage was directed by Harry Revier, with the new dialogue written by Helen Leighton. *Planet Outlaws* is rarely seen today. A second, completely different *Buck Rogers* feature version, running 91 minutes and entitled *Destination Saturn*, was re-edited for television distribution in the late 1960s. *Destination Saturn*, is often misleadingly distributed on videocassette as *Planet Outlaws*, and picked up another bogus title in the early 1980s when it was distributed by Magnetic Video as *Buck Rogers Conquers the Universe*. In the late 1960s, the original serial version of *Buck Rogers*, along with the three *Flash Gordon* serials, was released to TV by ABC Films, Inc. The serial was complete, although the re-made main titles read *Buck Rogers vs. the Planet Outlaws*. When the rights to the serial were acquired by Crystal Pictures, *Buck Rogers* received limited play at revival theaters after the release of *Star Wars*. It was again distributed to television, and again the prints were complete, although bearing Filmcraft re-release main titles. It is this print that currently appears on videocassette.

There was a very low-budget TV series, *Buck Rogers in the 25th Century*, broadcast live on ABC in 1950 and 1951, starring Robert Pastene as Buck and Lou Prentis as Wilma Deering. A 1979-1981 NBC-TV series, starring Gil Gerard as Buck and Erin Gray as Wilma, also spawned a 1979 feature film. This was *Buck Rogers* in name only, for both the TV show and the theatrical feature had far more in common with *Star Wars* than the titular source material.

Video availability: VCI.

The Phantom Creeps

(Universal, 1939)

Associate producer: Henry MacRae. Directors: Ford Beebe, Saul A. Goodkind. Screenplay: George Plympton, Basil Dickey, Mildred Barish. Original story: Willis Cooper. Photography: Jerry Ash, A.S.C., William Sickner, A.S.C. Art director: Ralph DeLacy. Film editors: Alvin Todd, Irving Birnbaum, Joseph Gluck. Dialogue director: Lyonel Margolies. Sound: Western Electric. Feature version: *The Phantom Creeps* (79 minutes), released theatrically.

Cast: Bela Lugosi (Dr. Alex Zorka), Robert Kent (Capt. Bob West), Dorothy Arnold (Jean Drew), Edwin Stanley (Dr. Fred Mallory), Regis Toomey (Jim Daly), Jack C. Smith (Monk), Edward Van Sloan (Jarvis), Dora Clement (Mrs. Zorka), Anthony Averill (Rankin), Eddie Acuff ("Mack"), Hugh Huntley. Monte Vandergrift. Frank Mayo. James Farley. Reed Howes. Lee J. Cobb.

Chapter Titles

(1) *The Menacing Power.* (2) *Death Stalks the Highway.* (3) *Crashing Timbers.* (4) *Invisible Terror.* (5) *Thundering Rails.* (6) *The Iron Monster.* (7) *The Menacing Mist.* (8) *Trapped in the Flames.* (9) *Speeding Doom.* (10) *Phantom Footprints.* (11) *The Blast.* (12) *To Destroy the World.*

Story

Dr. Alex Zorka, a mad scientist, conducts bizarre experiments in his secret laboratory, assisted by his henchman Monk, an ex-convict. A devisualizer belt that renders its wearer invisible and a frightening eight-foot-tall robot are among Zorka's inventions, which include small mechanical spiders that induce a state of suspended animation when they explode. The secret of Zorka's scientific power is a weird meteorite fragment that he has recovered from Africa; it contains almost unlimited energy. Capt. Bob West of military intelligence is assigned to investigate Zorka's activities. Concurrently, a group of foreign spies headed by the mysterious Jarvis, operating under the guise of the International School of Languages, is also attempting to learn Zorka's secrets. Matters are complicated further when Jean Drew, a pretty newspaper reporter, also develops an interest in the case.

Dr. Mallory, Zorka's former associate, suspects Zorka of treason. Bob West and his assistant Jim Daly attempt to question Zorka, but he eludes them and fakes his own death in a staged auto crash. Jean Drew stows away in the airplane in which Bob and Jim are taking Zorka's wife to identify her "husband's" body. To prevent exposure of his faked death, the invisible Zorka plants a mechanical spider in the plane and it explodes, causing the plane to crash. Bob West, Jim Daly and Jean Drew survive, but Mrs. Zorka is killed. Dr. Zorka

The Phantom Creeps poster.

The Phantom Creeps exhibitor's pressbook cover.

secretly uses his devisualizer belt to prevent the authorities from discovering his many other scientific inventions.

Bob pursues a fugitive automobile into the hills, believing it is being driven by someone who has learned Zorka's secrets. Jean is with Bob when he finds a strange disc (which is used to attract Zorka's mechanical spiders) planted by the invisible Zorka in his deserted car. Zorka, unseen, knocks Bob unconscious and sends the car hurtling toward the edge of a cliff with West in it. West is thrown clear of the car and saved just in time.

Zorka is desperately trying to guard the priceless meteorite fragment. Dr. Mallory invents a "neometer," an instrument he believes will detect the presence of Zorka's meteorite. Bob and Jim Daly, using Mallory's neometer, capture Zorka's assistant Monk, who is trying to escape with the meteorite. Driving Monk to headquarters for interrogation, Bob attempts to open the heavily insulated case containing the meteorite, but the volatile energy within, suddenly unleashed, causes nearby power lines to explode. The car crashes off the road and Monk escapes. West and Jim survive the accident, retaining possession of the meteorite.

The foreign spy ring captures Jim, Jean and Dr. Mallory, who were in the process of taking Zorka's confiscated meteorite to Mallory's laboratory for analysis. Jean, through a clever ruse, prevents the spies from stealing the meteorite, but she and her companions are taken to the spies' private airfield. Zorka, enraged over the loss of his meteorite, is trailing the others with vengeance in mind. Bob, learning of his friends' capture, follows them to the spies' airfield, and as he enters a hangar

a gun battle erupts and Bob retreats into a waiting plane with Jean. The plane then takes off and nearly crashes before Bob gains control of it and saves them. The spies, however, escape, and are now in possession of Zorka's meteorite.

Dr. Mallory, held prisoner by the spies and forced to experiment with Zorka's meteorite, succeeds in sending a radio message to Bob, who hurries to Mallory's aid. Zorka, still trailing the stolen meteorite, enters Mallory's laboratory while invisible and manages to reclaim the meteorite, escaping with it. Bob rescues Mallory, but is pursued by the spies, who mistakenly believe that West has the meteorite. The chase runs parallel to a railroad; and as the spies close in, Bob swerves across the tracks. He is nearly killed in a collision with the train, but survives the accident, and escapes the pursuing spies. Jean is trapped by the spies in their hideout, but is able to convince them that she wants to help them in their search for Zorka's secrets. Jim, seeing Jean leave the spies' hideout, wrongly suspects her of being involved with them.

Bob and Dr. Mallory discuss the mysterious disappearance of Zorka's meteorite, and conclude the supposedly dead Zorka is still alive. Using the neometer, Bob goes to Zorka's laboratory and investigates. When Zorka, unseen behind a secret panel, discovers Bob in the lab, he unleashes his giant robot, which nearly kills him. Bob is saved when Jean and Jim arrive, forcing Zorka to recall the robot in order to conceal it. Zorka then rents an office (under the alias "Dr. Zane") as a hiding place for the meteorite.

The foreign spies overpower Zorka, steal the meteorite and hurry to board

The Phantom Creeps—Bela Lugosi admires his creation.

a yacht anchored at a pier. Jean, learning of this, notifies Bob, and he races to the pier with Jim. Pursuing the spies in a speedboat, Bob and Jean are nearly killed in a collision, but survive, and the spies escape. Bob trails the spies by plane, but is hampered by a dense fog. The spies fire on the plane but Bob manages to bail out and save himself just before the plane crashes. Bob traces the meteorite to the spies' chemical laboratory near the river. During the terrific fight that ensues, Zorka, again invisible, escapes with the meteorite. An explosion and resulting fire disrupt the fight and the spies escape, leaving a desperate Bob struggling frantically to save

Jim. The two government agents survive the fire when they fall into the river.

For the second time, the foreign spies succeed in stealing Zorka's meteorite. Bob flies over the ship in which the spies attempt to take it out of the country, and drops a message threatening instant destruction unless the meteorite is surrendered. Pretending to surrender, the spies trick Jim and Jean into a dangerous situation. Bob is forced to withdraw, allowing the spies to escape.

His plans for world conquest threatened, Zorka uses Monk to lure the spies into his laboratory, then activates the giant robot and orders it to attack them. Seeing the spies escaping with the meteorite, Bob and Jean pursue them aboard a train, only to discover that the spies have tricked them and the meteorite is not aboard. Zorka, also believing the meteorite is aboard, races to the signal tower to stop the train. Fighting desperately, he hurls the tower man against the control lever that operates the derail switch. The switch is opened, hurling the oncoming train to destruction, but Bob and Jean escape the wreckage unharmed.

Zorka, frantic over the loss of his meteorite, leaves Monk in his laboratory and once again becomes invisible to search for it. Bob, Jim and Jean hurry to meet a Federal Communications truck in an attempt to trace an elusive wavelength broadcasting a mysterious code. Discovering that their broadcast is being traced, the spies try to escape with the meteorite, unaware that the invisible Zorka is riding in their car with them. Bob and Jean, pursuing the spies' car, see a construction barricade ahead. Believing that the warning cries of the workmen is a trick to stop them, they crash through and are nearly killed by a dynamite explosion, but escape unharmed. Jarvis and the spy ring are captured by Bob, but Zorka recovers his meteorite and escapes with it while still invisible.

Returning to visibility, Zorka, intoxicated by the volatile power at his command, now intends to conquer the world. When his laboratory is surrounded by government troops who destroy his menacing robot, Zorka escapes with the meteorite and boards a plane with Monk. From the plane, Zorka gleefully hurls vials of concentrated explosive at the world below, cackling maniacally as factories and

government installations are destroyed. Seeing a dirigible, Zorka bombs it, laughing insanely as the aircraft erupts in billowing flames.

A vast formation of government fighter planes commanded by Bob suddenly appears in the sky, pursuing Zorka. Bob's plane closes in, and Zorka, trying to evade it, loses control of his plane and crashes into the sea. The unstable meteorite explodes in a titanic blast, destroying Zorka, Monk and Zorka's dreams of world conquest.

Comments

After he attained stardom in *Dracula* (Universal, 1931), Bela Lugosi's film career began an almost immediate and irreversible slide downhill, partially due to his being typecast in horror films and partially due to Lugosi's less-than-acute business sense. After Lugosi inadvertently created his own competition in Boris Karloff by refusing to play the Monster in *Frankenstein* (Universal, 1931), he seemingly never turned down another role, no matter how dubious, and by 1933 he had already starred in his first serial, *The Whispering Shadow*. Actors like Boris Karloff and John Wayne appeared in serials early in their careers and went on to better things, but moving from features to serials was hardly a recommended professional move. By 1939, though, Lugosi was in no position to be choosy, and in the '40s he would find himself permanently mired in a cinematic bog of grade-Z turkeys at Monogram.

The Phantom Creeps isn't a great (or even a *good*) serial, but it does have Lugosi, who contributes one of his most enjoyably hammy portrayals as Dr. Alex Zorka. Despite his professional misfortunes and frequent exploitation as a camp figure, Lugosi was an excellent actor, capable of impressive work in his commanding, larger-than-life theatrical style, as his better films prove. When he was stuck in junk, though, Lugosi's over-the-top theatrics were somehow even more of an asset, and often his grand performances were the only worthwhile quality to be found in these cheaper films. *The Phantom Creeps* is one such film, and Lugosi is a riot to watch as he chews the economical scenery in this demented hodgepodge of mad scientist horror movie clichés and science fiction gimmickry.

The one other cast member in the serial worth mentioning is more of a prop than an actor — Lugosi/Zorka's menacing eight-foot-tall robot, its clawed hands pawing the air and a perpetual sneer on its bald, over-sized head. This robot is one of the most deranged creations ever seen in a horror or science fiction movie, and was used in this serial for the first and only time. Like innumerable other "mad scientist" inventions in cheap movies, the robot is (Zorka claims) only a prototype; he plans to create a vast army of similar mechanical men. Of course, neither the plot nor the serial's budgetary restrictions will allow him to realize his threat, and the robot is eventually destroyed by soldiers in the last chapter.

The rest of the cast, including leading man Robert Kent and sidekick Regis Toomey, is mostly negligible, although blonde Dorothy Arnold (the real-life wife of baseball great Joe DiMaggio) registers well as a brassy girl reporter. It's also a treat for film buffs to see Edward Van Sloan (Prof. Van Helsing from *Dracula*); Lee J. Cobb makes a brief early film appearance as the foreman of a construction gang. Jack C. Smith, as Zorka's assistant and chauffeur Monk, is such an untrustworthy character that Zorka's constant and repeated dependence on him is ludicrous.

The bulk of the serial's music is from Franz Waxman's score for *Bride of Frankenstein* (Universal, 1935). The special effects in *The Phantom Creeps* are rudimentary and unremarkable, with many props from Universal's *Frankenstein* movies and *Flash Gordon* serials reused. In one scene, as Zorka describes how he obtained the volatile meteorite fragment while on an expedition to Africa, footage from the 1936 Karloff/Lugosi feature *The Invisible Ray* is used to illustrate the narration, with a scene of Karloff wearing a hooded radiation suit representing Lugosi. Thus, through an economical editing move, Lugosi inadvertently found himself impersonated by his rival Karloff. Uncommonly choppy editorially, *The Phantom Creeps*, like many Universal serials, suffers from an over-abundance of stock footage and obvious post-production voice-over dubbing.

Video availability: VCI

Flash Gordon
Conquers the Universe

(Universal, 1940)

Associate producer: Henry MacRae. Directors: Ford Beebe, Ray Taylor. Screenplay: George H. Plympton, Basil Dickey, Barry Shipman. Photography: Jerome H. Ash, A.S.C., William Sickner, A.S.C. Art director: Harold MacArthur. Supervising film editor: Saul A. Goodkind. Film editors: Alvin Todd, Louis Sackin, Joe Gluck. Electrical properties: Kenneth Strickfaden. Dialogue director: Jacques Jaccard. Sound: Western Electric. Assistant directors: Edward Tyler, Charles Gould. Feature versions: *The Purple Death from Outer Space* (97 minutes), *Perils from the Planet Mongo* (91 minutes), both edited for television distribution.

Cast: Larry [Buster] Crabbe (Flash Gordon), Carol Hughes (Dale Arden), Charles Middleton (Emperor Ming), Anne Gwynne (Sonja), Frank Shannon (Dr. Zarkov), Lee Powell (Roka), Roland Drew (Barin), Shirley Deane (Aura), Donald Curtis (Capt. Ronal), Don Rowan (Capt. Torch), Sigurd Nilssen (Count Korro), Michael Mark (Karm), William Royle (Capt. Sudin), Victor Zimmerman (Thong), Edgar Edwards (Turan), Tom Chatterton (Mr. Arden), Harry C. Bradley (Keedish), Mimi Taylor (Verna), Byron Foulger (Drulk), Benjamin Taggart (Gen. Lupi),

Earl Dwire (Zandar), Luli Deste (Queen Fria), Jack Roper (giant), Charles Sherlock, Paul Reed, Harold Daniels, Edward Payson, Reed Howes, Clarice Sherry, Jack Gardner, Joey Ray, Paul Douglas, Ernie Adams, Edward Mortimer, Robert Blair, Bill Hunter, Charles Waldron, Jr., Pat Gleason, Frank Hagney, Ray Mala, Chief Yowlatchie, John Hamilton, Herbert Rawlinson, Jeanne Kelly [Jean Brooks], Allan Cavan, John Elliott, Roy Barcroft, Carmen D'Antonio.

Chapter Titles

(1) *The Purple Death.* (2) *Freezing Torture.* (3) *Walking Bombs.* (4) *The Destroying Ray.* (5) *The Palace of Terror.* (6) *Flaming Death.* (7) *The Land of the Dead.* (8) *The Fiery Abyss.* (9) *The Pool of Death.* (10) *The Death Mist.* (11) *Stark Treachery.* (12) *Doom of the Dictator.*

Story

Ming, dictator of the planet Mongo, sends a rocketship to Earth and orders his soldiers, led by the ruthless Capt. Torch, to expel a virulent "death dust" that spreads a fatal world-wide plague called the Purple Death. Instantly fatal, the disease leaves a purple spot on the

Opposite: Flash Gordon Conquers the Universe poster.

foreheads of its victims. Flash Gordon and Dr. Zarkov, believing that their old foe Ming the Merciless is behind the Purple Death, set out with Dale Arden in Zarkov's rocketship for the planet Mongo.

Arriving in the forest kingdom of Arboria to enlist the aid of Prince Barin, they meet Fria, Queen of the ice kingdom Frigia, who is also seeking Barin's aid against Ming. Joining forces, they journey by rocketship to Ming's laboratory just in time to prevent a fiendish test on human subjects. A fight breaks out, and Flash, pitted against a huge opponent of tremendous strength, falls into a deep pit.

Flash is rescued by Zarkov. Ronal, Barin's captain, learns there is an antidote for the Purple Death, a mineral known as polarite which can be found only in frozen, unlivable Frigia. Flash and Zarkov, accompanied by Dale and the others, promptly embark on an expedition into Frigia, protected against the intense cold by an invention of Zarkov's. A Ming rocketship, sent to destroy them, approaches, and the soldiers aboard, led by Capt. Torch, see Flash, Dale, Barin, Roka and one of the miners climbing a huge mountain searching for the polarite. The rocketship drops a bomb. It misses, but starts an avalanche that nearly kills Flash and his friends.

Emperor Ming, rejoicing in the belief that Flash's party has been destroyed, intercepts a radio message from Flash to his father on Earth, informing him that he has discovered the polarite and will use it to counteract the death dust threatening Earth. Ming is enraged, but realizes that his soldiers cannot survive the brutal subzero temperatures of Frigia. He sends Officer Torch against

the expedition with an army of "annihilatons," mechanical men charged with explosives, which Torch can control and explode from the safety of his ship. Deep in the frozen wastes, the walking bombs attack the expedition. Flash and most of his men survive the attack by Ming's robots, but Dale and Zarkov are captured and taken to Ming's palace. Flash and Roka then capture a Ming rocketship and force the crew to fly them to Ming's palace, where they hope to rescue Dale and Zarkov. Disguised as Ming guards, they make their way through the palace corridors.

Spying on two palace guards, they learn that Zarkov is about to be executed in the arena. Flash races up the stairs leading to the arena, and through a window sees Zarkov manacled helplessly between two stone pillars as Ming and his retinue watch. As Ming's voice sentences Zarkov, a death ray erupts from a clock on the wall and moves slowly toward the doomed scientist. Flash valiantly leaps through the window and shields Zarkov from the burning ray with his own body. Roka then arrives and destroys the clock emitting the death ray with a blast from his ray gun, saving Flash and Zarkov.

Flash and Roka, forced to leave Zarkov behind, escape from the arena. While Ming's soldiers frantically search for them through the winding palace corridors, they find their way to the laboratory and rescue Dale and Zarkov. After a further encounter with Ming's guards, followed by a hazardous mid-air rescue of Roka from a burning rocketship, Flash and his party finally escape Ming's clutches in one of the dictator's rocketships.

An approaching rocketship under the command of Prince Barin suddenly

Flash Gordon Conquers the Universe— Buster Crabbe and Carol Hughes battle an annihilation.

opens fire on them. Flash, immediately realizing that Barin is mistaking them for his enemy Ming, tries desperately to signal Barin's ship, and at the last minute succeeds in sending a code message with ray cannon blasts. Ming then orders his daughter Princess Aura, now married to Barin, removed from Barin's kingdom, which he intends to destroy with a fiery projectile. Flash, trying to prevent this, takes off with Dale and Ronal in a rocketship equipped with Zarkov's untested "thermal control," devised to combat the incendiary effects of Ming's fiendish invention. Dale and Ronal, operating the thermal control of the ship, watch anxiously as Flash, wearing a fire-proof uniform, fights his way into the blazing inferno as the first projectile falls. The thermal control resists the terrific heat as planned, but suddenly the high temperature melts a connection, the thermal control fails and Flash is nearly killed.

Flash is saved at the last minute when the malfunctioning thermal control suddenly begins operating again. Ming's barbaric attack on Barin's kingdom prompts Zarkov to create an "N" ray, to be discharged from a powerful "nullitrion," to neutralize and render useless Ming's power plant. Barin informs Flash that the nullitrion can best be directed at Ming's palace from the Devil's Dome, a high peak located in the Land of the Dead, a wasteland inhabited by the Rock Men, a bizarre race of nomads. The Rock Men wear costumes designed to blend in with the rock terrain, in order to camouflage themselves against attack by the giant reptiles inhabiting the region. Officer Torch and his soldiers, along with Ming's beautiful spy Sonja, plant a powerful bomb on the Devil's Dome, but are promptly captured by the Rock Men.

Flash and his party land in their rocketship, unaware of the bomb. They are attacked by the Rock Men, and during the struggle Torch's bomb explodes. Flash, Dale, Roka and two of Roka's soldiers are nearly killed by the explosion, but they survive and are taken prisoners by the Rock Men along with Torch, Sonja and Ming's soldiers. The Land of the Dead has become a battleground in a scientific war against Ming. With Flash and his party, as well as Ming's soldiers in captivity, the Rock King condemns all of them to death, blaming them for the disappearance of his son in the explosion.

Flash and Zarkov escape from their cell and discover the rock prince helpless in the magnetic grip of a powerful lodestone. Flash attempts to rescue the Rock Prince while Zarkov hurries to the Rock King with this information. Flash succeeds in freeing the Rock Prince from the lodestone and returning the prince to his father just as Dale and the others are about to be sacrificed.

Meanwhile, Emperor Ming is still holding his daughter, Princess Aura, as a hostage in his struggle against Barin. Flash, Zarkov and the others, leaving the Land of the Dead with Torch and

Sonja prisoners, accompany Barin in his rocketship to Ming's palace in a desperate attempt to rescue Princess Aura. Through the cooperation of Capt. Sudan, one of Ming's guards (secretly in league with them), they enter the tunnels beneath the palace, but they are attacked by a garrison of Ming's soldiers, who sound an alarm. Ming, realizing his enemies are in the subterranean tunnels, opens a water valve, nearly drowning Flash and his friends, but with Capt. Sudan's help, they survive.

Torch and Sonja, Ming's agents, now confined in prison cells in Barin's palace, escape to the radio room, overpower the operator and communicate with Ming. Ming instructs Torch to send out a false order grounding Barin's rocketship fleet in order to clear the way for Ming's bombers, and to then destroy the radio to prevent Barin countermanding the order. Dale overhears this and is captured by Torch and Sonja, who flee with her to the roof of Barin's palace. Flash pursues and corners them, and is fighting with Torch when Ming's bombers attack the palace.

Ming's air attack on the palace is beaten off, and Torch is recaptured by Flash, but the escaping enemy soldiers have kidnapped Dale. Zarkov is tricked into Ming's power, and with Dale and Princess Aura already his prisoners, Ming is now apparently in control of the situation. Flash leads a rescue party into Ming's palace through an abandoned tunnel and, stealthily entering the palace, locates the chamber where Dale and Aura are being held, unaware that the chamber is wired with a deadly electrical charge activated by Ming. Flash avoids the trap, rescuing Dale and Aura.

When Ming constructs the prototype for a new "Z-O" rocketship armed with

***Flash Gordon Conquers the Universe—*Lee Powell, Buster Crabbe, Carol Hughes, Frank Shannon, Rock Men.**

a powerful explosive called "solarite," Flash commandeers the Z-O ship, aiming it at the tower of Ming's palace after Ming and his followers have been locked inside by an accomplice of Zarkov's. Flash bails out in mid-air and is picked up safely by Dale and Zarkov in their rocketship. From their ship, Flash and his friends watch as the explosive-laden Z-O ship crashes into Ming's tower, destroying the evil tyrant and his warped dreams of conquest in a single powerful blast. Their mission finally accomplished, Flash, Dale and Zarkov return to Earth.

Comments

After the release of *Buck Rogers*, Universal briefly considered filming a sequel, but after noting that serial's acceptable but relatively lukewarm box office receipts, decided to produce a third *Flash Gordon* serial instead. The third and last *Flash Gordon* serial, *Flash Gordon Conquers the Universe* was an improvement over *Flash Gordon's Trip to Mars*, boasting what is undoubtedly the prettiest art direction ever lavished on a serial. Although not as physically substantial as *Buck Rogers*, *Flash Gordon Conquers the Universe* is in the same league, with bright, glossy photography and excellent sets, a few of which were originally constructed for the Universal features *Tower of London* (1939) and *Green Hell* (1940). The miniature work, always a weak point in Universal serials, is generally better than that in the first two Gordons, with improved rocket-ships that are more carefully manipulated and photographed. An expansive glass shot of Ming's throne room is stunning, and would be acceptable for any "A" budget feature. Some of the better rocketship footage from the first serial is reused here, augmented with superimposed elements like snow or a "space port" archway. Only the cut-rate ray gun blasts, achieved by simply scratching the film emulsion, and Ming's unconvincing "annihilaton" robots (looking like men in metallic pajamas) disappoint.

Excellent use is made, in Chapters 2 and 3, of mountain-climbing footage lifted from the Leni Riefenstahl docu-drama *White Hell of Pitz Palu*, which had been distributed by Universal in 1930. These scenes are awesome and spectacular, but the degraded negative quality doesn't blend with the carefully matched new scenes filmed for the serial, making the stock footage too obvious. Musical themes from other Universal features (like *Bride of Frankenstein* and *Son of Frankenstein*) are re-orchestrated for *Flash Gordon Conquers the Universe*, with an almost inspired application of Franz Liszt's *Les Preludes* as a main title overture.

In *Flash Gordon Conquers the Universe*, new-to-the-series actors portrayed Princess Aura and Prince Barin, and Carol Hughes replaced Jean Rogers (then under contract to 20th Century-Fox and unavailable) as Dale Arden. Hughes is very lovely, and an excellent choice for the role. No reference to the events in *Flash Gordon's Trip to Mars* is made in *Flash Gordon Conquers the Universe*, and in fact the narratives of the three serials make slightly more sense if *Flash Gordon Conquers the Universe* is

placed second in the trilogy and *Flash Gordon's Trip to Mars* third. *Flash Gordon Conquers the Universe* proves that Universal's designers and technicians were carefully studying Alex Raymond's comic strips. The first serial had been a faithful reproduction of Raymond's strip as it had appeared at the time, but in the intervening years Raymond's artwork had matured, growing more detailed and realistic. *Flash Gordon Conquers the Universe* reflects the changing artwork of the strip and, like the first serial, draws inspiration from Raymond's work published at the time of filming.

Flash Gordon Conquers the Universe, although profitable, was the least successful of the *Flash Gordon* serials. According to Buster Crabbe, a few years after the release of *Flash Gordon Conquers the Universe*, there was some talk at Universal of producing a fourth *Flash Gordon* serial but these plans never materialized. A cheap *Flash Gordon* TV show, starring Steve Holland, was produced in West Germany in the early 1950s, and a regrettably campy, multi-million dollar feature film remake starring Sam J. Jones was released by Universal in 1980. Even with a production schedule spanning years, a budget of over $30 million and a spate of mysteriously favorable reviews, the movie failed to equal the cheaply made serials. The newer film was quickly forgotten and its transience proves how good the original serials were, and still are. The naiveté and charm of the serials is neither forced nor calculated, and this is the main reason for their continuing appeal with film buffs. It's a priceless quality that all the hi-tech special effects in the world could never duplicate.

Video availability: VCI

Flash Gordon Conquers the Universe— Carol Hughes, Shirley Deane, Charles Middleton.

Mysterious Dr. Satan

(Republic, 1940)

Associate producer: Hiram S. Brown, Jr. Directors: William Witney, John English. Screenplay: Franklyn Adreon, Ronald Davidson, Norman S. Hall, Joseph Poland, Sol Shor. Photography: William Nobles. Film editors: Edward Todd, William Thompson. Music: Cy Feuer. Production manager: Al Wilson. Unit manager: Mack D'Agostino. Sound: RCA. Feature version: *Dr. Satan's Robot* (100 minutes), edited for television distribution.

Mysterious Dr. Satan—Edward (Eduardo) Ciannelli with his robot.

Cast: Edward Ciannelli (Dr. Satan), Robert Wilcox (Bob Wayne), William Newell (Speed Martin), C. Montague Shaw (Scott), Ella Neal (Lois Scott), Dorothy Herbert (Alice Brent), Charles Trowbridge (Governor Bronson), Jack Mulhall (chief of police), Edwin Stanley (Col. Bevans), Walter McGrail (Stoner), Joe McGuinn (Gort), Bud Geary (Halett), Paul Marion (the stranger), Archie Twitchell (airport radio announcer), Lynton Brent (Scarlett), Kenneth Terrell (Corwin), Al Taylor (Joe), Alan Gregg (Red).

Chapter Titles

(1) *Return of the Copperhead.* (2) *Thirteen Steps.* (3) *Undersea Tomb.* (4) *The Human Bomb.* (5) *Doctor Satan's Man of Steel.* (6) *Double Cross.* (7) *The Monster Strikes.* (8) *Highway of Death.* (9) *Double Jeopardy.* (10) *Bridge of Peril.* (11) *Death Closes In.* (12) *Crack-up.* (13) *Disguised.* (14) *The Flaming Coffin.* (15) *Doctor Satan Strikes.*

Story

Dr. Satan, a brilliant but warped master criminal, embarks on a reign of terror using a powerful robot he has created in order to achieve his ends. Dr. Satan needs an advanced remote-control cell to perfect his robot and increase its power, and attempts to steal the cell from its inventor, Thomas Scott. The theft is prevented when an athletic masked hero known only as the Copperhead suddenly appears. The Copperhead is, in reality, Bob Wayne, who has donned an old mask used by his father when the elder Wayne was a wrongly accused fugitive from justice in the Old West. As the Copperhead, Bob Wayne vows to clear his father's name by fighting for justice in opposition to Dr. Satan's plans.

Still trying to obtain the elusive remote-control cell, Dr. Satan plants a time bomb aboard a yacht being robotically piloted by the remote-control cell in a test run. Thomas Scott's daughter Lois is aboard the yacht; Dr. Satan informs Scott of the time bomb in an effort to blackmail the inventor into surrendering the remote-control cell. The Copperhead races onto the scene in a speedboat, and rescues Lois just as the yacht explodes, sinking with the remote-control cell aboard.

Thomas Scott plans to test a second remote-control cell using it to pilot a supposedly empty airplane, but the Copperhead secretly stows aboard the plane to prevent sabotage by Dr. Satan. After Scott pilots the test plane using the remote-control cell, sending the plane on a bombing run, two of Dr. Satan's henchmen chase after it in another plane; lowering a ladder, one of the hoods boards Scott's plane. Dr. Satan's henchman disconnects the remote-control cell and commandeers the plane, but the Copperhead emerges from a rear compartment and attacks the man, trying to stop him. Dr. Satan's henchman tumbles from the plane to his death and the Copperhead lands the plane safely in a field just as a carload of Dr. Satan's men arrives to meet it. The Copperhead removes his mask before the men approach the plane, and Bob Wayne is taken prisoner by Dr. Satan's hoods, who also remove the remote-control cell from the plane. Bob is held captive in a room located in Dr. Satan's laboratory, but overpowers the man left to guard him and escapes before Dr. Satan can interrogate him. The enraged Dr. Satan electrocutes the guard in reprisal. As Dr. Satan's other men dispose of the body, Bob returns in his Copperhead disguise and surprises Dr. Satan, holding a gun on the madman.

The Copperhead takes the remote-control cell from Dr. Satan; when Dr. Satan's men return, the Copperhead holds them off with his gun and disarms them. Backing away from the men to phone the police, the Copperhead stumbles into Dr. Satan's electrical apparatus, and Dr. Satan attempts to

Mysterious Dr. Satan— Robert Wilcox, Ella Neal.

throw a switch that releases a powerful electrical charge. The Copperhead stops him with a shot from his gun that strikes the switch. A violent fight erupts between the Copperhead and Dr. Satan's men. The Copperhead escapes by crashing through a window and running away. The remote-control cell is destroyed in the struggle.

Dr. Satan and his men go to a storage area on the twelfth floor of a downtown building, unaware that the Copperhead is hiding in the trunk of one of their cars. Finding the building doorways guarded by Dr. Satan's men, the Copperhead enters by climbing to the twelfth floor on the outside of the building. The Copperhead is surprised by

Dr. Satan's men after he enters a window; exiting through the window, he climbs the outside of the building to the roof. Dr. Satan and his men follow up the stairs, and after a tense struggle with the hoods, the Copperhead breaks away and quickly descends to the ground floor by sliding down elevator shaft cables.

Learning that Dr. Satan plans to salvage the original remote-control cell from the wreckage of the sunken yacht, Bob intends to prevent this by destroying the wreckage with a depth charge after locating the sunken yacht with a diving bell. Bob and Lois Scott descend to the wreck in a diving bell as Thomas Scott, along with reporter Speed Martin and Scott's secretary Alice Brent, lower an explosive charge along a separate cable from the schooner above. Dr. Satan's men silently approach the schooner in a launch and, boarding, try to take over the ship, holding a gun on Scott. Alice Brent surprises the hoods by swinging into them on a rope. As a violent fight rages, the switch leading to the submerged depth charge is accidentally thrown and the diving bell containing Bob and Lois is damaged in the explosion, filling with water.

On the schooner above, Dr. Satan's men are beaten off and driven back to their own boat, but they manage to take Speed Martin prisoner as they escape. Bob and Lois are pulled to the surface in their crippled diving bell and are saved. Dr. Satan outfits the captive Speed Martin with an electronic chest panel containing a television camera and a powerful explosive. Injecting Martin with a mind-controlling drug, Dr. Satan orders Martin, now a human robot, to Thomas Scott's house. Watching Scott and his daughter Lois through

the television apparatus, Dr. Satan orders Scott to follow Speed Martin and surrender the plans for his remote-control cell.

Unknown to Dr. Satan, Bob enters the room behind Martin and, unseen, instructs Scott via a hastily scribbled note to stall while he calls the police. Bob phones the police and convinces them to turn off the city's power supply for 30 seconds at exactly 3:10 p.m. so that Dr. Satan's machinery will fail. Waiting for the power to be shut off, Bob follows Scott and the robotized Speed Martin unseen as they leave Scott's home. As the electrical power fails, Bob is able to disconnect the bomb from Speed Martin and hurl it away before the power is restored and Dr. Satan explodes the bomb. Bob and Scott are surprised by Dr. Satan's men, who have been watching nearby. They overpower Bob and kidnap Scott. Bob shoots at them as they speed away in a car and one of his shots punctures their gas tank.

Leaving the still-robotized Speed standing on the grounds of Scott's estate, Bob hurries to his own car and trails the leaking gasoline. Dr. Satan's men, discovering that their gas tank has been punctured, steal a fuel truck when they pull into a service station. Learning this, Bob, now disguised as the Copperhead, follows the truck. Dr. Satan's men open the tank valve on the truck, spilling the fuel on the road, and the fuel is ignited, engulfing the Copperhead's car in a sea of flames. The Copperhead saves himself by jumping out of the car just before it explodes.

Dr. Satan's men take the captive Scott to a waterfront hideout. Scott tries to bribe the man guarding him, but learns that Dr. Satan's hoods all wear an electronic control disc that can electrocute them at Dr. Satan's command. The disc cannot be removed without killing the person who wears it, but the guard agrees to help Scott escape if Scott can remove the disc, which Scott is able to do by using the electrical equipment in the hideout. Dr. Satan arrives to interrogate Scott just after the hood has been released from the control disc. Dr. Satan's former underling, now safe from electrical reprisal, rebels, pulling a gun on the madman. As Scott watches, horrified, Dr. Satan summons his robot from another room and orders it to kill the man.

His hopes for escape dashed, the captive Scott is then forced to work on installing a new remote-control cell in Dr. Satan's robot. Working in the madman's lab, the resourceful Scott is able to send a secret radio message to Bob, telling him where Dr. Satan's men will pick up a vital electronic component needed for the remote-control cell. Catching up to Dr. Satan's men, Bob trails them back to the waterfront lab where Scott is being held. Wearing his Copperhead mask, Bob enters the building and overpowers the hoods. Dr. Satan is alerted to the Copperhead's presence by a warning device, and when the Copperhead arrives to rescue Thomas Scott, Dr. Satan orders his powerful robot to attack the masked vigilante. The Copperhead is nearly killed by the automoton, but Scott is able to deactivate the robot just in time to save the Copperhead.

Dr. Satan manages to escape with Scott before the Copperhead can stop them. Dr. Satan administers a mind-controlling drug to Scott, and learns from the mesmerized scientist that the secret of his remote-control cell is a rare mineral called tungite, a supply of which is controlled by Scott's secretary, Alice Brent. Dr. Satan immediately dispatches his men to Scott's home, where they force Alice to give them the tungite. Bob arrives and fights the men, but he is overpowered and they escape with the tungite. Lois Scott then arrives as the hoods leave, and is kidnapped by them.

Using Lois as bait, Dr. Satan tries to lure the Copperhead into a trap, but the Copperhead is able to rescue Lois. Scott finally installs one of his remote-control cells in Dr. Satan's robot, and Dr. Satan decides to test the improved mechanical man by using it to rob a bank. A bank guard alerts the police as the theft is in progress, but Dr. Satan's henchmen escape with the robot.

Bob deduces that Dr. Satan will strike next at the Metropolitan Drug Company warehouse where tungite is stored, and instructs Speed to meet him there. Speed arrives, followed immediately by Bob Wayne in his Copperhead identity, as two of Dr. Satan's men try to rob the warehouse, assisted by the robot. A fight erupts, with Speed and two of Dr. Satan's henchmen knocked unconscious as the Copperhead battles the robot. The robot knocks out the Copperhead and tries to topple a shelf containing acid bottles on top of him. The Copperhead rolls out of the way just as the falling acid bottles smash. Carrying the unconscious Speed from the warehouse, he escapes.

Finally tracking Dr. Satan to his lair, the Copperhead frees Scott, now recovered from Dr. Satan's mind-controlling drug. Scott and the Copperhead then overpower Dr. Satan in a violent struggle, and the Copperhead, revealing his true identity to Scott, then takes his mask off and places it on the unconscious Dr. Satan. When Dr. Satan's hoods appear, Scott tells them he has caught the Copperhead. Dr. Satan's men, believing the unconscious Satan to be the Copperhead, lock him in a room with the robot, planning to use it to kill him. Dr. Satan regains consciousness just as the robot seizes him. He struggles desperately in the metallic grip of his own creation, shrieking for his life. The evil genius crashes through a window with his monstrous invention, plunging to his doom.

Comments

Any dramatic honors to be claimed in Republic's *Mysterious Dr. Satan* are won hands down by veteran character actor Eduardo Ciannelli (his first name is Americanized to "Edward" in the credits here), who easily outshines the rest of the cast as the villainous title figure. The stage is set for Ciannelli's entrance by the following dialogue exchange between hero Bob Wayne (Robert Wilcox) and the doomed Governor Bronson (Charles Trowbridge), who has been threatened by Dr. Satan:

> BOB WAYNE: Then some of the rumors about this mysterious Dr. Satan are true!
> GOVERNOR BRONSON: All of them are probably true! Dr. Satan's spies have penetrated even the police department! The situation is so serious that I'm going to call four companies of the National Guard!

Dr. Satan is introduced as he tinkers with his monstrous robot, Ciannelli's dour features thrown into craggy relief by melodramatic under-the-chin lighting. "Scott's remote-control cell is all I need," Satan tells an underling. "Once I've equipped that robot with that device, there is no limit to the power and wealth I can command!" "But Dr. Satan ... the police!" the underling cautions. "The police will be fast, but I'll be faster!" Dr. Satan retorts. Later, as Dr. Satan confronts inventor Thomas Scott (C. Montague Shaw), the following dialogue establishes the madman's ruthlessness:

> SCOTT: Dr. Satan! What do you want with me?
> SATAN: I want a complete set of plans for your remote-control cell. If you care to be reasonable in the matter, you'll be handsomely rewarded.
> SCOTT: I refuse to give them to you at any price!
> SATAN: You're testing that invention tonight on Turner's yacht. Your daughter is aboard that yacht. My men have wired explosives into the fuel tanks. The fuse is connected with the speed indicator. When the boat attains a speed of 25 knots, those charges will be fired.
> SCOTT: I don't believe it! I still refuse to give you the plans!
> SATAN: I anticipated you might be stubborn. Perhaps a little time might change your mind, particularly when you realize that each minute will bring your daughter a minute closer to death!

Ciannelli's sinister manner and low, rasping voice combine with atmospheric lighting to impart a tangible feeling of menace that is difficult to convey in print. The year before, Ciannelli had played the murderous leader of the Thugs in R.K.O.'s *Gunga Din*, and in *Mysterious Dr. Satan* he lends real class to a serial that, although well produced, is otherwise very bland in the acting department.

Mysterious Dr. Satan resurrected one of the "Volkite" robots (re-designed and slimmed down) from *Undersea Kingdom* (q.v.) as Dr. Satan's primary instrument of destruction. After this serial, the robot would appear in other Republic cliffhangers, including *Zombies of the Stratosphere* (q.v.). Although enjoyable in its own right, *Mysterious Dr. Satan* is also interesting for what it was originally intended to be, and very nearly was. The wildly successful Superman character had been introduced to comic book readers only two years before, and Republic, negotiating for the screen rights, had begun work on a Superman serial script. When negotiations with National Periodical Publications fell through due to the comic book publisher's excessive licensing demands, Republic (never a studio to waste any-thing) hastily re-tooled the existing Superman script, changing Superman to the Copperhead and altering other character names and scenes wherever necessary. For instance, in a scene where Superman had entered a building by *flying* into it in the original script, the Copperhead, lacking superhuman pow-ers, entered the building by *climbing* the outer wall in the rewrite. The re-worked script plays better than one would expect, with *Mysterious Dr. Satan* emerging from the rubble of failed con-tract negotiations as one of Republic's slickest cliffhanger entries. Eduardo Ciannelli and the serial's glossy produc-tion values more than compensate for the bland actors cast in the leading "heroic" roles, including Robert Wilcox and his co-stars Ella Neal and Dorothy Herbert.

Video availability: Republic Home Video.

Dick Tracy vs. Crime, Inc.

(Republic, 1941)

Associate producer: William J. O'Sulli-van. Directors: William Witney, John English. Screenplay: Ronald Davidson, Norman S. Hall, William Lively, Joseph O'Donnell, Joseph Poland. Photogra-phy: Reggie Lanning. Film editors: Tony Martinelli, Edward Todd. Special effects: Howard Lydecker. Music score: Cy Feuer. Production manager: Al Wil-son. Unit manager: Mack D'Agostino. Sound: RCA. Re-release title: *Dick Tracy vs. The Phantom Empire*. Feature version: *Dick Tracy vs. Crime, Inc.*, released to home video.

Cast: Ralph Byrd (Dick Tracy), Michael Owen (Billy Carr), Jan Wiley (June Chandler), John Davidson (Luci-fer), Ralph Morgan (Morton), Kenneth

Dick Tracy vs. Crime, Inc. — The Ghost, John Davidson.

Harlan (Lt. Cosgrove), John Dilson (Welden), Howard Hickman (Chandler), Robert Frazer (Brewster), Robert Fiske (Cabot), Jack Mulhall (Wilson), Hooper Atchley (Trent), Anthony Warde (Corey), Chuck Morrison (Trask).

Chapter Titles

(1) *The Fatal Hour.* (2) *The Prisoner Vanishes.* (3) *Doom Patrol.* (4) *Dead Man's Trap.* (5) *Murder at Sea.* (6) *Besieged.* (7) *Sea Racketeers.* (8) *Train of Doom.* (9) *Beheaded.* (10) *Flaming Peril.* (11) *Seconds to Live.* (12) *Trial by Fire.* (13) *The Challenge.* (14) *Invisible Terror.* (15) *Retribution.*

Story

A master criminal known as the Ghost, who is able to become invisible when his assistant Lucifer aims a beam of light at a medallion he wears, is responsible for a massive crime wave, and desperate government officials assign Dick Tracy to investigate. Unknown to Tracy and everyone else, the Ghost is really a member of the Council of Eight, a select group of leading citizens dedicated to the eradication of crime; the Ghost has already murdered three of his fellow council members while still keeping his own identity a secret. With his assistants Billy Carr and June Chandler,

Tracy immediately goes to work. The Ghost, bombing a fault line on the Atlantic Ocean seabed, creates huge tidal waves that heavily damage New York City.

Interfering with the Ghost's criminal activities at every turn, Tracy discovers a unique medal at one crime scene that had been presented only to the Council of Eight members. When an astonished Tracy confronts the Ghost after his suspicions have focused on the surviving Council members, he sees the masked criminal vanish before his eyes, and uses bloodhounds to track his invisible quarry. Tracy finally lures the Ghost into a room outfitted with a special light bulb; when the bulb is turned on, the polarity of the light waves is reversed and the Ghost becomes visible.

After a desperate fight between Tracy and the Ghost, the Ghost breaks free, with Tracy in pursuit. As he flees, the Ghost, again invisible, tries to escape across high tension wires and is electrocuted. The power feedback also kills Lucifer, who was operating the invisibility machine from afar. The Ghost is revealed to be Morton, a respected Council of Eight member, and Tracy deduces that Morton had turned to crime in order to avenge the death of his brother, who was also a criminal.

Comments

Republic's fourth and last *Dick Tracy* serial, *Dick Tracy vs. Crime, Inc.* was the second to feature a science fiction element in the plot, in this case the power of invisibility employed by the Ghost. The Ghost, wearing a skin-tight dark metallic mask, is introduced as he whirls around in a chair to confront his assistant, the aptly named Lucifer (John Davidson), who comments on his master's activities.

LUCIFER: I begin to see your plan! By creating a reign of terror, you can force the city to accept any demands you make!

Opposite and above: Dick Tracy vs. Crime, Inc.— **Ralph Byrd.**

Commenting on the opposition, Lucifer observes:

> LUCIFER: This Dick Tracy is a dangerous adversary.
> THE GHOST: He's clever, I'll grant him that. But he can't fight an invisible man!

The invisibility scenes are quickly and economically done, with the Ghost holding a medallion that reflects a spotlight beam, then fading away via a simple dissolve. The camera then typically pans across an empty set, accompanied by a high-pitched electronic whine on the soundtrack to indicate the Ghost's presence.

The serial gets off to a rousing start in Chapter 1, as the Ghost threatens to destroy New York City unless his ransom demands are met. The Ghost kidnaps Dr. Jonathan Martin (an unbilled C. Montague Shaw) and tortures the scientist (off-screen) by inserting bamboo splinters under his fingernails and setting them on fire. Tracy and his men are able to track the captive Martin to one of the Ghost's hideouts, and after a gun battle with the Ghost's henchmen, Tracy learns that Martin was forced to reveal how New York could be destroyed.

> MARTIN: The Amsterdam Fault, a volcanic fissure opening into the subterranean fires miles below New York. Sea erosion has sealed up that vent, but a few depth charges will smash through, and bring about an earthquake and a tidal wave that will be catastrophic. The Ghost isn't bluffing! He *can* destroy New York!

Tracy is off in a flash to prevent the disaster, but not before the Ghost has already started the tidal wave and destroyed New York's harbor area. These impressive tidal wave destruction scenes were lifted from the feature film *Deluge*, an independently produced doomsday thriller distributed by R.K.O. in 1933. The special effects for *Deluge*, involving large-sized miniature replicas of New York buildings filmed at high speed to slow the action and create an illusion of mass, were created by Ned Mann, who also handled the special effects for the Alexander Korda production *Things to Come* (1936). These same scenes were also used in Republic's *S.O.S. Tidal Wave* (1938) and their serial *King of the Rocket Men* (1949) (q.v.).

Slicker and more quickly paced than the first *Dick Tracy* (q.v.), *Dick Tracy vs. Crime, Inc.* opens and closes each chapter with a fast-motion point-of-view scene showing a car rushing through dark city streets, establishing the serial's hyperactive tone from the outset. Republic's usual technical gloss is in full evidence, and the cast, from lead Ralph Byrd on down, is in top form. As usual in Republic's serials, the violence, though sanitized and not graphic in detail, is still virile, with plenty of the usual fistfights and gunplay. In one scene, as Tracy is attempting to trail and rescue Dr. Martin, he poses as a door-to-door salesman as he approaches the gang's hideout. "Is the lady of the house in?" Tracy politely inquires of a thug leaning out of a window, just before drawing his gun and using it.

The final scene in the film, with the Ghost unmasked by Tracy, is handled with clever economy as Tracy reverses the polarity of the light waves in a room by using a special light bulb, thus revealing the invisible Ghost. The effect is cheaply achieved by simply printing the scene in negative as Tracy and the Ghost engage in a fistfight, but the effect is sufficiently weird and believable. Inexplicably, *Dick Tracy vs. Crime, Inc.* was re-titled *Dick Tracy vs. the Phantom Empire* when re-released by Republic in the mid–1950s.

Video availability: VCI

Batman

(Columbia, 1943)

Producer: Rudolph C. Flothow. Director: Lambert Hillyer. Screenplay: Victor McLeod, Leslie Swabacker, Harry Fraser. Photography: James S. Brown, A.S.C. Film editors: Dwight Caldwell, Earl Turner. Music: Lee Zahler. Sound engineer: Jack Goodrich. RCA sound. Assistant director: Gene Anderson. Re-release title: *An Evening With Batman and Robin*.

Cast: Lewis Wilson (Batman/Bruce Wayne), Douglas Croft (Robin/Dick Grayson), J. Carrol Naish (Dr. Tito Daka), Shirley Patterson [Shawn Smith] (Linda), William Austin (Alfred), Charles C. Wilson (Capt. Arnold), Charles Middleton (Ken Colton), Robert Fiske (Foster), Michael Vallon (Preston), Gus Glassmire (Martin Warren).

Chapter Titles

(1) *The Electrical Brain.* (2) *The Bat's Cave.* (3) *The Mark of the Zombies.* (4) *Slaves of the Rising Sun.* (5) *The Living Corpse.* (6) *Poison Peril.* (7) *The Phoney Doctor.* (8) *Lured By Radium.* (9) *The Sign of the Sphinx.* (10) *Flying Spies.* (11) *A Nipponese Trap.* (12) *Embers of Evil.* (13) *Eight Steps Down.* (14) *The Executioner Strikes.* (15) *The Doom of the Rising Sun.*

Story

Nineteen-forty-three, during World War II: Millionaire Bruce Wayne and his young ward Dick Grayson battle criminals and Axis fifth columnists in their costumed secret identities of Batman and Robin. An underground Japanese agent, Dr. Daka, is sent to America to sabotage the war effort, and maintains a secret headquarters inside a dilapidated carnival "Cave of Horrors" exhibit that depicts, ironically, Japanese war crimes. Martin Warren, the uncle of Linda Page, Bruce Wayne's girlfriend, was wrongly imprisoned for crimes he did not commit, and when he is released from prison he is kidnapped by Dr. Daka and transformed into a zombie. Using an army of hoods blackmailed into following his orders and a group of mind-controlled zombies like Warren created in his laboratory, Daka uses his evil genius to aid the Axis powers.

Batman—Shirley Patterson, Lewis Wilson.

Although unaware of Daka's identity, Batman and Robin arrive on the scene when the Japanese spy's gang attempts to steal the city's radium supply to power a destructive radium ray gun invented by Daka.

Beginning to suspect that Batman and Bruce Wayne are the same man, Daka kidnaps Linda Page and destroys her will with the mind-control device in his laboratory. Batman and Robin are lured to Daka's headquarters behind the carnival chamber of horrors, and Batman is overpowered by Daka's zombie guards. He is nearly made into a zombie himself before he escapes with Robin's help. Daka is killed when he attempts to flee, stumbling into his own alligator pit. Using Daka's lab equip-

ment, Batman and Robin restore the memories of Linda and her Uncle Martin. They also discover evidence clearing Martin's name and implicating the rest of the Japanese spy ring. Batman and Robin quickly disappear and Bruce Wayne returns with Dick Grayson, offering to escort the unsuspecting Linda home.

Comments

One of the greatest comic book characters, second only to Superman in popularity and durability, Batman premiered in issue #27 of National Periodicals' *Detective Comics* in 1939, drawn by creator Bob Kane. Batman was awarded his own comic book the next year; daily and Sunday newspaper

***Batman*— Lewis Wilson, Douglas Croft.**

strips were distributed by the McClure Syndicate from 1943 to 1946. Although Bob Kane was the primary creator of the Batman character, which combined elements of Zorro and Sherlock Holmes, other contributors to the strip included writer Bill Finger and artists Jack Burnley, Charlie Paris, Dick Sprang and Jerry Robinson. *Batman* comic books are still published today, and in the last six decades have inspired two movie serials, a radio show, a wildly popular 1960s TV show with Adam West, a feature film with West and four recent big-budget feature films.

The first live-action adaptation of *Batman* was produced as a serial by Columbia Pictures in 1943. Reflecting its period, the screenwriters opted for a wartime menace and injected a villainous Japanese spy into the proceedings, but otherwise maintained a general fidelity to the early Kane comics in terms of atmosphere and character detail. Both Lewis Wilson as Batman and Douglas Croft as Robin are reasonable facsimiles of their comic book originals, at least as they were drawn at the time. J. Carrol Naish, an excellent character actor, makes a rare serial appearance as the Japanese spy Dr. Daka, contributing some enjoyably hammy, over-the-top villainy. The serial's direction was by Lambert Hillyer, a veteran of B-westerns who had also directed the Universal horror movies

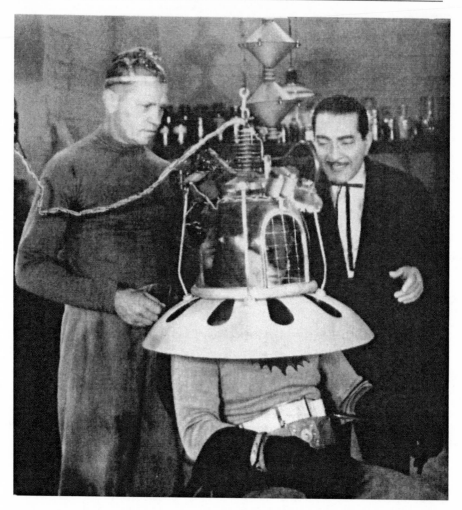

Batman— Lewis Wilson (center), J. Carrol Naish.

The Invisible Ray and *Dracula's Daughter* (both 1936). In *Batman*, Hillyer maintains a brisk pace and manages some nice atmospheric touches. The sets are solid and believable and the photography is excellent. Overall, *Batman* stands as one of the better Columbia serials of the period.

Today, however, *Batman* is generally criticized as being one of the lesser 1940s serials, and is even occasionally derided as camp. There is an acute disparity between the actual quality of the film and most published opinions of it, and there are several reasons for this. To begin with, the serial was re-released, in its 15-chapter entirety, as *An Evening with Batman and Robin* in 1965, during the camp craze that would be exploited so thoroughly by the Adam West *Batman* TV series. A condescending attitude toward the serial was established

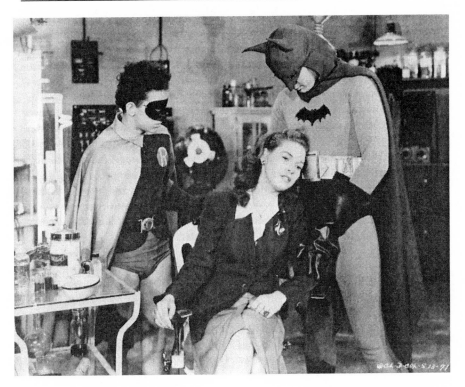

Batman— Douglas Croft, Shirley Patterson, Lewis Wilson.

by reviews in leading publications like *Time* and even encouraged by studio publicity materials. Secondly, the serial's wartime setting, and even the serial format itself, seemed outdated and ridiculous in 1965, especially with all 15 chapters strung end-to-end in a marathon four-and-a-half-hour screening. Finally, the serial's "low-tech" motif—there are none of the gadgets and paraphernalia so popular at the time in the *Batman* TV show and the James Bond movies—disappointed many younger viewers.

Additionally, the serial's racism—there are many anti-Japanese slurs throughout—did not go over well with mid-'60s viewers, who seemed to disregard the serial's year of origin in their critical reaction. All of these factors, along with certain qualities that tend to make *Batman* a very atypical serial—and therefore disappointing to many serial fans and commentators—have combined to lessen the film's reputation over the years. But, as noted, *Batman* is one of the better serials of its time, and those who criticize it should compare this 1943 serial with the truly awful sequel *Batman and Robin* (q.v.), produced by Sam Katzman in 1949.

Although there are plenty of fistfights, the 1943 *Batman* serial tends to emphasize plot and atmosphere, and this understandably disappoints serial fans enamored of the more action-oriented Republic cliffhangers. Yet the atmosphere in *Batman* is precisely what makes it so enjoyable today, with director Hillyer and cameraman James S. Brown creating a believably gritty, East Coast urban environment on Columbia's back lot. (A minor geographical error does crop up, though, when Bruce Wayne receives a letter in one scene and a close up of the address reads: "Mr. Bruce Wayne—1918 Hill Road—Los Angeles, California.") Although there is no familiar bat-signal in the film, there is a nice melodramatic scene in which a powerful flashlight projects a bat symbol into a darkened room, frightening a group of Daka's henchmen as a discordant note of Lee Zahler's virile music underscores the action on the soundtrack. This same loud blast of music is used throughout to highlight Batman's appearances, which tend to be sudden and dramatic. In fact, *Batman* often uses music scoring as effectively as some of the early Republic serials. The interior of Batman's subterranean cave, with the rough-hewn walls thrown into sharp relief by exaggerated lighting as bats flutter through the air, is also memorable.

As Batman, Columbia contract actor Lewis Wilson imparts considerable depth to the role, projecting charm as Bruce Wayne and also *film noir*-ish toughness when interrogating criminals in his Batman disguise. Wilson's personality suggests the young William Holden. Wilson did not enjoy much of a film career, appearing in a couple of Columbia B-pictures and a low-budget exploitation item in the '50s before fading into obscurity. Douglas Croft, as Robin, was an experienced juvenile actor who had appeared briefly in the James Cagney musical *Yankee Doodle Dandy* the previous year; to date, he is the only actor cast as Robin who was the correct age, playing the character in a resourceful, street-smart and believable manner. There is a determined effort throughout the serial to make both Batman and Robin as believable as possible, with Batman even recruited as a government agent in the struggle against Axis spies.

J. Carrol Naish as Dr. Daka injects the only intentional humor. Naish is clearly enjoying himself in this role, performing with the same type of likable, melodramatic hamminess that Charles Middleton brought to the *Flash Gordon* serials. In fact, Middleton himself appears in *Batman*, somewhat miscast and wasted in a tame supporting role as a rustic miner. Shirley Patterson, a young and pretty Columbia contract starlet, lends a great deal of charm to this serial. Patterson corresponded with the author in 1986, and recalled how she became ill when Daka's smoke-producing mind-control helmet was placed over her head for a scene in the film. Patterson also recalled that she left the film industry after her stint at Columbia, then returned in the 1950s under the name Shawn Smith, appearing in films like *The Land Unknown* and *It! The Terror from Beyond Space*.

The frequent anti-Japanese dialogue in *Batman* is the most troubling aspect of the film for modern viewers, but it should be noted that *Batman* is a product of its time, and that it certainly isn't the only 1940s wartime film to employ this jingoism. Nevertheless, when the serial was released on videocassette by Goodtimes Home Video in 1989, a "politically correct" censored version was prepared, with the racial slurs in the dialogue eliminated and overdubbed, and the opening and closing voice-over narration on each chapter replaced with new narration by announcer Don Pardo. The complete, unexpurgated original release version has been telecast on the American Movie Classics (AMC) cable TV network. *Batman* was re-released by Columbia in 1954; after the 1965 re-release *An Evening with Batman and Robin*, it was issued to home movie collectors in the Super 8mm format.

Like many comic book characters that have enjoyed longevity, Batman has evolved over the years. In the 1960s, the character was spoofed and ridiculed by the campy Adam West TV show during a widespread "pop art" craze that, in retrospect, seems facile and immature. The current big-budget features, starring leading men like Michael Keaton, Val Kilmer and George Clooney as Batman, present a far darker and far more violent treatment, reflecting the modern comic books and presenting Batman as a dangerous (and even psychologically troubled) hi-tech vigilante.

The original *Batman* serial, like these later television and big-screen incarnations of the character, was based on the comic books of its period, and (like all commercial films) it reflected its time and the popular attitudes of that turbulent wartime era. It should be judged only from a proper historical perspective, with a fair and open-minded attitude.

Manhunt of Mystery Island

(Republic, 1945)

Associate producer: Ronald Davidson. Directors: Spencer Bennet, Wallace A. Grissell, Yakima Canutt. Screenplay: Albert DeMond, Basil Dickey, Jesse Duffy, Alan James, Grant Nelson, Joseph Poland. Photography: Bud Thackery. Film editors: Cliff Bell, Harold R. Minter. Special effects: Howard Lydecker, Theodore Lydecker. Musical director: Richard Cherwin. Set decorator: Charles Thompson. Unit manager: R.G. Springsteen. Sound: Ed Borschell. RCA Sound. Feature version: *Captain Mephisto and the Transforma-* *tion Machine* (100 minutes), for television distribution.

Cast: Richard Bailey (Lance Reardon), Linda Stirling (Linda Forrest), Roy Barcroft (Mephisto), Kenne Duncan (Brand), Forrest Taylor (Prof. Forrest), Forbes Murray (Hargraves), Jack Ingram (Armstrong), Harry Strang (Braley), Edward Cassidy (Melton), Frank Alten (Raymond), Lane Chandler (Reed), Russ Vincent (Ruga), Dale Van Sickel (Barker), Tom Steele (Lyons), Duke Green (Harvey).

Chapter Titles

(1) *Secret Weapon.* (2) *Satan's Web.* (3) *The Murder Machine.* (4) *The Lethal Chamber.* (5) *Mephisto's Mantrap.* (6) *Ocean Tomb.* (7) *The Death Drop.* (8) *Bombs Away.* (9) *The Fatal Flood.* (10) *The Sable Shroud.* (11) *Satan's Shadow.* (12) *Cauldron of Cremation.* (13) *Bridge to Eternity.* (14) *Power Dive to Doom.* (15) *Fatal Transformation.*

Story

Prof. Forrest, inventor of a powerful radiatomic power transmitter, is missing under mysterious circumstances, and his daughter Claire searches for him with the aid of criminologist Lance Reardon. Analyzing unique dust found on the clothes of a murdered man who had been on a radium expedition with Forrest, Reardon determines that the man had been on remote Mystery Island in the Pacific. He goes there with Claire on the assumption that they will find her father on the island.

Mystery Island is owned by four men, all of whom are descendants of Capt. Mephisto, the tyrannical pirate who ruled Mystery Island two centuries earlier. Lance and Claire are unaware that one of their four hosts is secretly keeping Prof. Forrest prisoner on the island, and that the fiend is capable of changing himself into the living image of the long-dead Capt. Mephisto through the use of a scientific device called the "transformation chair." The ruthless Mephisto plans to use Prof. Forrest's radiatomic power transmitter for his own personal gain, and he desperately tries to prevent Lance and Claire from discovering his scheme.

The captive Prof. Forrest and his assistant Raymond, also a prisoner, try to escape from Mephisto, but are recaptured by the pirate. Discovering Prof. Forrest's hidden radiatomic power transmitter, Reardon disconnects the vital power control unit and confiscates it so the machine cannot be used. Mephisto and his henchman Brand scheme to retrieve the power unit. When Reardon hatches a plot to nab Mephisto by planting a dummy package supposedly containing the power unit in Claire's room, Mephisto and Brand confront the girl, only to discover the package is a phony.

Mephisto and Brand kidnap Claire and take her through a hidden door to a secret passage, but Claire manages to alert Reardon, who is outside on the grounds of the estate, by breaking a window to get his attention. As she is taken into the secret passage by her abductors, she unwinds a spool of thread to leave a trail that Reardon can follow. Exiting the secret passage, Mephisto and Brand force Claire into a car and speed away with her, followed closely by Reardon in his own car. Mephisto stops his car and Brand stretches a rope across the road, which forces Reardon's car to crash off the road and fall into the ocean. Reardon saves himself by leaping to safety at the last instant.

Finding a warehouse imprint on a block and tackle attached to the rope, Reardon traces Mephisto and Brand to a waterfront sponge warehouse, where Claire is held captive in a fishnet suspended from a rope as Mephisto and Brand torture her in an effort to learn the location of the power control unit. Reardon surprises Mephisto and Brand, a fight erupts, and the rope suspending Claire unreels from its spool, lowering Claire through a trap door into the ocean, where she nearly drowns. Reardon drives away Mephisto and Brand, saving Claire by rewinding the rope and reeling her back up through the trap door.

Mephisto learns that the power control unit was in Reardon's car when it crashed into the ocean, and that Reardon plans to use diving equipment to retrieve the device. Mephisto sends Brand to steal the island's only diving equipment before Reardon can obtain it, but Reardon uses the diving equipment to search underwater for the power control unit, while Claire waits in a motorboat. Reardon salvages the power control unit, but two hoods, under orders from Brand, pursue Reardon and Claire in another boat, trying to steal the device for Mephisto.

Meanwhile, Prof. Forrest and Raymond, working in the lab, plan to explode the power unit by remote control, unaware that it is in Reardon's possession. As Reardon and Claire flee the attacking hoods in a high-speed boat chase, Reardon notices the increasing power build-up in the unit and quickly tosses it overboard; the unit explodes the pursuing boat, killing the hoods.

Mephisto attempts to coerce Prof. Forrest and Raymond into building another power control unit. When Brand arrives to report that the two hoods pursuing Reardon and Claire have been killed, Mephisto, enraged, lashes Brand with a ship and stalks out of the room. The resentful Brand then makes a deal with Prof. Forrest to help him escape from the island, and delivers a note from Forrest to his daughter Claire, telling her to meet Brand for further instructions.

Claire hurries to meet Brand; Reardon, learning of this, trails her. Claire is captured by one of Mephisto's henchmen and held in a warehouse. Reardon surprises the man and they fight. Reardon overpowers the man and, freeing Claire, sends her away to safety. Aware that Capt. Mephisto will arrive soon, Reardon stays behind in the warehouse to ambush him. When Mephisto appears, they engage in a gun battle, but when Reardon steps on a hidden trap door, Mephisto pulls a lever that opens the door, and Reardon falls into a small room that begins to fill with deadly gas. Reardon nearly suffocates, but Claire returns with a gun, drives Mephisto away and frees Reardon.

Beginning to suspect that Mephisto must be one of the island's owners in disguise, Reardon lifts one of Mephisto's fingerprints from the trap door control knob, then tricks the island's owners into leaving their prints on wine glasses during a discussion with them. Reardon tries to match the prints, but Brand arrives and overpowers Reardon in a fight, stealing the evidence. When Reardon and Claire return to the warehouse to lift more comparison prints, Brand and an accomplice wait to ambush them as Reardon and Claire investigate a secret tunnel.

Melton, one of the island's four owners, also arrives. After Brand becomes involved in a gun battle with Reardon and Claire, he helps Melton to escape, believing that Melton must be Mephisto. Reardon leaves Claire to guard Brand's accomplice, wounded in the gunfight, and follows Brand and Melton. Brand traps Reardon in a wine press chamber and starts the machinery, nearly crushing Reardon, but Claire arrives and opens a door on the side of the chamber, freeing him. Reardon shoots at Brand, driving him off. Reardon and Claire eventually learn that

Melton isn't Captain Mephisto, but had only pretended to be in an effort to learn more information from Brand.

Melton phones Claire and instructs her to meet him with Reardon at a secret rendezvous point if she wants to learn her father's whereabouts. The real Mephisto discovers this, and, killing Melton, ambushes Reardon and Claire as they arrive at a warehouse to meet Melton. A fight develops between Mephisto, Brand and Reardon. Reardon overpowers Brand, but Mephisto escapes with Claire, bound by ropes, in a speedboat. Reardon pursues them in another boat. Reardon leaps into Mephisto's boat, and they both fall into the ocean as they fight. Claire is now alone in the boat as it races toward the rocky shoreline. The boat crashes on the rocks and Claire is thrown into the ocean, but Reardon is able to rescue her before she drowns. Mephisto escapes by swimming ashore.

Learning that an old chart depicting the secret passageways beneath the mansion exists on the mainland, Reardon and Claire plan to fly over and retrieve it. Mephisto, learning of their plans, conceals a bomb in their plane. Reardon and Claire discover the bomb and throw it out of the plane just before it explodes. Discovering that Reardon and Claire have survived, Mephisto orders Brand to the mainland, instructing him to get the tunnel chart before Reardon does. Reardon acquires the tunnel chart from a curio dealer, but Brand arrives and tries to steal it. A fight develops, and Reardon is hurled from a window several stories above the street; he survives when he grabs a firehose mounted on the wall before falling out the window. Using the firehose as a rope, Reardon climbs back into the building. Reardon gives the tunnel chart to Claire

for safekeeping while he searches for Brand, but Brand finds Claire first and takes the map from her.

Brand takes Claire to a ship, intending to set out for Mystery Island, but Reardon appears and surprises him. Reardon frees Claire, but discovers that Brand has burned the tunnel chart. Reardon turns Brand over to the police and subjects him to a lie-detector test in an effort to get more information about Mephisto and Prof. Forrest. As the test is administered, one of Mephisto's henchmen appears and frees Brand at gunpoint. A fight develops and the henchman is killed, but Brand escapes in the confusion.

Brand returns to Mystery Island, informing Mephisto that Reardon has learned Prof. Forrest is working with radium and plans to trail him with a radium detector. Brand, acting on Mephisto's orders, follows Reardon and Claire in their car by plane and tries to bomb them, but he is unsuccessful. As Reardon searches Mystery Island for Prof. Forrest using the radium detector, Mephisto sends Brand to stop him. Brand and a henchman attack Reardon and Claire on a wharf, trying to take the radium detector from them. Reardon succeeds in overpowering Brand, but the henchman snatches the radium detector from Claire and flees in a speedboat. Reardon jumps into the boat, attacking the man, and Claire follows in another boat. As Reardon and the man fight, a gun goes off, rupturing the engine's fuel line, and the boat explodes in flame. Reardon, grabbing the radium detector, leaps to safety aboard Claire's boat.

Removing the radium supply from the radiatomic power transmitter, Mephisto is able to lure Reardon and Claire

Manhunt of Mystery Island— Roy Barcroft.

into a trap inside a cave, which is then flooded by Mephisto. The rushing waters force them into a tunnel with an opening high on a mountainside; Claire and Reardon are swept out through the opening and they fall into the ocean below. The radium detector is ruined, though. Keeping this a secret, Reardon tries to set a trap to catch Mephisto, using the radium detector as bait, but he fails.

Armstrong, one of the island's three remaining owners, is suspected of being Mephisto. Armstrong disappears from the estate and phones Reardon, informing him that he isn't Mephisto, but can prove who is if Reardon will bring some film developer and meet him at a shack

on the beach. Reardon hurries with Claire to meet Armstrong, but Brand learns of this and reports it to Mephisto. Reardon arrives at the shack with Claire. Armstrong informs Reardon that he has managed to take an infrared photo of Mephisto and will develop the film in Reardon's presence, revealing Mephisto's true identity. As the lights are turned out so that Armstrong can develop the film, Mephisto and Brand enter the room, turning on the light. A fight erupts and Claire is knocked unconscious. As Armstrong struggles with Brand, Mephisto flees the shack with Reardon in pursuit. After a furious chase up a mountainside, Reardon falls after grappling with Mephisto, but his fall is broken by a fishnet suspended on a wooden frame.

At the shack, Brand kills Armstrong and escapes. Claire regains consciousness as Reardon returns, but they find that the film Armstrong was developing has been ruined. Brand picks up Mephisto in his car, and Mephisto hatches a plan to lead Reardon on a wild goose chase so that Claire can be kidnapped and used to force Prof. Forrest into finishing the radiatomic power transmitter. Reardon is ambushed in a cave by Mephisto's men, but survives. Mephisto takes Claire to her father, and forces Prof. Forrest to continue working on the radiatomic power transmitter by threatening his daughter with death. Having captured Brand, Reardon contacts Mephisto by radio and offers to exchange Brand for Claire. Mephisto agrees, giving Reardon his location, and Reardon arrives, parking his car with Brand tied up inside.

As Reardon, on foot, approaches the cabin where Mephisto waits, Brand loosens the ropes binding him and manages to inform Mephisto over Reardon's car radio. The treacherous Mephisto ambushes Reardon at gunpoint as he enters the cabin and starts to free Claire. Mephisto disarms Reardon, but the resourceful Claire kicks a chair, throwing Mephisto off balance, and Reardon engages Mephisto in a fight. A wood-burning stove is knocked over and the cabin is set afire. Reardon escapes the burning cabin with Claire. They chase Mephisto across a rickety suspension bridge; when Mephisto reaches the other side, he cuts the ropes. Reardon and Claire plummet downward with the bridge, but survive when they fall into the water below.

Reardon and Claire trick Mephisto into revealing the location of a secret passage leading to the crafty pirate's hidden lair. Reardon follows Mephisto, but is knocked unconscious in a tense struggle with the murderer. Mephisto then devises a seemingly perfect plan to end Reardon's persistent interference. He intends to seat the unconscious Reardon in the transformation chair, transform Reardon into Mephisto, and leave him to take the blame for the real Mephisto's dastardly crimes. Before he can accomplish this, Claire shoots him. The villainous pirate is revealed as Braley, one of the island's two remaining owners. With the madman defeated and his accomplice Brand captured, Reardon leaves Mystery Island with Claire and her father, now freed from Mephisto's clutches.

Comments

Molecular transformation is the science fiction premise behind *Manhunt of Mystery Island*, a concept that would not be dealt with again in films until the original version of *The Fly* appeared in 1958. The exact mechanics of the evil Capt. Mephisto's "transformation chair" (consisting of a revolving dynamo wheel and crackling electrical effects) are never fully explained, although the villainous reincarnated pirate does offer a cursory explanation to an inquisitive underling in Chapter 1:

"I've often wondered how you change from one person to another," the lackey asks in a conversational tone.

"No doubt you have," Mephisto replies. "I'll tell you this much. The appearance of human beings' stature, complexion and pigmentation is controlled by the molecular arrangement of the blood corpuscles. I have found a means of altering that arrangement."

"I understand," The lackey remarks.

"If I thought you really did," Mephisto answers, "I'd *kill* you! Remember, any attempt to discover which one of the owners is my true personality will result in your immediate destruction!"

"Don't lose your head — dead men don't walk!" cautions hero Lance Reardon (Richard Bailey) in *Manhunt of Mystery Island*, but they do in this serial in the person of Capt. Mephisto as played by Roy Barcroft. Barcroft, a stocky B-Western veteran and a good actor with an imposing presence, cuts a menacing figure in his flamboyant pirate garb, peering through secret peepholes in the walls, menacing his underlings and attacking his role with aplomb. At one point, Mephisto grows impatient with the captive Prof. Forrest, who is taking too long to perfect his "radiatomic power transmitter."

"You wouldn't dare trick me?" Mephisto inquires.

"Trick you?" Forrest retorts. "I'd *kill* you if I thought I could escape afterwards. As it is, I'm obeying orders."

"Don't tax my patience too far!" Mephisto bellows, stalking off-camera.

The much-discussed "radiatomic power transmitter" itself— a device that will supposedly transmit power to ships and trains from a central base in order to counter any potential world fuel shortage — is a disappointing prop considering its importance to the story, and looks like nothing more than a black box mounted on a tripod. The power transmitter is outfitted with a spray nozzle at one point so that it can spray a jet of "radium vapor" and serve as a weapon, but the supposedly flammable radium vapor is obviously nothing more than ordinary steam.

The usual "guessing game" involving four suspect characters — Prof. Hargraves, Mr. Armstrong, Fred Braley and attorney Paul Melton — any one of whom may actually be Captain Mephisto — is a tiresome plot device used too often in serials, but it is at least handled well in this instance. Once the basic premise and general plot are established, *Manhunt of Mystery Island* settles into the usual progression of fistfights and chases, with the tropical resort island location providing a welcome change of setting.

Aside from the serial's basic premise and Roy Barcroft's enjoyable performance, the other major asset of *Manhunt of Mystery Island* is Linda Stirling, a classically beautiful young actress who had starred in Republic's *The Tiger Woman* serial the previous year. Republic, with its bread-and-butter output of B-Westerns and serials, was hardly considered a "glamour" studio, but if the serials ever produced the equivalent of Elizabeth Taylor, Linda Stirling was it, and she may well have gone on to major stardom if she hadn't been overexposed in B-Westerns and cliffhangers.

Leading man Richard Bailey is a barely competent actor with the personality of a tree stump, and is not entirely believable as Lance Reardon, a supposedly brilliant criminologist; he regularly pontificates in the usual Sherlock Holmes deductive reasoning manner, detecting vital clues that the other characters are apparently too dense to notice. Despite his best efforts, the unemotional Bailey is easily overshadowed by Roy Barcroft's over-the-top villainy and Linda Stirling's glamour.

Video availability: Republic Home Video.

The Monster and the Ape

(Columbia, 1945)

Producer: Rudolph C. Flothow. Director: Howard Bretherton. Screenplay: Sherman Lowe, Royal K. Cole. Photography: L.W. O'Connell. Film editors: Dwight Caldwell, Earl Turner. Music: Lee Zahler. Assistant director: Leonard J. Shapiro.

Cast: Robert Lowery (Ken Morgan), George Macready (Ernst), Carole Mathews (Babs Arnold), Ralph Morgan (Prof. Arnold), Willie Best (Flash), Jack Ingram (Nordik), Anthony Warde (Flint), Ted Mapes (Butler), Eddie Parker (Blake), Stanley Price (Mead), Ray "Crash" Corrigan (the ape).

Chapter Titles

(1) *The Mechanical Terror.* (2) *The Edge of Doom.* (3) *Flames of Fate.* (4) *The Fatal Search.* (5) *Rocks of Doom.* (6) *A Friend in Disguise.* (7) *A Scream in the Night.* (8) *Death in the Dark.* (9) *The Secret Tunnel.* (10) *Forty Thousand Volts.* (11) *The Mad Professor.* (12) *Shadows of Destiny.* (13) *The Gorilla at Large.* (14) *His Last Flight.* (15) *Justice Triumphs.*

Story

Prof. Arnold of the Bainbridge Research Foundation invents a robot called "the metalogen man," and proudly exhibits his creation for Prof. Ernst. Arnold then leaves to meet Ken Morgan, who represents a large company that commissioned the robot. When Arnold and his daughter Babs return to his laboratory with Morgan, they find that the robot has been stolen.

Morgan finds the robot, but Ernst, at his home, activates the robot by remote control; the automoton seizes Morgan and throws him into an electronic energizer. Fortunately, Morgan lands on an insulated mat and is saved. Learning that a supply of metalogen needed for the robot is at the Graystone Museum, Ernst uses his trained gorilla Thor in an attempt to steal the rare metal. Morgan trails Ernst, but is nearly killed when his car plunges over an embankment.

In his lair, Ernst discovers that the containers he has stolen do not contain the metalogen. Morgan, unharmed, learns where the metalogen has been hidden. Meanwhile, Prof. Arnold and Babs have been imprisoned by Ernst, who also learns, from Arnold, where the metalogen is hidden. He goes to retrieve it with Blake, a henchman. In a fight with hoods, Morgan, unconscious, falls on a conveyer belt that inches toward a flaming oven. Morgan revives in time to save himself and then frees Prof. Arnold and Babs.

Having procured the metalogen, Ernst has returned home, but Arnold uses a radio detector to track the stolen metal. Ernst, tipped off by Blake, transfers the metalogen to another location, his old workshop. Morgan enters the deserted workshop alone and is nearly

The Monster and the Ape—Robert Lowery with robot.

trapped in a powerful blast when gunshots strike a drum filled with explosives.

Morgan saves himself by leaping out of a window just before the detonation. Dr. Draper, a geologist who has in-

vented a machine capable of locating buried meteorites containing metalogen, agrees to help Morgan. Ernst, however, imprisons Draper, stealing his credentials. Disguising himself as Draper, he lures Morgan to a remote

stone quarry. The gorilla Thor then starts a rock avalanche, nearly killing Morgan, who narrowly escapes by hiding in a crevice.

The metalogen detector leads Morgan to a paint factory and he becomes embroiled in a tense struggle with Flint and Butler, two of Ernst's hoods. The metalogen detector is smashed during the fight; Butler starts a fire as Morgan battles Flint on a catwalk above a paint vat. The robot then appears, trapping Morgan on the catwalk over the rising flames. Morgan pulls himself to safety and, deftly avoiding the robot's grasp, manages to disconnect a metalogen disc from the automoton's body, without which it cannot function. Morgan learns that the real Dr. Draper has been in a hospital since Ernst attacked him. Meanwhile, Babs Arnold is working at the lab when Thor the gorilla arrives and begins to strangle her. Nordik, one of Ernst's henchmen, stops Thor from killing Babs, then steals the robot and the metalogen disc. The ape escapes while Nordik is taking him back to Ernst, but is captured by Morgan, who places an announcement in the newspapers that Thor is being held at the laboratory. Babs is imprisoned and Morgan is captured by Ernst, and both are locked in a room with movable walls that close together. Morgan and Babs are saved by the police, who arrive just in time.

Morgan then discovers a map depicting the paint factory and goes there, but the robot knocks Morgan unconscious. An explosion, nearly buries him alive, but he revives just in time and is able to escape the blast. Finding the robot, Morgan once again removes the Meta-

logen disc and the robot collapses, inert. Morgan is about to take the disc and some rocks away for analysis, but is nearly killed when Ernst throws an electrical switch. He is saved at the last moment when a policeman waiting outside appears and shuts off the current. Trailing Ernst to his house, Morgan falls into a deep well, but he escapes by climbing up the stone wall. Learning that the metalogen is about to be sent to a bank vault in an armored car, Ernst sends a shortwave radio message and, pretending to be the vault manager, instructs the armored car driver to take his cargo to the brick works. Searching for the armored car, Morgan's taxi cab is destroyed in a collision with a truck.

Morgan and the cab driver emerge unharmed from the accident. Meanwhile, Ernst reveals that he plans to manufacture an army of metalogen robots in a foreign country. Captured by Morgan, Ernst's henchman Butler escapes and warns Ernst that Morgan is on the way. Leaving the gorilla Thor to handle Morgan, Ernst and his men flee, but Prof. Arnold arrives and kills Thor, saving Morgan's life. Using his metalogen detector to track Ernst, Arnold is captured by Ernst's gang, and Morgan learns that Ernst's men have already left in a plane for the West Coast with the metalogen. Morgan charters a plane in pursuit. Army anti-aircraft batteries open fire because the planes are flying without authorization, and score a direct hit.

Morgan bails out of his plane before it explodes, but the other plane crashes, killing Ernst's gang and destroying the metalogen. Morgan and Babs free Prof.

Opposite: The Monster and the Ape— Carole Matthews, Ted Mapes.

Arnold and learn that the treacherous Ernst is en route to the airport. Morgan and the police chase Ernst's car, which topples out of control off a steep cliff, hurling Ernst and the robot to destruction.

Comments

Columbia's *The Monster and the Ape* wasn't based on a comic strip, but with its outlandish plot it might just as well have been. Columbia had begun serial production late in the day, in 1937, and from the outset their serials were less serious and more intentionally humorous in nature than the rival products turned out by Republic and Universal. Columbia serial actors, under the supervision of directors like James W. Horne, were often allowed (and even encouraged) to ham shamelessly, and scenes would be intentionally slanted for a comic effect as if to let the audience in on the joke. Villains would gesture broadly and heroes would run around in fast motion like they were in a comedy (James W. Horne *was* a comedy specialist, having directed Laurel and Hardy). Evidently, the Columbia studio brass felt that, since the serials (in their opinion) were nothing but junk anyway, why not just relax and play them for what they were worth? This overt tongue-in-cheek approach, while generally disliked by serial fans at the time, gave the Columbia serials a lighter and more playful tone that makes them enjoyable to watch through adult eyes today. *The Monster and the Ape*, with its pulp script full of mad scientists and killer gorillas, fits snugly into this mold; it was virtually the last Columbia serial with any consistent entertainment value.

After the release of *The Monster and the Ape*, Sam Katzman took over as producer of Columbia's serials, establishing tighter-than-usual budgetary restrictions that squeezed the last vestige of creativity out of the studio's chapterplays. Katzman, one of the most artless and insensitive men ever to produce movies, was cynical at best and downright contemptuous at worst, and he evidently just didn't care about the serials he produced, assuming that the audience for such fare was either too young or too unsophisticated to notice the drop in quality. For 11 years, from 1945 until the very last serial made, *Blazing the Overland Trail*, was released by the studio in 1956, Columbia had the richly deserved reputation of producing the worst serials of the sound era. Aside from *Superman* (q.v.) in 1948, and its sequel *Atom Man vs. Superman* (q.v.) in 1950, Katzman's serial unit produced little of merit. Although some of his cliffhangers, like *The Adventures of Sir Galahad* (1949), exhibited some ambition in terms of subject matter and a certain degree of rough-hewn charm, Katzman's serial product at Columbia is largely forgettable.

The Monster and the Ape was at least an enjoyable farewell to the better, pre-Katzman Columbia serials. Produced by Rudolph C. Flothow and directed by Howard Bretherton, the film has a goofy, comic book edge with some nice atmospheric touches. Dependable leading man Robert Lowery, four years away from playing Batman in the Katzman-produced *Batman and Robin* (q.v.), is good in his role opposite aristocratic villain George Macready, who appeared in Columbia's subdued horror film *The Soul of a Monster* the same year. Ray "Crash" Corrigan is on hand in his ape suit as the trained gorilla Thor, and the serial's robot is, for once, a believable one. Even the more expensive serial *Flash Gordon Conquers the Universe* (q.v.) had been unable to present convincing robots, and the automotons on display in other serials like *The Phantom Empire* were even worse. Aside from the robot in *The Monster and the Ape*, the only other convincing mechanical men seen in serials were those created for *The Vanishing Shadow* (q.v.) and *The Phantom Creeps* (q.v.). Inasmuch as the robot is a central figure in *The Monster and the Ape*, a convincing robot costume was essential, and Columbia's designers succeeded with their creation. The robot's head, incidentally, repainted with a "glitter" finish, later serves as the "Atom Man's" mask in *Atom Man vs. Superman* (q.v.).

The Purple Monster Strikes

(Republic, 1945)

Associate producer: Ronald Davidson. Directors: Spencer Bennet, Fred Brannon. Screenplay: Royal Cole, Albert DeMond, Basil Dickey, Lynn Perkins, Joseph Poland, Barney Sarecky. Photography: Bud Thackery. Film editors: Cliff Bell, Harold Minter. Special effects: Howard Lydecker, Theodore Lydecker. Set decorators: John McCarthy, Jasper Cline. Art director: Fred A. Ritter. Makeup: Bob Mark. Musical director: Richard Cherwin. Sound: Ed Borschell. RCA sound. Unit manager: Roy Wade. Feature version: *D-Day on Mars* (100 minutes), for television distribution.

Cast: Dennis Moore (Craig Foster), Linda Stirling (Sheila Layton), Roy Barcroft (The Purple Monster), James Craven (Dr. Cyrus Layton), Bud Geary (Hodge Garrett), Mary Moore (Marcia), John Davidson (Emperor of Mars), Joe Whitehead (Stewart), Emmett Vogan (Saunders), George Carlton (Meredith), Kenne Duncan (Mitchell), Rosemonde James (Helen), Monte Hale (Harvey), Wheaton Chambers (Benjamin), Frederick Howard (Crandall), Anthony Warde (Tony), Ken Terrell (Andy).

Chapter Titles

(1) *The Man in the Meteor.* (2) *The Time Trap.* (3) *Flaming Avalanche.* (4) *The Lethal Pit.* (5) *Death on the Beam.* (6) *The Demon Killer.* (7) *The Evil Eye.* (8) *Descending Doom.* (9) *The Living Dead.* (10) *House of Horror.* (11) *Menace from Mars.* (12) *Perilous Plunge.* (13) *Fiery Shroud.* (14) *The Fatal Trial.* (15) *Takeoff to Destruction.*

Story

Investigating the arrival of a strange meteor on Earth, Dr. Cyrus Layton, famed astronomer and head of the Scientific Foundation, discovers that it is actually a spacecraft piloted by a Martian calling himself the Purple Monster. Returning to his observatory with the interplanetary visitor, Dr. Layton is startled to learn that the Purple Monster intends to conquer the Earth. Layton's protestations are cut short when the Purple Monster kills him with a vial of poison gas and, through a scientific process, becomes transparent and inhabits Layton's dead body.

Now disguised as Layton, the Purple Monster is able to operate undetected, hiring a cheap thug, Hodge Garrett, to aid him in his schemes. The world at large, including Layton's niece Sheila and her friend Craig Foster, legal counsel for the Scientific Foundation, remain unaware of the Purple Monster's cunning masquerade.

The ruthless would-be conqueror intends to construct a rocketship much larger than the single-passenger craft that he first arrived in, so that he will be able to make numerous trips between Earth and Mars in order to transport the invasion force. The Purple Monster determines that he must obtain a series of complicated devices invented by other members of the Scientific Foundation to complete the rocketship. Craig and Sheila, aware of this, struggle tirelessly in opposition to the Martian's plans.

The Purple Monster summons an accomplice, Marcia, from Mars; she murders a secretary at the Scientific Foundation, inhabiting her body as a disguise. Marcia's secret is discovered by Sheila, and Marcia dies in an accident when she tries to escape. When Sheila informs Craig of this, they realize that the Purple Monster has the same

power, and trap him when Craig plants a hidden movie camera and films the Martian as he momentarily leaves the dead body of Dr. Layton. His secret revealed, the Purple Monster blasts off for Mars in his newly constructed rocketship, intending to return with an invasion force. Craig, arriving just as the Martian blasts off, aims an "electroannihilator" ray gun at the rocketship as it streaks away from Earth. The Purple Monster is blown into oblivion along with his plans for world conquest.

Comments

The first movie (serial or feature) about interplanetary travel since 1940's *Flash Gordon Conquers the Universe* (q.v.), *The Purple Monster Strikes* also pre-dates the influential feature *Destination Moon* by five years. The Purple Monster character, accurately described in the film as "a weird-looking person dressed in tights and a helmet," is shown brandishing a dagger in a still picture beneath the opening credits. The serial begins with a brief but credible scene of a spacecraft zooming toward Earth as a melodramatic off-screen announcer intones, "Out of the infinite distances beyond the stratosphere, a strange weird object is hurtling through interstellar space toward the Earth." The benign Dr. Cyrus Layton (James Craven), peering through his telescope, notices "a strange purple-colored meteor headed toward the Earth, apparently from the direction of Mars." Layton hurries to the landing site, just as the small, torpedo-shaped craft lands and the Purple Monster (Roy Barcroft) leaps from the exploding wreckage. The following dialogue exchange between Prof. Layton and the Purple Monster neatly establishes the serial's basic premise

The Purple Monster Strikes— Dennis Moore.

and emphasizes the titular antagonist's ruthless nature with admirable economy.

LAYTON: Why, who are you?

MONSTER: My name would mean nothing to you. I've come from the planet which people on Earth call Mars.

LAYTON: From Mars? But you speak our language.

MONSTER: I speak all languages. Many years ago, my people invented and perfected a remarkable instrument known as the distance eliminator. With the aid of this device, I've been able to see and hear everything that happens on Earth.

LAYTON: But this is splendid! Science has been attempting for years to find a method of communicating with Mars. As a matter of fact, I myself have been working on something that will eventually enable us to fly to your planet.

MONSTER: I know. You are Dr. Cyrus Layton. We've watched the progress of your work and have come to you for help. My own projectile, you see, has no provision for a return journey. I am very anxious to see the plans for your jet plane.

LAYTON: Why, I'll show them to you immediately. The observatory is close by and my car is right here.

MONSTER: Thank you.

After a quick transitional dissolve, the conversation continues at Layton's observatory as the Purple Monster examines Layton's jet plane blueprints:

LAYTON: I'm highly flattered, sir. I was afraid that my humble efforts might seem childish to a scientist from Mars.

MONSTER: On the contrary, this is just what I need. Your launching rocket is far superior to ours, and your anti-gravity device, which assures a safe landing, is superb. Are there other copies of the plans?

LAYTON: No, this is the only copy. My project is backed by the Scientific Research Foundation. We've tried to keep it more or less a secret until we're ready to let the public know.

MONSTER: That is a very wise precaution. Do any of the members of the Foundation know the details of the plans?

LAYTON: Only one, our attorney Craig Foster. He was formerly an officer of the United States Secret Service. I expect him here soon with my niece Sheila. I'll be proud to introduce them to you. This is really the greatest day of my life!

MONSTER: Unfortunately for you, Doctor, it is also the *last* day of your life!

LAYTON: I beg your pardon ... I—I'm afraid I don't quite understand.

MONSTER: My people have planned for a long time to invade the Earth and enslave its inhabitants, destroying all those who resist us. I am a forerunner of that invasion, the advance guard.

LAYTON: You must be insane! You must have injured your head when you landed. You'd better let me get you a drink.

MONSTER: Stay where you are. I am not mad. The invasion has only been delayed because of our inability to build ships that could safely land and return to Mars. Your plans have supplied that need.

LAYTON: Then you landed in the wrong country, my friend. Do you think the American people will sit by and do nothing while you build a jet plane for the purpose of bringing in an army of conquest?

MONSTER: Yes—because they won't know I'm building it. I intend to build it in the personality of Dr. Cyrus Layton. You see, I have the ability to kill you, enter your body, and use it for my own purposes.

LAYTON: Now I know you're insane!

MONSTER: This capsule contains a specimen of the atmosphere surrounding Mars, a highly concentrated form of carbo-oxide gas. Harmless for me to breathe, of course, but it will be instantly fatal to *you*!

The Purple Monster immediately murders the hapless scientist and inhabits his

The Purple Monster Strikes— Roy Barcroft.

dead body. A lot of footage is repeatedly expended on the subject of corpse possession and reanimation, which involves a simple double-exposure shot of the transparent Martian stepping into the lifeless body. It is used again when the Purple Monster's girl assistant (played by Mary Moore, wife of "Lone Ranger" Clayton Moore) murders a female lab worker and inhabits her body. The potentially repulsive subject of decomposition is tactfully avoided.

The general plot of Republic's subsequent "Martian invasion" serials, including *Flying Disc Man from Mars* (q.v.), *Radar Men from the Moon*—which featured lunar invaders (q.v.)—and *Zombies of the Stratosphere* (q.v.), was established in *The Purple Monster Strikes*, with the alien invader arriving on Earth, smugly announcing his grandiose plans for conquest, and then proceeding as cheaply and as economically as possible, hiring an unimpressive group of thugs and petty crooks as henchmen. In this case, The Purple Monster's chief assistant is the improbably named cretin Hodge Garrett (Bud Geary), who proves to be more of a hindrance than an asset. Republic's mundane approach to their science fiction serials with this type of plot seems motivated less by monetary considerations than by a general lack of imagination. *The Purple Monster Strikes*, being the first of its kind, at least plays better than its subsequent imitators.

Video availability: Republic Home Video.

The Crimson Ghost

(Republic, 1946)

Associate producer: Ronald Davidson. Directors: William Witney, Fred C. Brannon. Screenplay: Albert DeMond, Basic Dickey, Jesse Duffy, Sol Shor. Photography: Bud Thackery. Film editors: Harold R. Minter, Cliff Bell. Special effects: Howard Lydecker, Theodore Lydecker. Art director: Fred A. Ritter. Set decorator: John McCarthy, Jr., Earl Wooden. Makeup: Bob Mark. Sound: William E. Clark, RCA sound. Feature version: *Cyclotrode "X"* (100 minutes), for television distribution.

Cast: Charles Quigley (Duncan Richards), Linda Stirling (Diana Farnsworth), Clayton Moore (Ashe), I. Stanford Jolley (Blackton), Kenne Duncan (Chambers), Forrest Taylor (Van Wyck. Emmett Vogan (Anderson), Sam Flint (Maxwell), Joe Forte (Parker), Stanley Price (Fator), Wheaton Chambers (Wilson), Tom Steele (Stricker), Dale Van Sickel (Harte), Rex Lease (Bain), Fred Graham (Zane), Bud Wolfe (Gross).

Chapter Titles

(1) *Atomic Peril.* (2) *Thunderbolt.* (3) *The Fatal Sacrifice.* (4) *The Laughing Skull.* (5) *Flaming Death.* (6) *Mystery of the Mountain.* (7) *Electrocution.* (8) *The Slave Collar.* (9) *Blazing Fury.* (10) *The Trap That Failed.* (11) *Double Murder.* (12) *The Invisible Trail.*

Story

The brilliant Prof. Chambers, working for the United States government, has developed a futuristic machine called the Cyclotrode that can neutralize all electrical current within the range of its rays. Unknown to Chambers, one of the associates in whom he has confided is actually the Crimson Ghost, a ruthless master criminal who hides his identity behind a gruesome skull mask. Chambers is threatened by the Crimson Ghost's henchmen, led by Ashe, but destroys the Cyclotrode before they can steal it. The Crimson Ghost's men then try to kidnap Chamber so that he can be forced to build another Cyclotrode, but they are stopped by Duncan Richards, a resourceful criminologist and Chambers' friend.

Later, the Crimson Ghost does succeed in kidnapping Chambers and forces the scientist to wear a slave collar, a metal neck band containing a mind-control device that cannot be removed without killing the person wearing it. Richards learns of Chambers' disappearance from Diana Farnsworth, a secretary for Chambers and his associates. At a bank vault where a duplicate Cyclotrode is stored, Richards finds a mesmerized Chambers and the Crimson Ghost's men attempting to steal the machine.

Richards trails the criminal gang to a secret hideout where the captive Prof. Chambers has rigged a trap to kill the Crimson Ghost; Richards almost stumbles into the trap himself. Chambers, however, valiantly sacrifices his own life to save Richards. With Chambers dead, the Crimson Ghost plans to build a larger, more powerful version of the Cyclotrode himself by copying Chambers' duplicate machine. Needing money

to accomplish this, the Crimson Ghost and his henchmen use the Cyclotrode already in their possession to disable a payroll car. The Crimson Ghost's men shoot both of the payroll car guards, killing them, but one of the guards is able to send an alarm to the police before he dies. The Crimson Ghost disables the approaching police car with the Cyclotrode, and his men break into the payroll car and rob it.

Learning of this, Richards correctly surmises that Prof. Chambers' Cyclotrode was used to commit the theft. Knowing that heavy water is necessary to operate the Cyclotrode, and that the compound is manufactured only by the Cornwall Chemical Company, Richards instructs the Cornwall officials not to release any heavy water without his authorization. The Crimson Ghost sends Richards a message on a phonograph record, but when Richards tries to play it in his lab, the disc exudes a powerful gas that knocks Richards unconscious.

Ashe, the Crimson Ghost's henchman, then enters the lab with an accomplice, and they take the unconscious Richards to a hotel room where the Crimson Ghost is waiting. The Crimson Ghost is about to attach a mind-controlling slave collar to Richards when the criminologist suddenly revives and leaps to his feet, grabbing a nearby gun that had been carelessly left on a table. One of the henchmen suddenly grabs a pistol, but he is fatally shot by Richards, who then becomes involved in a violent struggle with both the Crimson Ghost and Ashe.

Trapped in the hotel room when the key falls out of the locked door and is lost in the confusion of the fight, the Crimson Ghost exits through the window while Richards fights Ashe. The

Ghost manages to get to the building across the street by traveling hand-over-hand across an electrical wire, high above the city street. Having beaten Ashe unconscious, Richards follows across the same wire in pursuit of the Crimson Ghost, but the Ghost, now safely on the roof of the other building, cuts the electrical wire, and Richards plummets toward the street below. Richards saves himself by hanging onto the wire and swinging back against the hotel, entering through a window.

Now suspecting that one of the late Prof. Chambers' associates is secretly the Crimson Ghost, Richards proves his theory when he plants a story about an anonymous phone call informing him to pick up a letter with information about the Crimson Ghost. Traveling to a remote location with Diana to pick up the fictitious letter, they are trailed by Ashe and an accomplice, who attack them in an attempt to retrieve the letter. As Ashe tries to run down Richards with his car, Diana shoots and kills Ashe's accomplice. Ashe is driven off by gunfire.

In the conference room used by Chambers' associates, Richards discovers a hidden microphone and stages a phony conversation with Diana in which he remarks that the only available supply of heavy water is hidden in a bottle within the conference room safe. Richards and Diana hide, waiting for the guilty party to appear and steal the heavy water. Anderson, one of chambers' associates, enters the room and removes the bottle of heavy water from the safe.

Richards and Diana emerge from hiding and accuse Anderson of being the Crimson Ghost. When Anderson tries to kill Richards, they realize that Anderson is wearing a slave collar and is only acting under the control of the Crimson Ghost, who is waiting in a car outside with Ashe. Anderson's slave collar is exploded by remote-control, killing him, and Ashe suddenly runs into the room, surprising Richards and Diana and stealing the bottle of heavy water.

Ashe and the Crimson Ghost speed away in their car with the vital compound, but Richards and Diana chase them in their own car. The Crimson Ghost's car screeches to a halt, and the villain runs into a building with Ashe just as Richards pulls up behind them and follows. The Crimson Ghost and Ashe trick Richards into entering a locked room, where the Crimson Ghost taunts Richards by speaking to him through a microphone concealed in an illuminated skull. When the room is suddenly filled with deadly gas, Richards nearly suffocates, but Diana, who had been waiting outside, saves him when she enters the building and opens the door to the gas-filled room, allowing Richards to escape.

After the gas has cleared, Richards and Diana search the room for clues. Examining the skull containing the microphone, Richards finds a unique type of radio condenser, and intends to track down the Crimson Ghost by finding out who purchased it. Discovering that the heavy water stolen by Ashe is only plain ordinary water substituted by Richards, the Crimson Ghost plans to steal more heavy water from the Cornwall Chemical Company. To crack the company safe, the Crimson Ghost sends Ashe to Snyder's Radio Shop to pick up a stethoscope device to be used in the theft. Richards, tracking down the source of the radio condenser, surprises Ashe at Snyder's.

During a fight with Ashe and a crooked technician in league with the Crimson Ghost, Richards is knocked unconscious. Ashe and the other man tie Richards to a chair and Ashe, taking the stethoscope, leaves to rob the Cornwall Chemical safe. Ashe's accomplice remains behind; when Richards revives, he tricks the man into removing a cigarette case from his coat pocket. When the hood opens the specially rigged case, it emits a gas that knocks him out. Activating a grinding wheel on a nearby workbench, Richards cuts the ropes binding him and escapes.

Meeting the Crimson Ghost and another henchman at the Cornwall Chemical Company, Ashe and his accomplice steal the heavy water after the Crimson Ghost leaves. Richards suddenly appears and surprises them. In the gun battle that follows, the second hood is killed and Ashe escapes in his car, with Richards in pursuit. Ashe, racing ahead of Richards, delivers the bottle of heavy water to the pilot of a waiting plane. As the pilot taxis, attempting to take off, Ashe shoots at Richards' approaching car. A bullet strikes Richards' windshield, momentarily blinding him, and Richards' car, out of control, explodes into flame as it collides with the plane. Richards saves himself by leaping clear just in time.

The Crimson Ghost plans to manufacture his own supply of heavy water by stealing a government shipment of refined uranium. The Crimson Ghost orders Ashe to steal the uranium shipment from the Federal Atomic Plant near Owl Creek Bridge. Meanwhile, Richards has discovered a map of the Fernando Hills among the effects of the dead airplane pilot, with an unregistered landing site clearly marked. Convinced that the Crimson Ghost has a secret airstrip in that area, Richards plans to investigate by air. Learning of this, the Crimson Ghost radios Ashe to shoot down Richards' plane with the Cyclotrode when he appears over the area.

As Diana flies a plane over the Fernando Hills and reports back to Richards by radio, Ashe disables her plane with the Cyclotrode. Diana bails out, parachuting to safety just before the plane crashes, as Richards hurries to meet her. Ashe and an accomplice spot Diana's parachute and reach her before Richards does. Ashe leaves to blow up Owl Creek Bridge with a bomb, as his accomplice takes Diana away at gunpoint. Richards arrives and spots them, killing the hood in a fight and freeing Diana. Realizing that Ashe intends to destroy an approaching uranium truck and rob it by blowing up the bridge, Richards hurries to stop him after sending Diana to warn the truck.

Richards surprises Ashe as he operates the bomb controls. As Diana races across the bridge in her car to warn the oncoming radium truck, the bridge suddenly explodes, but Diana, jumping from her car just before the blast, survives. Ashe overcomes Richards in a fight and, fleeing, runs into Diana and kidnaps her, taking her to the Crimson Ghost. The ruthless Crimson Ghost outfits Diana with a slave collar and sends the mesmerized girl to spy on Richards. Richards eventually discovers the plot and, through a delicate operation, is able to remove the slave collar without harming Diana.

Diana is restored to normalcy and Ashe is captured by Richards, but the hood is freed by the Crimson Ghost, who is unaware that Richards has allowed Ashe to escape so that he could

be secretly trailed by television. Richards follows Ashe to a secret tunnel, where Ashe meets the Crimson Ghost. Richards is ambushed by the Crimson Ghost, who has learned that Ashe has been trailed. As a fight erupts and Richards battles the Crimson Ghost, Ashe and another henchman, volatile fuel leaks from a storage tank. The Crimson Ghost knocks Richards unconscious and escapes with Ashe and a flask of heavy water just as the leaking fuel explodes. Reviving and leaping behind some heavy machinery, Richards is shielded from the explosion. Ashe is apprehended after a fight with Richards.

The Crimson Ghost soon manages to build a larger Cyclotrode, and Duncan and Diana continue in their struggle against the fiendish mastermind. They finally run down the madman and unmask him as Prof. Parker, one of the late Prof. Chambers' most trusted associates. With the Crimson Ghost defeated and his criminal organization eradicated, the powerful Cyclotrode is finally secured by the United States government.

Comments

Although *the Crimson Ghost* is a slick, well-made serial, it suffers from the same overall blandness that afflicted most Republic serials from the mid-'40s on. Technically, and in terms of basic quality — the casting, direction, editing and music scoring — it can't be faulted, but there is something vital missing that prevents *The Crimson Ghost* from achieving the total effectiveness of preceding Republic efforts. The music score, although professional and serviceable enough, is perhaps the weakest ingredient. The main title music in particular is ineffective, with some passages sounding more appropriate to a Shirley Temple movie than an action-adventure yarn. A little more melodramatic punch in the scoring would have helped.

What *The Crimson Ghost* does have (and this is the one factor that makes it so memorable) is its title character, one of the single greatest menaces in serial history. The Crimson Ghost's monstrous skull-face visage, complete with blackened eye sockets and several missing teeth, surrounded by a hooded cloak, must have given plenty of youthful serial fans nightmares in 1946. The title fiend's unrelenting menace falters only once, when the Crimson Ghost delivers what may well be the worst line of dialogue in serial history. "We've been tricked by cleverness!" he solemnly intones at one point to his henchmen, after their machinations have been foiled by the hero. But it's hard to laugh at bad dialogue, even dialogue that bad, when it's being delivered by someone wearing that mask. The Crimson Ghost's skull mask is so frightening that a photographic image of the face, unattributed to the serial, currently appears on T-shirts sold to teenagers (who are, of course, completely unaware of the source).

Charles Quigley, cast as hero Duncan Richards, is good in his one-note role, and certainly handles dialogue better than most Republic leading men. Linda Stirling is on hand as girlfriend Diana Farnsworth, lending some badly needed pulchritude to the proceedings, and contributing a welcome human dimen-

Opposite: The Crimson Ghost— Clayton Moore, "The Crimson Ghost," Stanley Price.

sion to what could have been an incon-
sequential character. When Diana is
outfitted with a mind-controlling slave
collar by the Crimson Ghost, a device
that cannot be removed without causing her death, it is one of the few
instances in a Republic serial when the
viewer actually *cares* about a supporting
character's life-threatening peril. Kenne
Duncan was a likable and dependable
character actor who appeared in many
films of the 1930s, '40s and '50s, but he
was not a polished actor and is somewhat miscast here as Prof. Chambers,
inventor of the Cyclotrode. The Cyclotrode itself is somewhat disappointing,
consisting of little more than a black
box with a spiraled neon tube mounted
on it.

The other memorable cast member in
The Crimson Ghost is Clayton Moore as
one of the villain's henchmen. Referred
to only by his character's surname, Ashe,
Moore was still a couple of years away
from attaining cultural immortality as
The Lone Ranger on television, and it
seems odd in retrospect that Republic
cast him in villainous roles just as often
as in heroic roles. Moore played a
heroic leading role in Republic's 1942
serial *Perils of Nyoka* and had been
very effective, but he is just as effective as a villain in *The Crimson Ghost*,
demonstrating that he had a far wider
range as an actor than is commonly
believed.

In the early 1990s, *The Crimson Ghost*
was re-edited into a feature version and
computer-colorized for cable television
and video distribution.

Video availability: Republic Home
Video.

Brick Bradford

(Columbia, 1947)

Producer: Sam Katzman. Director:
Spencer G. Bennet. Screenplay: George
H. Plympton, Arthur Hoerl, Lewis
Clay. Photography: Ira H. Morgan,
A.S.C. Film editor: Earl Turner. Music:
Mischa Bakaleinikoff. Assistant direc-
tor: R. M. Andrews. Second unit direc-
tor: Thomas Carr.

Cast: Kane Richmond (Brick Brad-
ford), Linda Johnson (June Sanders),
Pierre Watkin (Prof. Salisbury), Charles
Quigley (Laydron), Jack Ingram
(Albers), Fred Graham (Black), John
Merton (Dr. Tymak), Leonard Penn
(Byrus), Wheeler Oakman (Walthar),
Carol Forman (Queen Khana), Charles
King (Creed), John Hart (Dent), Helene
Stanley (Carol Preston), Nelson Leigh
(Prescott), Robert Barron (Zontar),
George DeNormand (Meaker), Noel
Neill (Indian girl).

Chapter Titles

(1) *Atomic Defense.* (2) *Flight to the Moon.* (3) *Prisoners of the Moon.* (4) *Into the Volcano.* (5) *Bradford at Bay.* (6) *Back to Earth.* (7) *Into Another Century.* (8) *Buried Treasure.* (9) *Trapped in the Time Top.* (10) *The Unseen Hand.* (11) *Poison Gas.* (12) *Door of Disaster.* (13) *Sinister Rendezvous.* (14) *River of Revenge.* (15) *For the Peace of the World.*

Story

An official of the United States government assigns the heroic Brick Bradford to guard the "interceptor ray," a powerful anti-guided missile weapon invented by Dr. Tymak, a Britain scientist. The villainous Laydron, who plans to steal the interceptor ray, learns of this by spying on Bradford and his friends Prof. Salisbury, June Saunders and Sandy Sanderson.

A rare element called "lunarium," found only on the Moon and necessary to operate the interceptor ray, is obtained by Dr. Tymak when he is transported instantly to the surface of the Moon through "the crystal door," one of his many fabulous scientific inventions. Tymak is captured by the Lunarians while on the Moon. Brick Bradford follows by transporting himself to the Moon through the crystal door in a rescue attempt. Arriving on the Moon, Brick discovers that an exiled group of Lunarians are desperately trying to overthrow the Moon's rulers; Brick successfully aids their revolutionary cause while rescuing Tymak in the process.

After Bradford returns to Earth with Dr. Tymak, Laydron and his gang attempt to kidnap Tymak repeatedly, but they are constantly thwarted by Brick. Tymak then determines that, as a vital component in his scientific work, he must have a secret formula that has been lost for 200 years. Traveling back through time in the whirling "time top," another Tymak invention, Bradford and his friends are able to retrieve the valuable formula. After valiantly battling savages and pirates, they return to the present, eventually defeating Laydron and his gang.

Comments

The *Brick Bradford* newspaper comic strip was created by writer William Ritt and artist Clarence Grey. First distributed by Central Press Association and later by King Features Syndicate, the strip made its debut in August 1933, running until 1957. *The Brick Bradford* strip was noted for its sweeping adventure stories that often lasted years before the extended plotline was resolved and a new continuity established. Brick Bradford was initially presented as a daring but down-to-earth soldier of fortune, but science fiction elements soon crept into the strip; even though the science fiction angle did not dominate the stories, *Brick Bradford* was a sort of precursor to Alex Raymond's more robust *Flash Gordon* strip. William Ritt left the daily strip in 1952 along with Clarence Grey, although Grey continued to draw the Sunday color installment until his death in 1957.

Brick Bradford certainly would have made a fascinating movie serial in the tradition of *Flash Gordon*, but the strip was (unfortunately) adapted for the serials by Columbia Pictures under producer Sam Katzman's supervision in 1947. Kane Richmond, an excellent and underrated actor, was cast as Bradford, and was a standout in a largely

***Brick Bradford*—Kane Richmond, Linda Johnson and the "time top."**

undistinguished cast. The main problem with the serial is its lopsided plot construction. The first half is a science fiction adventure very much like *Flash Gordon*, as Bradford travels to the Moon and through time, but the story soon collapses into a tedious succession of chases and rescues when Bradford returns to Earth.

The special effects, such as they are, present another serious problem. When Bradford travels to the Moon through

the "crystal door," his transportation is represented by a field of cheaply animated cartoon explosions and starbursts superimposed over the image. This low-cost technique of relying on cartoon animation in special effects scenes was a ploy that Sam Katzman repeatedly fell back on in Columbia serials, most notoriously for the flying scenes in *Superman* (q.v.). When Bradford arrives on the Moon, he is obviously in familiar Bronson Canyon, a popular serial and B-Western location, with some very Earth-like cloud formations clearly visible in the sky. The time-traveling "time top" is unconvincing as well, but it is at least a three-dimensional miniature (with a life-size counterpart) instead of a cartoon. Combining cartoon animation with live-action footage can be a valid technique; it was used previously in serials by Mascot producer Nat Levine, who superimposed cartoon flames onto crashing airplanes in his 1933 cliffhanger *The Mystery Squadron*. In that case, the animation had been used only to supply peripheral detail; Katzman used cartooning like a crutch,

employing cheap animation for scenes that could have been shot economically with rear projection and a variety of other special effects techniques. Worse yet, Katzman used the cartoon animation in his serials without any taste or cleverness, almost as though he was daring the audience to notice his cut-rate production methods.

As a result, *Brick Bradford*, which could have been an outstanding adventure fantasy, soon degenerates into bland, tepid, juvenile fare. The serial finally sputters to a tame conclusion with the hero and heroine (Linda Johnson) in a romantic clinch with Katzman's cartoon starbursts superimposed over the image, bringing one of Columbia's most disappointing serials to an ignominious conclusion.

The *Brick Bradford* newspaper strip reappeared in a series of comic books published by King Comics, beginning in 1936. Ace Comics began a series of reprints in 1947, and *Brick Bradford Comics* began a short run as its own title in 1948, possibly due to the Columbia serial's release.

Superman

(Columbia, 1948)

Producer: Sam Katzman. Directors: Spencer G. Bennet, Thomas Carr. Screenplay: Arthur Hoerl, Lewis Clay, Royal Cole. Adaptation: George H. Plympton, Joseph F. Poland. Photography: Ira H. Morgan, A.S.C. Film editor: Earl Turner. Music: Mischa Bakaleinikoff. Art director: Paul Palmentola. Set decorator: Sidney Clifford. Sound engineers: Josh Westmoreland,

Phillip Faulkner. Assistant director: R.M. Andrews. Second unit director: Thomas Carr.

Cast: Kirk Alyn (Superman/Clark Kent), Noel Neill (Lois Lane), Tommy Bond (Jimmy Olsen), Carol Forman (The Spider Lady), George Meeker (Driller), Jack Ingram (Anton), Pierre Watkin (Perry White), Terry Frost (Brock), Charles King (Conrad), Charles Quigley (Dr. Hackett), Herbert Rawlinson (Dr. Graham), Forrest Taylor (Leeds), Stephen Carr (Morgan), Rusty Wescoatt (Elton), Nelson Leigh (Jor-El), Luana Walters (Lara), Edward Cassidy (Eben Kent), Virginia Carroll (Martha Kent), Alan Dinehart III (Clark Kent as a boy), Ralph Hodges (Clark Kent as a teenager), Robert Barron (Rozan), Gene Roth (train conductor), Jack North (track walker), Tom London (Pop Andrews), Frank Ellis (mine guard), Stanley Price (Grandall), Paul Stader (Irwin), Leonard Penn (Ward), Peggy Wynn (Flo, the operator), Emmett Vogan (Secretary of National Security).

Chapter Titles

(1) *Superman Comes to Earth.* (2) *Depths of the Earth.* (3) *The Reducer Ray.* (4) *Man of Steel.* (5) *A Job for Superman.* (6) *Superman in Danger.* (7) *Into the Electric Furnace.* (8) *Superman to the Rescue.* (9) *Irresistible Force.* (10) *Between Two Fires.* (11) *Superman's Dilemma.* (12) *Blast in the Depths.* (13) *Hurled to Destruction.* (14) *Superman at Bay.* (15) *The Payoff.*

Story

Jor-El, a scientist on the distant planet Krypton, predicts that a natural disaster will soon cause the planet to explode, but his frantic warnings go unheeded by Krypton's leading scien-

tists. Disaster strikes exactly as Jor-El had warned but, before Krypton is destroyed, the doomed scientist and his wife Lara place their infant son in a rocketship and launch the craft toward Earth. The last survivor of this advanced race, the extra-terrestrial orphan is found by a childless farm couple, the Kents, after the rocket lands in a rural area of the United States. The Kents raise the boy as their own son, naming him Clark; as he grows to maturity, Clark discovers that he possesses superhuman powers, including x-ray vision, invulnerability, enormous strength and the ability to fly through the air. As an adult, Clark Kent works as a reporter for the Metropolis *Daily Planet* newspaper and, costumed in his true identity as Superman, uses his extraordinary powers to aid mankind and battle evil.

The Spider Lady, a glamorous, ruthless criminal, coerces the brilliant scientist Dr. Graham into constructing a "reducer ray" and threatens to destroy Metropolis with the device if her ransom demands are not met. Clark and his fellow *Daily Planet* reporters Lois Lane and Jimmy Olsen attempt to track down the Spider Lady, who has gained possession of kryptonite, a radioactive fragment of the planet Krypton that is deadly to Superman. Superman, after nearly being destroyed once by kryptonite, shields himself by lining his costume with lead and trails the Spider Lady to her headquarters after she kidnaps Lois and Jimmy. In the ensuing struggle, the Spider Lady is disintegrated by her own reducer ray and Lois and Jimmy, still unaware of Clark's secret, are rescued by Superman.

Comments

In the pantheon of comic book superheroes, Superman is the great original,

the inspiration for all of the similar pulp paper icons who would follow; with Sherlock Holmes and Tarzan, he is one of the greatest fictional characters in popular culture. Created by two teenagers, writer Jerry Siegel and artist Joe Schuster, Superman made his debut in *Action Comics* #1 in June 1938. The innovative strip was a wildfire success, and the character was given his own comic book the following year. A daily newspaper strip, distributed by the McClure Syndicate, appeared in January 1939, followed by the introduction of a color Sunday page later that year. Early artists involved in the strip included Wayne Boring and Jack Burnley, with Al Plastino and Curt Swan drawing the comic book in later years. Read by millions every month, *Superman* was a natural for movie treatment from the beginning, but it would be a full decade after the character's print debut before the first live-action adaptation came to theater screens.

There had been a *Superman* radio series starring Bud Collyer in the 1940s, and an excellent series of 17 Technicolor cartoons animated by the Max Fleischer studio from 1941 to 1943. Republic Pictures had made an abortive attempt at filming a Superman serial in 1940, only to balk at the excessive licensing demands made by the comic book publisher, National Periodical Publications (now DC Comics); they hastily revamped their script as *Mysterious Dr. Satan* (q.v.). By 1948, though, comic book sales were sagging in the post-war economy, and National Periodicals, trying to stimulate new interest in their flagship property, finally sold the Superman movie rights to Columbia Pictures.

The resulting 15-chapter serial, produced by Sam Katzman, suffers from the usual deficiencies of any Katzman production, although it is a slight cut above the run-of-the-mill Katzman effort. Possibly, Katzman *had* to try harder, simply because the unusual subject matter demanded more. Still, there are plenty of flaws. Spencer Bennet, who

Opposite: Superman — Kirk Alyn. *Above:* Noel Neill as Lois Lane.

directed with Thomas Carr, could be a dynamic filmmaker at times, as his energetic, often imaginative direction of Republic's serial *Secret Service in Darkest Africa* 1943) amply demonstrates. Bennet was an experienced serial hand whose career stretched back to the silent era, but his considerable talent and expertise couldn't be proven by his work for Katzman at Columbia. His direction for *Superman* is flat and uninspired, with most of the scenes playing out at a leaden pace. This may be due in part to the disparate production methods between Republic and Columbia, but the end result is the same: a serial that lacks the excitement it could and should have had.

Producer Katzman's regrettable decision to use cartoon animation superimposed over real scenery whenever Superman flies is also a disappointment. Although the technique might have worked if the cartooning had been more polished and had been used more sparingly, Katzman opted for cheap, flat animation. Every time Superman flies through the air, or even performs a relatively mundane feat like crashing through a wall, he is suddenly transformed into an unconvincing cartoon figure. Even the flight of the infant Superman's rocketship from Krypton, and a tornado menacing the Kents' farm in Chapter 1, are represented by cartoon animation. Reportedly, Katzman's technical crew had attempted to depict Superman flying by suspending actor Kirk Alyn from wires in front of a rear-projection screen, but the resulting footage was so inept that even the undemanding Katzman abandoned the idea. For very little extra expense, Superman could have been represented by a three-dimensional stop-motion animated

figure in the flying scenes; this would have been more convincing. But the cartoon technique that Katzman finally chose was (expectedly) the cheapest, easiest and least preferable solution.

Superman is at least well cast. As Superman and alter ego Clark Kent, Kirk Alyn, although not a versatile actor, is competent, and visually he is the perfect flesh-and-blood counterpart of the comic book original. Befitting the serial's juvenile target audience, Alyn was not even given screen billing, and was listed in the credits as "Superman." As Lois Lane, Noel Neill contributes a lot of vitality to what could have been a mundane role; she is a lot more fun in this serial than she was when she played the character in the later 1950s George Reeves TV series. *Little Rascals* graduate Tommy Bond plays cub reporter Jimmy Olsen as somewhat aggressive and insolent, very different from Jack Larson's tamer interpretation in the TV series. Pierre Watkin is properly acerbic as *Daily Planet* editor Perry White. The chief antagonist, the Spider Lady, is played by Carol Forman. Although not a very good actress, Forman is both attractive and menacing as she plots against Superman from a hidden lair decorated with a huge, electrically charged spider web.

Columbia Pictures' original agreement with National Periodicals stipulated that *Superman* and its 1950 sequel *Atom Man Vs. Superman* (q.v.) would be withdrawn after the initial release, with no theatrical re-release or later television distribution allowed. As a result, both serials were unseen for nearly four decades, with only a short preview trailer and a very choppy, re-edited feature version of *Superman* available in bootleg form. When the serials finally did reappear, issued on videocassette by Warner Home video in 1989, disappointment was pronounced and widespread, largely due to the cheapness of the films. While this reaction is understandable and perhaps even justified, the 1948 *Superman* serial gains a little in stature when placed in its original context. As mentioned, the film was a cut above the usual Sam Katzman serial, and in 1948, with the original release prints tinted sepia, it was a genuine thrill for young moviegoers to see Superman as a live-action figure for the first time. The serial was very popular and, unlike other serials, was booked for evening performances at first-run theaters. Paradoxically, this long-unseen serial was one of the most financially successful sound cliffhangers. Its many flaws aside, the original live-action *Superman* is a likable film, and few movies, from this or any other period, have succeeded as well at bringing the cherished, juvenile world of comic books and comic book superheroes to life on the screen.

Video availability: Warner Home Video.

Batman and Robin

(Columbia, 1949)

Producer: Sam Katzman. Director: Spencer Bennet. Screenplay: George H. Plympton, Joseph F. Poland, Royal K. Cole. Photography: Ira H. Morgan, A.S.C. Film editors: Earl Turner, Dwight Caldwell. Art director: Paul Palmentola. Set decorator: Sidney Clifford. Musical director: Mischa Bakaleinikoff. Sound: RCA. Production manager: Herbert Leonard. Assistant director: R.M. Andrews.

Cast: Robert Lowery (Batman/Bruce Wayne), John Duncan (Robin/ Dick Grayson), Jane Adams (Vickie Vale), Lyle Talbot (Commissioner Gordon), Ralph Graves (Harrison), Don Harvey (Nolan), William Fawcett (Prof. Hammil), Leonard Penn (Carter), Rick Vallin (Barry Brown), Michael Whalen (Dunne), Greg McClure (Evans), House Peters, Jr. (Earl), Jim Diehl (Jason), Rusty Wescoatt (Ives), Eric Wilson (Alfred), Marshall Bradford (Roger Morton).

Chapter Titles

(1) *Batman Takes Over.* (2) *Tunnel of Terror.* (3) *Robin's Wild Ride.* (4) *Batman Trapped.* (5) *Robin Rescues Batman.* (6) *Target—Robin.* (7) *The Fatal Blast.* (8) *Robin Meets The Wizard.* (9) *The Wizard Strikes Back.* (10) *Batman's Last Chance.* (11) *Robin's Ruse.* (12) *Robin Rides the Wind.* (13) *The Wizard's Challenge.* (14) *Batman vs. The Wizard.* (15) *Batman Victorious.*

Story

A remote-control machine invented by the government is stolen, and masked crimefighters Batman and Robin are assigned by Police Commissioner Gordon to find the device. Batman and Robin are in reality millionaire Bruce Wayne and his teenage ward Dick Grayson, a secret known only to their loyal butler Alfred. The remote-control machine was invented by Prof. Hammil, a brilliant invalid confined to a wheelchair, cared for by his faithful servant Carter. A hooded mastermind calling himself the Wizard has installed the stolen remote-control machine in a secret underground cavern, and instructs his gang of hoodlums that they must steal some diamonds, which the machine uses as a power source. When the robbery occurs, Bruce and Dick are with Vickie Vale, a photographer. After getting rid of Vickie, they change into their Batman and Robin costumes. Batman and Robin catch the diamond robbers in the act and overpower three of the men, but the others escape.

Radio newscaster Barry Brown reveals on the air that the remote-control machine will be used to rob a plane with diamonds aboard. Batman, however, is piloting the plane with Robin. When it takes off, the remote-control machine takes over the plane and forces it down. Batman throws the package of diamonds out of the plane, and the Wizard, using the remote-control machine, explodes the plane. The two heroes escape just before the blast.

Batman and Robin trail Dunne, a private detective, from Barry Brown's home to the railroad yards and see two hoods attempting to learn from a freight clerk which train is loaded with X-90, a new type of explosive. Brown has already broadcast a prediction that the Wizard's gang will rob a train, and Batman, aware of Brown's tip, boards the speeding train and fights the Wizard's men atop one of the cars. Knocked off as the train enters a tunnel, Batman saves himself by grabbing a ladder on the train car. Nolan, one of the Wizard's henchmen, is able to seize a box of the X-90 explosive, but leaves the necessary detonator behind. Brown reveals on a radio broadcast that Roger Morton, who knows where more X-90 detonators are in storage, is in town, and Morton is kidnapped by the Wizard, who forces Morton to reveal where the detonators are hidden. Learning this, Batman and Robin go to the research plant containing the detonators; Batman is hurled over a cliff when the Wizard fires a powerful electrical charge at him. Batman's fall is broken by a tree.

Captured by the Wizard's men, Robin punctures a sack of cement in the Wizard's truck, and the leaking powder leaves a trail that Batman follows. Batman, rejoining Robin, then rescues Morton, who has suffered minor injuries. Bugging Morton's hotel room, the Wizard is able to learn the location of Morton's secret formula. Discovering the bugging microphone, Batman rushes to Morton's laboratory, but finds that the Wizard's men have already arrived. A terrific fight ensues, and an electrical short circuit starts a fire, trapping Batman in the flames. Robin is able to rescue Batman, and Vickie Vale manages to photograph the Wizard's gang as they flee.

Vickie learns that her brother Jimmy,

*Opposite: **Batman and Robin**—newspaper ad.*

Batman and Robin—"The Wizard" in his lair.

who has been missing, is in the gang, and a check of police files confirms that another gang member is Mac Lacey, a waterfront character. Lacey is captured by Batman, who then tries to rescue Vickie after she has been lured to the waterfront by her brother. Vickie and Batman are knocked off a pier into the water, and the water is covered with leaking gasoline, which is then ignited by a flare, trapping Batman and Vickie beneath a sea of flames. By swimming underwater, Batman is able to save himself and Vickie.

Batman disguises himself as Mac Lacey, and in the Wizard gang's hideout he is accepted as Lacey. But the masquerade is revealed when newscaster Brown remarks, on a broadcast, that the real Lacey is being held by the police for

questioning. Batman, his ruse discovered, manages to escape with Robin's help. The Wizard then traps Batman and Robin in a locked room. A toxic gas is injected into the room and Batman and Robin begin to lose consciousness. By using emergency breathing equipment from their utility belts, they escape.

Harrison, president of Associated Railroads, arrives in town and offers to pay a ransom that the Wizard has demanded, so that the criminal mastermind will not interrupt rail traffic with the remote-control machine, as he has threatened. This turn of events is broadcast by Brown, and Batman and Robin hurry to protect Harrison. Fleeing the Wizard's gang, Batman and Harrison hide in a cabin, which is then blown

***Batman and Robin*—** Robert Lowery, John Duncan.

asunder in a huge explosion. But Batman, having discovered the time bomb just before the explosion, manages to shield himself and Harrison in a small basement area.

Pretending to pay the Wizard's ran-som, Harrison delivers $5 million to the Wizard, but uses cash treated with radioactivity. Using a Geiger counter, Batman and Robin are able to trail the radioactive cash to a warehouse and they surprise the Wizard's men. In the ensuing fight, Robin is knocked unconscious and Batman is trapped in a fire that erupts when the tainted money bursts into flame. Batman is able to escape the fire by hiding in a large packing crate.

The Wizard's remote-control machine breaks down, and the Wizard determines that a fresh supply of diamonds is needed to reactivate the device. In pursuit of this goal, the Wizard decides to rob a research plant where synthetic diamonds have been developed. Batman and Robin get wind of the plan after their capture of Vickie's brother Jimmy, and race to prevent the theft, but their car is disabled by the Wizard. Borrowing another car form a passing motorist, they continue their pursuit, but are nearly killed when the car hurtles over a cliff into a lake. Having jumped from the car before it plunged into the water, Batman and Robin survive.

The caped crusaders learn that Vickie Vale has been kidnapped by the Wizard and, allowing one of the Wizard's hoods to escape, trail him to a rendezvous with the Wizard in an office building. Batman is knocked out after grabbing an electrified doorknob in the office building, and Jimmy unmasks him and learns his true identity. Regaining consciousness, Batman rescues Vickie from the Wizard's men, but is hurled out of a high window during a fight and falls to his death on the street below. But it is revealed that the dead man is really Jimmy Vale, who had taken Batman's costume when Batman had been knocked unconscious, in an attempt to rescue his sister.

Bruce Wayne, recovering his Batman costume, tells Prof. Hammil that he is meeting Vickie that night. The Wizard then kidnaps Bruce Wayne, but Robin,

dressed as Batman, helps Wayne escape. Batman and Robin then follow the Wizard's car, only to see it disappear in a smoke screen. Unable to see in the smoke, Batman's car is hurled from the road toward a huge rock, but he and Robin avoid a collision.

Barry Brown learns that Prof. Hammil has constructed a device that will neutralize the remote-control machine, and that it is being transported from the research plant by an armored car. While Robin hides inside the armored car to guard the neutralizer device, the Wizard tries to destroy the car and the neutralizer. Batman, following in a plane, is misled by a decoy armored car as the Wizard bombs the real car with Robin inside, sending it into a violent, fiery crash. At the last minute, Robin managed to jump from the armored car before it was completely destroyed.

Stealing Prof. Hammil's neutralizer, the Wizard learns that when the electronic beams of the neutralizer and the remote-control machine are combined, a zone of invisibility is created. Barry Brown then reveals in a broadcast that the Wizard himself will rob the research plant. The Wizard, now invisible, slips unseen past the guards and, using the stolen X-90 explosive, blasts open the plant's vault. Batman, hiding in the vault to surprise the Wizard, is trapped in the explosion, but he survives by using an oxygen inhaler.

The Wizard's machine falters and he returns to visibility. He is seen and wounded slightly on one hand by a guard. Investigating his list of suspects, Batman discovers that Prof. Hammil, Barry Brown and Dunne all have minor wounds on their hands. Then Hammil's servant Carter and Barry Brown are both killed just as Brown is about to reveal the Wizard's true identity on the air. Posing as Commissioner Gordon, Batman serves as bait in an attempt to trap the Wizard, who has become invisible again. Vickie prepares to shoot an infra-red photo that will reveal the killer despite his invisibility, just as the Wizard fires a gun through the window, apparently killing Batman. Batman, though, quickly dives to the floor, dodging the shot. Vickie's infra-red photo finally reveals the Wizard's true identity. He is Carter, Prof. Hammil's servant.

At Hammil's mansion, Batman captures Carter after Hammil falsely confesses to being the Wizard because he had been threatened by Carter. Batman learns that the man they all thought was Carter, killed earlier, had actually been Carter' twin brother (and an accomplice). The Wizard's gang is also rounded up and jailed. Vickie, who has suspected that Batman is really Bruce Wayne, tries to prove it by phoning Bruce in Batman's presence, but is startled to hear Bruce's voice on the phone. She is unaware that she is listening to a recording prepared by Batman to protect his dual identity.

Comments

One of Columbia producer Sam Katzman's cheapest and dullest serials, *Batman and Robin* is disappointing enough on its own terms, but suffers even more in comparison to the studio's original 1943 *Batman* serial (q.v.). The sets are flimsy and unconvincing, mood and atmosphere are entirely absent, and even the wardrobe is third-rate, with the two title characters wearing the most ill-fitting superhero costumes ever seen on film. Although Robert Lowery, a capable B-movie leading man, is acceptable as Batman, he looks less than impressive

in his comic book disguise, struggling to see through a mask with misaligned eye holes. John Duncan is badly miscast as Robin, being at least a decade too mature for the role. Duncan's Robin costume is even more badly designed than Lowery's Batman outfit, bearing only a passing resemblance to the pulp-paper original.

These are not the only deficits. The rest of the cast, including Jane Adams as Vickie Vale and Lyle Talbot as Commissioner Gordon, are competent in their roles, but are nearly defeated by a hackneyed script and unimaginative direction. The only good qualities to be found are in the professionalism of these actors and the usual sharp cinematography seen in studio product of the era. But the ultra-low budget and indifferent execution nullifies even these minimal assets. Bruce Wayne is supposedly a millionaire, but the furnishings in his none-too-opulent home look like standard issue Sears-Roebuck merchandise. At one point, Batman falls out of an office building window, and the shot of Batman falling is actually a stock shot of Lewis Wilson in a similar plunge to doom from the first *Batman* serial. In an introductory montage of Batman and Robin going about their crimefighting duties in Chapter 1, a brief stock shot of Douglas Croft as Robin from the first serial is included, despite the fact that Croft looks nothing like John Duncan, nor does the earlier Robin costume resemble Duncan's.

Commissioner Gordon uses the now-familiar bat-signal to summon Batman when he is needed, a gimmick not in the first serial, but the device shown — a large, box-like opaque projector that Gordon stores in his office and must clumsily wheel to an open window for use — looks dubious and unconvincing, like nearly everything else in the film. (And why is a dense bank of clouds always conveniently overhead every time Gordon projects the signal?) The script is a major liability, the worst sort of Saturday matinee paint-by-the-numbers tripe, with the science fiction angle introduced by the Wizard's remote-control machine and his brief foray into invisibility. Early on in the proceedings, the invalid Prof. Hammil is shown furtively regaining his ability to walk by sitting in some sort of futuristic electronic chair resembling a similar device in Republic's *Manhunt of Mystery Island* (q.v.), but this serves no real narrative purpose, and is only included as a "red herring" device so that Hammil can be included in the list of Wizard suspects.

Three of the principals in *Batman and Robin* are best known to film buffs for their roles in other movies: Robert Lowery for his appearances in the Universal horror films *The Mummy's Ghost* (1944) and *House of Horrors* (1946), Jane Adams for her role as a mad scientist's deformed assistant in Universal's *House of Dracula* (1945), and Lyle Talbot for appearing in the notorious Ed Wood film *Plan 9 from Outer Space* (1959).

Batman and Robin was issued to home movie collectors in the 1970s in the Super 8mm sound format, with all of the chapters intact except for Chapter 1, which was abridged by eight minutes. Curiously, this same version, with the slightly abridged first chapter, was later released on videocassette by Goodtimes Home Video. The complete serial has been televised on the American Movie Classics (AMC) cable TV network.

King of the Rocket Men

(Republic, 1949)

Associate producer: Franklin Adreon. Director: Fred C. Brannon. Screenplay: Royal Cole, William Lively, Sol Shor. Photography: Ellis W. Carter. Special effects: Howard Lydecker, Theodore Lydecker. Film editors: Cliff Bell, Sam Starr. Art director: Fred Ritter. Set decorators: John McCarthy, Jr., James Redd. Sound: Earl Crain, Sr. RCA Sound. Music: Stanley Wilson.

Makeup: Bob Mark. Unit manager: Roy Wade. Optical effects: Consolidated Film Industries. Feature version: *Lost Planet Airmen* (65 minutes), released theatrically.

Cast: Tristram Coffin (Jeff King), Mae Clarke (Glenda Thomas), Don Haggerty (Tony Dirken), House Peters, Jr. (Burt Winslow), James Craven (Prof. Millard), I. Stanford Jolley (Prof.

Bryant), Douglas Evans (chairman), Ted Adams (Martin Conway), Stanley Price (Gunther Von Strum), Dale Van Sickel (Martin), Tom Steele (Knox), David Sharpe (Blears), Eddie Parker (Rowan), Michael Ferro (Turk), Frank O'Connor (Guard), Buddy Roosevelt (Phillips).

Chapter Titles

(1) *Dr. Vulcan — Traitor.* (2) *Plunging Death.* (3) *Dangerous Evidence.* (4) *High Peril.* (5) *Fatal Dive.* (6) *Mystery of the Rocket Man.* (7) *Molten Menace.* (8) *Suicide Flight.* (9) *Ten Seconds to Live.* (10) *The Deadly Fog.* (11) *Secret of Dr. Vulcan.* (12) *Wave of Disaster.*

Story

Dr. Vulcan, an evil scientific genius, kills Prof. Drake of Science Associates and nearly succeeds in killing Prof. Millard, another member of the organization. Vulcan's crimes are being investigated by Glenda Thomas, a magazine photographer, when she meets two other members of Science Associates, Burt Winslow, the publicity director, and Jeff King. After King foils an attack by Vulcan's henchmen, he visits a secret cave where Prof. Millard, having survived Vulcan's attempt on his life, is in hiding. Millard gives King an experimental jet-propelled flight suit; King, wearing a metal helmet and calling himself Rocket Man, uses the flying suit to oppose Vulcan's scheme of controlling Science Associates and conquering the world.

After several encounters between Rocket Man and Dr. Vulcan's henchmen, Prof. Millard invents a machine called "the decimator," capable of disintegrating solid rock. The powerful device is stolen by Dr. Vulcan. By aiming the decimator at a fault line on the Atlantic Ocean floor, Vulcan plans to dissolve the rock strata (creating an earthquake that will destroy New York with a giant tidal wave) unless the city meets his ransom demand of one billion dollars.

Using detection equipment, King locates the decimator and Dr. Vulcan's headquarters on a small island off the East Coast and flies there as Rocket Man. Vulcan has already started the decimator and immense waves are destroying New York's waterfront, but Rocket Man crashes through a window, overcomes Vulcan and his henchman Dirken after a terrific fight and stops the decimator before the city is completely destroyed.

Comments

Even Republic's usually polished cliffhangers, while never losing their production gloss, had suffered a noticeable loss of quality by 1949. But, as they always had been in the past, Republic's serials were superior to the rival product, which by this point consisted solely of the Sam Katzman-produced Columbia chapterplays. With the relatively exorbitant licensing fees demanded by the publishers of comic strip heroes in mind, Republic created its own original character, Rocket Man, a masked vigilante, his identity hidden by a bullet-shaped steel helmet, who zooms through the air in a jet-propelled flying suit. Although the title seemingly implies an entire army of such characters, this is not the case; Republic occasionally used the ploy of naming the leading character King (in this case Jeff King) to suggest more than the studio's limited budgets were capable of delivering.

Rocket Man is an ingenious creation

King of the Rocket Men— Mae Clarke, Tristram Coffin.

with his silver helmet, futuristic jet pack and leather flying jacket. A small control panel strapped to his chest reads simply "up," "down," "slow," "fast," in juxtaposition to a couple of switches. The character is designed to attract the comic book crowd of the era, Rocket Man, who would prove amazingly resilient for the studio, is the serial's greatest asset.

The casting for *King of the Rocket Men* is offbeat, to say the least. Tristram Coffin, in the role of Rocket Man/Jeff King, had a slightly devious face with a pencil-thin mustache; he was usually cast as villains. Coffin wasn't the heroic type at all; although he was a good

actor, he seems like an odd choice for the role. The leading lady, Mae Clarke, was a dependable actress whose film career went back to early talkies, but she is past 40 in *King of the Rocket Men* and too mature for even the limited romantic interest usually found in a Republic serial. The remaining cast members are competent but unremarkable.

Technically, *King of the Rocket Men* ranks with the best of Republic's product. The New York destruction footage from *Deluge*, previously used by Republic in *Dick Tracy vs. Crime, Inc.* (q.v.), is seen again here in Chapter 12, but the real special effects treat is the footage of Rocket Man in flight, shot with a light-

King of the Rocket Men— Tristram Coffin.

weight, full-size dummy gliding on wires in the same manner as the flying scenes shot for Republic's *Adventures of Captain Marvel* (1941). If anything, the flying scenes in *King of the Rocket Men* are even more convincing, since the artificial face of the Captain Marvel dummy was sometimes visible when it flew too close to the camera and Rocket Man's helmet eliminates that problem here. The flying sequences were filmed outdoors against real scenery for maximum believability, and are far more convincing than the serviceable but flatly done rear-projection close-ups of Rocket Man shot in the studio.

The Rocket Man character, re-named and played by different actors, would reappear in two other Republic serials, *Radar Men from the Moon* (q.v.), in which the character was named Commando Cody; *Zombies of the Stratosphere* (q.v.), in which the character was referred to simply as Larry Martin; and a series of 12 *Commando Cody, Sky Marshall of the Universe* shorts released to theaters and television by Republic in 1953 (see comments on *Radar Men from the Moon* for the titles of these shorts). The Rocket Man character has also unofficially inspired the comic book *The Rocketeer* by Dave Stevens, and the Walt Disney feature film *The Rocketeer*, based on Stevens' comic book.

Video availability: Republic Home Video.

The Invisible Monster

(Republic, 1950)

Associate producer: Franklin Adreon. Director: Fred C. Brannon. Screenplay: Ronald Davidson. Photography: Ellis W. Carter. Special effects: Howard Lydecker, Theodore Lydecker. Film editors: Cliff Bell, Sam Starr. Art director: Fred A. Ritter. Set decorators: John McCarthy, Jr., James Redd. Music: Stanley Wilson. Sound: Earl Crain, Sr. RCA Sound. Makeup: Bob Mark. Unit manager: Roy Wade. Optical effects: Consolidated Film Industries. Feature version: *Slaves of the Invisible Monster* (100 minutes), for television distribution.

Cast: Richard Webb (Lane), Aline Towne (Carol), Lane Bradford (Burton), Stanley Price (Phantom Ruler), John Crawford (Harris), George Meeker (Long), Keith Richards (doctor), Dale Van Sickel (Martin), Tom Steele (Haines), Marshall Reed (police officer McDuff), Forrest Burns (guard), Ed Parker (Stoner), Frank O'Connor (Hogan), Charles Regan (Art), Charles Sullivan (Grogarty), Howard Mitchell (night watchman), Bud Wolfe (Harding), Mark Strong (watchman #1), Bert LeBaron (watchman #2), David Sharpe (watchman #3/guard #1), George Volk (guard #3), John Hamilton (Henry

The Invisible Monster—Stanley Price as the Phantom Ruler.

Miller), Guy Teague (Al), Roy Gordon (Moore), George Magrill (Sam).

Chapter Titles

(1) *Slaves of the Phantom.* (2) *The Acid Clue.* (3) *The Death Car.* (4) *Highway Holocaust.* (5) *Bridge to Eternity.* (6) *Ordeal by Fire.* (7) *Murder Train.* (8) *Window of Peril.* (9) *Trail of Destruction.* (10) *High Voltage Danger.* (11) *Death's Highway.* (12) *The Phantom Meets Justice.*

The Invisible Monster— Aline Towne, Richard Webb.

Story

A ruthless mastermind known as the Phantom Ruler plots the conquest of the world. To acquire manpower, he imports illegal aliens who are technical experts in their various fields, blackmailing them (under threat of deportation) into following his orders. Donning a black cloak treated with a special chemical, the Phantom Ruler is able to render himself invisible when he steps within a beam of light projected by a special lamp housed in the rear of a truck. After the Phantom Ruler stages a bank robbery to finance his crimes, insurance company investigator Lane Carson is assigned to the case. With the help of his capable assistant Carol Richards, he trails the Phantom Ruler.

After a series of crimes, the Phantom Ruler's henchmen try to steal a truckload of the chemical needed to maintain the Ruler's invisibility, but Carson intercepts the shipment, preventing the theft. The Phantom Ruler learns that drums of the chemical have been stored in a guarded warehouse, and manages to obtain the chemical by drilling through the warehouse wall while invisible, inserting a hose into a drum and siphoning off the chemical. Carson, realizing how desperate the Phantom Ruler is to acquire the chemical, analyzes it and discovers its amazing properties.

The Phantom Ruler, deciding that the illegal aliens he has smuggled into the country have become a liability, plans to kill them. Wiring the floor of his secret headquarters with high-voltage cables, he intends to electrocute the unsuspecting men, but before he can do so, Carson and several police officers locate the Ruler's lair and break in. When the madman attempts to escape in the hectic struggle that follows, he steps on the high-voltage cables and is electrocuted himself.

Comments

Invisibility has been a common science fiction theme in movies since the silent era, with the first screen adaptation of H.G. Wells' novel *The Invisible Man* appearing in 1906 under the title *The Invisible Thief*. Along with later

sound features like director James Whale's definitive version of *The Invisible Man* (Universal, 1933) and subsequent horror and comedy movies on the subject, serials dealing with invisibility have included *The Vanishing Shadow* (q.v.), *Flash Gordon* (q.v.), *The Phantom Creeps* (q.v.), *Dick Tracy vs. Crime, Inc.* (q.v.), *Batman and Robin* (q.v.) and *The Lost Planet* (q.v.).

In Republic's *The Invisible Monster*, invisibility is the serial's main theme, with veteran supporting actor Stanley Price given a rare leading role as the title fiend. As usual with Republic villains, especially in the studio's latter-day serials, Price as the Phantom Ruler has ambitions of global conquest that are decidedly small scale, in keeping with the film's limited budget. The Phantom Ruler turns invisible after donning a chemically impregnated hooded robe and stepping into a special beam of light. To remain invisible, one of the Phantom Ruler's henchmen must continuously track him with a spotlight concealed in the rear of a truck — a plan for world conquest that seems remarkably cumbersome and impractical. The required invisibility effects are simply executed, with the Phantom Ruler stepping into a spotlight and fading away through a simple optical dissolve. For other scenes, guns and various objects are suspended from wires to give the impression that they are being held by the unseen Phantom Ruler.

James Whale's *The Invisible Man*, with an excellent script by R.C. Sheriff, had exploited the subject of invisibility with genuine wit, intelligence and style. Even the lesser Universal sequels, like *The Invisible Man Returns*, *The Invisible Woman*, *Invisible Agent* and *The Invisible Man's Revenge*, managed to deal with the subject in amusing and inventive ways. Republic's *The Invisible Monster*, though, suffers from a general lack of imagination throughout, and the Phantom Ruler may well be the dullest "invisible man" in film history. The subplot dealing with the Phantom Ruler's scheme of importing illegal aliens (character actor John Hamilton, who played Perry White in the TV series *The Adventures of Superman* is among them), is extraneous and completely unnecessary. A little more imagination — or even just a little comedy, for that matter — would have expanded the story's possibilities and improved the serial considerably.

The acting of the two nominal stars, Richard Webb and Aline Towne, is a slight improvement over the usual Republic serial leads. Although Towne would play traditional girl sidekick roles in the Republic serials *Radar Men from the Moon* (q.v.) and *Zombies of the*

Stratosphere (q.v.), in *The Invisible Monster* her character exhibits relatively mature (for serials) feminist qualities; the part as written is definitely forward-looking and a rarity for serials. Republic's leading *men* were a generally wooden and colorless lot; and any sort of depth in its female characters was almost unheard of.

The Invisible Monster might have been a better serial if the writers had concentrated on mood and characterization, but this approach was rarely employed at Republic; as expected, the accent is on the usual succession of fistfights and car chases. The disappointing result, like so many other post-World War II serials, is an unimaginative cliffhanger dealing with a potentially imaginative and atmospheric subject in a pedestrian manner. *The Invisible Monster* is definitely one of Republic's lesser efforts.

Video availability: Republic Home Video.

Atom Man vs. Superman

(Columbia, 1950)

Producer: Sam Katzman. Director: Spencer G. Bennet. Screenplay: George H. Plympton, Joseph F. Poland, David Mathews. Photography: Ira H. Morgan, A.S.C. Film editor: Earl Turner. Music: Mischa Bakaleinikoff. Sound engineer: Josh Westmoreland. Assistant director: R.M. Andrews. Second unit director: Derwin Abrahams.

Cast: Kirk Alyn (Superman/Clark Kent), Noel Neill (Lois Lane), Lyle Talbot (Luthor/Atom Man), Tommy Bond (Jimmy Olsen), Pierre Watkin (Perry White), Jack Ingram (Foster), Don C. Harvey (Albert), Rusty Wescoatt (Carl), Terry Frost (Baer), Wally West (Dorr), Paul Stader (Lawson), George Robotham (Earl), William

Fawcett (the mayor), Stanley Blystone (man in the street), Fred Kelsey (the chief of police).

Chapter Titles

(1) *Superman Flies Again.* (2) *Atom Man Appears.* (3) *Ablaze in the Sky.* (4) *Superman Meets Atom Man.* (5) *Atom Man Tricks Superman.* (6) *Atom Man's Challenge.* (7) *At the Mercy of Atom Man.* (8) *Into the Empty Doom.* (9) *Superman Crashes Through.* (10) *Atom Man's Heat Ray.* (11) *Luthor's Strategy.* (12) *Atom Man Strikes.* (13) *Atom Man's Flying Saucer.* (14) *Rocket of Vengeance.* (15) *Superman Saves the Universe.*

Story

A masked criminal known as the Atom Man instigates a reign of terror in Metropolis and threatens to destroy the entire city. *Daily Planet* newspaper reporters Clark Kent (secretly the mighty Superman), Lois Lane and Jimmy Olsen are assigned to cover the story. Criminal genius Lex Luthor is released from prison and claims to have reformed, but it becomes apparent that Luthor and the Atom Man are one and the same person. Leading a seemingly respectable life after gaining his freedom, Luthor follows his criminal tendencies to their logical conclusion and goes into broadcasting as a front for his nefarious activities, opening a television station.

From this cover, Luthor begins a crime wave for which the fictional Atom Man is blamed. Even Superman is helpless when Luthor invents synthetic kryptonite, the one substance that can nullify the Man of Steel's awesome powers. Luthor then lures Superman into his secret headquarters and, using a futuristic machine to project Superman into another dimension called "the empty doom," imprisons the hero in a void. Operating a *Daily Planet* typewriter by sheer will power, the now-immaterial Superman communicates with Lois and Jimmy, telling them that he will soon reappear, which he does after escaping from "the empty doom."

Luthor threatens to destroy Metropolis with a machine called the "sonic vibrator." He prepares to do this from a safe vantage point, leaving Earth in a spaceship after he has taken Lois as a hostage. Superman is kept busy preventing death and destruction as Luthor's vibrator is trained on the city, but he is able to chase Luthor's ship through space. Crashing through the hull, Superman overpowers Luthor and flies back to Metropolis with Luthor and Lois Lane. With Luthor once again in prison, Metropolis is saved.

Comments

The success of Columbia's 1948 serial *Superman* (q.v.) demanded a sequel, and *Atom Man vs. Superman* was on theater screens two years later. Although touted in the industry trade press as a bigger and better production, there was little difference between *Atom Man vs. Superman* and its predecessor. Retaining the same principal cast from the first serial, *Atom Man vs. Superman* had a slightly better plot, introducing Superman's bald-headed comic book foe Lex Luthor to the live-action screen in the person of Lyle Talbot, a capable actor who, interestingly, had also played Commissioner Gordon in Columbia's *Batman and Robin* (q.v.) serial the previous year. The story is hampered somewhat by an unnecessary "masked villain" subplot, with Luthor posing as the titular "Atom Man," wearing a mask that

is really the robot head from Columbia's *The Monster and the Ape* (q.v.) serial. But once Luthor is revealed to be the Atom Man, the story proceeds at a fairly brisk pace.

Superman's flying scenes are slightly improved over those in the first serial, with live-action close-ups of Kirk Alyn used for the first time. But for the most part the same cheap cartoon animation is employed, and the low-budget technical work that hampered the first serial limits this one as well. At one point, Luthor constructs a flying saucer, but the spacecraft revealed turns out to be a cartoon animated in the same flat, unconvincing style as the Superman flying scenes. Like *Superman, Atom Man vs. Superman* was retired from exhibition after its initial theatrical run and was unseen until its release on videocassette in 1989.

Less than one year after the release of *Atom Man vs. Superman*, a new movie Superman appeared (as portrayed by veteran B-movie actor George Reeves) in a low-budget feature film called *Superman and the Mole-Men* (Lippert, 1951). Dark, somber and surprisingly mature in content and tone, *Superman and the Mole-Men* plays like a bizarre combination of *The Ox-Bow Incident* and *The Day the Earth Stood Still* as Superman protects subterranean creatures (who emerge from the shaft of an oil well) from persecution by ignorant townspeople. Reeves was a far better actor than Kirk Alyn, and went on to eclipse memories of his predecessor in 104 episodes of *The Adventures of Superman* TV series before his 1959 death (an apparent suicide). Since Reeves' death, other actors have played Superman, including Christopher Reeve in four feature films and Dean Cain in the recent TV series *Lois and Clark: The New Adventures of Superman*. There have also been TV shows and movies based on Superman's teenage incarnation as Superboy (and his cousin Supergirl as well). There was even a 1966 Broadway musical based on the Superman character. Superman seems well on his way to rivaling Tarzan in terms of the number of different actors cast in the role.

As flawed, simplistic and as disappointing as the Kirk Alyn serials may seem to modern viewers, it should be remembered that when these films were originally produced, audiences were less demanding of special effects, and budgetary shortcuts were commonplace and expected. Certainly, the Columbia *Superman* serials could have been better, even at the time. In 1941, Republic Pictures had filmed an excellent serial based on Superman's more fantasy-oriented comic book rival Captain Marvel, and the flying scenes in *Adventures of Captain Marvel*, using a combination of stuntmen, rear-projection and full-scale dummies suspended from wires and manipulated by a pulley system, were outstanding and generally convincing. Nevertheless, the cruder Kirk Alyn *Superman* serials were among the most popular live-action adaptations of comic book characters, and were appreciated as faithful and unpretentious translations of their pulp paper source by the audiences who originally saw them.

Video availability: Warner Home Video.

Opposite: Atom Man vs. Superman—**Kirk Alyn.**

Flying Disc Man from Mars

(Republic, 1951)

Associate producer: Franklin Adreon. Director: Fred C. Brannon. Screenplay: Ronald Davidson. Photography: Walter Strenge, A.S.C. Film editors: Cliff Bell, Sam Starr. Special effects: Howard Lydecker, Theodore Lydecker. Art director: Fred Ritter. Set decorators: John McCarthy, Jr., James Redd. Music: Stanley Wilson. Sound: Earl Crain, Sr. RCA Sound. Makeup: Bob Mark. Unit manager: Roy Wade. Optical effects: Consolidated Film Industries. Feature version: *Missile Monsters* (75 minutes), released theatrically in 1958.

Cast: Walter Reed (Kent Fowler), Lois Collier (Helen), Gregory Gay (Mota), James Craven (Bryant), Harry Lauter (Drake), Richard Irving (Ryan), Sandy Sanders (Steve), Michael Carr (Trent), Dale Van Sickel (watchman), Tom Steele (Taylor), George Sherwood (Gateman), Jimmy O'Gatty (Gradey), John DeSimone (Curtis), Lester Dorr (Crane), Dick Cogan (Kirk).

Chapter Titles

(1) *Menace from Mars.* (2) *The Volcano's Secret.* (3) *Death Rides the Stratosphere.* (4) *Execution by Fire.* (5) *The Living Projectile.* (6) *Perilous Mission.* (7) *Descending Doom.* (8) *Suicidal Sacrifice.* (9) *The Funeral Pyre.* (10) *Weapons of Hate.* (11) *Disaster on the Highway.* (12) *Volcanic Vengeance.*

Story

Aviator Kent Fowler is summoned by Dr. Bryant, a respected scientist, to investigate a UFO that Bryant has spotted hovering above his experimental plane factory. Fowler shoots down the mysterious craft; when Bryant investigates the crash site, he discovers a survivor, a Martian scientist named Mota. Mota explains to Bryant that the Martians are a scientifically advanced race, and offers to reward Bryant if the scientist will aid him in the conquest of Earth. Having secretly collaborated with the Nazis in World War II, the traitorous Bryant agrees, and keeps Mota's existence hidden from Fowler.

Mota establishes a secret base of operations in the crater of a dormant volcano, and uses a "semi-disc" Martian aircraft to periodically venture forth and steal the vital materials needed for his planned conquest. He is aided by two henchmen, Drake and Ryan, employed by Bryant.

After a series of robberies are committed by Bryant and Mota, Fowler begins to suspect Bryant's role in the crime wave, and eventually his suspicions are confirmed. Desperate now that Fowler knows the truth, Mota and Bryant embark on a ruthless campaign of destruction, dropping small-scale atomic bombs on bridges, factories and defense installations, attempting to force the government into surrender. Helen, Fowler's pretty assistant, is kidnapped by Mota and taken to his crater lair as a hostage, but Fowler discovers the hideout and arrives to rescue her. As

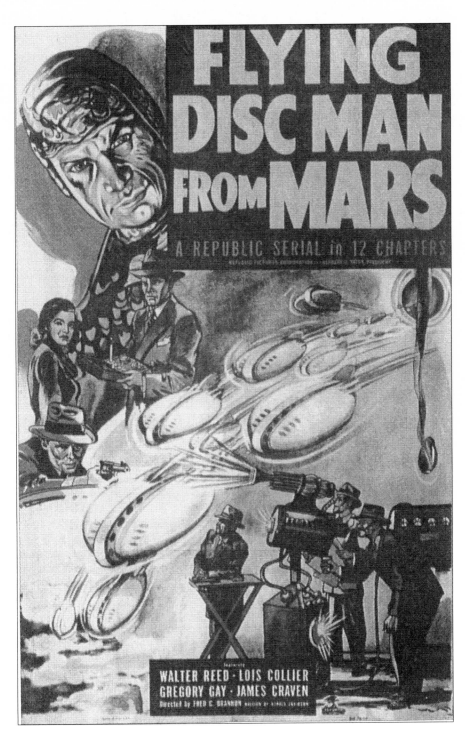

Flying Disc Man from Mars poster.

Fowler battles Mota's gang, an atomic bomb falls into the molten lava of the volcano and, exploding, starts a volcanic eruption. Hurriedly boarding the semi-disc plane, Kent and Helen escape just as the volcano explodes, killing Mota and Bryant and ending their dream of world domination.

Comments

The second of Republic's three "Martian invasion" serials, *Flying Disc Man from Mars* casts veteran character actor Gregory Gay as Mota (that's "atom" spelled backward), an emissary from the Red Planet out to conquer Earth. Mota arrives from space wearing Roy Barcroft's old costume from *The Purple Monster Strikes* (q.v.), giving Republic's overworked film editors an opportunity to lift clips of Barcroft's landing on Earth from the earlier film — a task made easier by the fact that actor James Craven is at the landing site to meet the alien invaders in both serials.

As the story progresses, Mota discards the Purple Monster duds, opting for a conservative business suit. After setting up his headquarters in a dormant volcano crater, he follows in the Purple Monster's unimaginative footsteps by hiring the usual band of petty thugs and two-bit crooks to assist in his plans. As Mota barks orders to his minions in a thick but indeterminate Middle-European accent, it gradually becomes apparent that *Flying Disc Man from Mars* is less about extra-terrestrial invasion than early 1950s Cold War McCarthyist paranoia. Mota is obviously one of *them*, and has to be defeated at all costs. Once the interplanetary origins of Mota have been established in Chapter 1, the potentially intriguing Martian angle moves into the background; afterwards,

for all intents and purposes, Mota could just as well be one of the Commie spies from *Big Jim McLain* or any of the many other red-baiting films made at the time.

The "disc" of the title refers to Mota's primary form of transportation used in carrying out his schemes, a futuristic "semi-disc" (as it's called in the film) plane. This full-size prop and its corresponding miniature is actually the "bat plane" (slightly modified with the addition of a tail fin) from Republic's 1942 serial *Spy Smasher*. Even though the aircraft had been designed by Republic's prop department almost a decade before, it bears enough resemblance to a traditional "UFO" to serve its purpose here. Flying saucer sightings were at a peak in 1951, with Hollywood quickly exploiting the newspaper headlines; *Flying Disc Man from Mars* was one of the earliest "alien invasion" films of the decade.

Aside from Gregory Gay's thoroughly professional work in the title role, the balance of the cast is largely forgettable, although former Universal pictures starlet Lois Collier makes a strong impression as the female lead. Despite Republic's promotion of Frances Gifford, Kay Aldridge and Linda Stirling as serial queens in the 1940s, in *Jungle Girl* (1941), *Perils of Nyoka* (1942) and *The Tiger Woman* (1944), respectively, strong female characters were a rarity at Republic, and the *supporting* female characters in the studio's Westerns and serials were particularly weak. This makes Lois Collier's performance in *Flying Disc Man from Mars* all the more unique.

Although *Flying Disc Man from Mars* should be included in any discussion of 1950s science fiction movies, the film is

Flying Disc Man from Mars— Gregory Gay.

regrettably weak conceptually. The viewer would expect at least a little awe and mystery to be associated with the arrival of a Martian on Earth, but certainly won't find these qualities in this serial. In fact, a comparison between *Flying Disc Man from Mars* and 20th Century–Fox's excellent feature *The Day the Earth Stood Still*, released the same year, throws the Republic serial's lack of imagination into even sharper relief.

The powerful tension and anticipation generated by the scenes of *The Day the Earth Stood Still*'s alien spacecraft arriving in Washington is entirely absent from *Flying Disc Man*; even a small fraction of the Fox feature's imagination would have improved the serial. *Flying Disc Man from Mars* does benefit from Republic's usual production finesse.

Video availability: Republic Home Video.

Mysterious Island

(Columbia, 1951)

Producer: Sam Katzman. Director: Spencer G. Bennet. Screenplay: Lewis Clay, Royal K. Cole, George H. Plympton, based on the novel *L'Ile Mysterieuse* by Jules Verne. Photography: Fayte Browne, A.S.C. Film editor: Earl Turner. Music: Mischa Bakaleinikiff. Set director: Sidney Clifford. Set continuity: Violet Newfield. Assistant director: R.M. Andrews. Production manager: Herbert Leonard.

Cast: Richard Crane (Capt. Harding), Marshall Reed (Pencroft), Karen Randle (Rulu), Ralph Hodges (Bert), Hugh Prosser (Gideon), Bernard Hamilton (Neb), Leonard Penn (Capt. Nemo), Terry Frost (Ayrton), Gene Roth (Capt. Shard), Rusty Wescoatt (Moley).

Chapter Titles

(1) *Lost in Space.* (2) *Sinister Savages.* (3) *Savage Justice!* (4) *Wild Man at Large!*

(5) *Trail of the Mystery Man.* (6) *The Pirates Attack!* (7) *Menace of the Mercurians.* (8) *Between Two Fires!* (9) *Shrine of the Silver Bird.* (10) *Fighting Fury!* (11) *Desperate Chances!* (12) *Mystery of the Mine.* (13) *Jungle Deadfall.* (14) *Men from Tomorrow!* (15) *The Last of Mysterious Island!*

Story

March 1865, toward the Civil War's end: Capt. Harding, a prisoner of the Confederates, escapes in a hot air balloon with war correspondent Gideon Spilett, sailor Jack Pencroft, Pencroft's adopted son Bert Brown and Harding's servant Neb. For five days, the balloon drifts aimlessly before settling on a deserted island. Harding, who had leapt overboard in an attempt to lighten the balloon's weight and save his compan-

Mysterious Island newspaper ad.

ions, is rescued from drowning in the sea by a bizarre figure who vanishes with him. An alien girl and two men from the planet Mercury land on the island in a spaceship. The castaways, hiding in a cave, are buried under tons of debris when the cavern roof collapses. Bert is excavated from the debris by Pencroft, and the others are revived.

The Mercurian girl Rulu and her alien companions have established a base on the island. Unconscious, Harding has been taken to the hidden grotto of Capt. Nemo. Ayrton, a former castaway who now lives as a wild man, savagely attacks Bert, who is rescued by his friends. Island tribesmen then pursue the castaways, who discover a crevice in the rock wall that leads outside. A witch doctor on the other side stops them by filling the crevice with flammable powder. Before the flames close in, Bert finds another way out of the crevice.

Rulu and her fellow Mercurians continue to search for a rare metal, which is the reason they have journeyed to Earth. The castaways discover Harding, still unconscious, lying in a jungle clearing, but Harding is carried off by tribesmen before his friends can reach him. Bert and Neb try to retrieve guns and ammunition from their balloon while Pencroft and Spilett trail after the tribesmen who carried Harding away. The tribesmen tie Harding to a pole and lower him into water, but the tribesmen are driven off by Bert and Neb, who save Harding from drowning. A call for help from Bert (attacked by Ayrton) alerts Harding and Pencroft, who restrain Ayrton. Ayrton tells the castaways that he has escaped from a band of pirates who use the island as a cache for stolen loot. When Ayrton offers to lead the castaways to food, Pencroft and Spilett

go with him. Ayrton double-crosses them and releases an overhead net, attempting to bury Pencroft and Spilett under tons of debris.

Pencroft leaps clear, but Spilett is knocked out. Pencroft fights off Ayrton, then revives Spilett. Two captured tribesmen lead the castaways to their chief. Ayrton and Moapi, the witch doctor, are already there, and the witch doctor declares that the castaways must be killed because the gods have been angered. Harding, Pencroft and Bert manage to escape from the tribesmen, and are led to Nemo's grotto by Ayrton, who then vanishes. The castaways are stunned into unconsciousness when the unseen Nemo electrifies the cave with one of his scientific devices.

The castaways are unharmed by Nemo's electrical shock. Meanwhile, the band of pirates, led by Capt. Shard, returns to the island; Ayrton is captured by them. The pirates then trap the castaways. While his friends battle the pirates, Bert seeks help from the mysterious figure who had rescued Harding, but he is trapped by the alien girl Rulu in Nemo's grotto. The other castaways are trapped in an explosion when Shard's aide Moley detonates a powder charge. The castaways, warned by Harding, avoid the explosion by running into a cave.

Harding and Neb exit the cave through a mysterious door, finding themselves in a tunnel. Pencroft and Spilett are taken prisoner. Rulu hypnotizes Bert with a futuristic device while Capt. Nemo aids the other castaways in escaping from the pirates. That night, the castaways are re-captured and placed in a boat that the pirates train their cannons on. Escaping the pirates' cannon-fire, the castaways return to the island,

and two pirates who trail Neb are captured. The island tribesmen form an alliance with the captives and the two captured pirates escape, informing Captain Shard of the tribe's decision. Shard, trailing the party of tribesmen and castaways, shoots one of the tribesmen. The tribal chief, believing the castaways are responsible, attacks them. As the castaways flee the pirates fire at them point blank.

Harding and his friends save themselves by dodging the bullets. When the pirates are repelled, the tribal chief is once again friendly with the castaways and leads them to a cavern known as "The Shrine of the Silver Bird." In the cavern, Harding discovers a mysterious plastic box. Bert, escaping from Rulu and taking one of her ray guns, is captured by Ayrton. The castaways and the tribal chief are surrounded by Rulu and her Mercurians, and Rulu destroys the plastic box found by Harding with a blast from her ray gun. Harding and Pencroft chase after Rulu, but the alien girl falls off a ledge. Harding and Pencroft are blasted off the same ledge when the other Mercurians detonate a concealed explosive charge. Rulu is captured by Harding and Pencroft when they land unharmed, but she escapes from them.

Harding follows her, but he is captured by Rulu's companions when they return. Harding tells Rulu that he and the other castaways are only trying to find Bert, and that after they have done so, they will leave the island. Convinced of this, Rulu agrees to help the castaways. Meanwhile, the pirates are led to Bert by Ayrton, who is made a prisoner and locked in a shack with Bert. The shack bursts into flame as they fight with one of their captors.

Bert and Ayrton escape the fire by crashing through the shack wall. Rulu arrives with Harding just before the pirates get there. As Spilett, Pencroft and Neb arrive, Rulu suddenly leaves. Harding learns that Capt. Shard plans to attack Rulu on the island, which gives Harding's party an opportunity to capture the pirate ship. Ayrton, injured in the fight, goes mad and decides to blow up the ship. Harding sees the crazed Ayrton throw a torch into the ship's hold, and he shouts a warning to Pencroft. They save themselves by diving overboard and swimming ashore, but Ayrton dies in the blast.

Pirates again capture Bert, but he is rescued by Rulu, who once again hypnotizes him. Rulu, Bert and tribesmen enslaved by the Mercurians are trailed to a mine by Harding and Pencroft, who learn that Rulu is mining radioactive metal that she needs. Suddenly, Harding and Pencroft are attacked by the other Mercurians, who fire on them. Bert, suddenly aroused from his hypnosis, rushes into the aliens and spoils their aim. Capt. Shard then suggests that the pirates and castaways form an alliance in an effort to escape from the island; Harding agrees. Rulu, learning that Capt. Shard plans to use tribal labor to aid his escape, puts the chief and his people under her spell in order to thwart Shard's plan. The tribesmen rig a jungle deadfall; Harding and Capt. Shard are nearly crushed by the huge weight but save themselves by rolling aside just in time.

Rulu discovers the radioactive metal she needs just as Harding and Capt. Shard reach her cave. She attempts to trick them, but they are rescued by the mystery man, who is revealed to be Capt. Nemo, a famous scientist who

Mysterious Island— Richard Crane.

commands the submarine *Nautilus*. Nemo informs them that Rulu has discovered a powerful explosive that could destroy the world. Another spaceship from Mercury then arrives on the island, and Harding and Capt. Shard are trapped in an explosion caused by the newly arrived Mercurians.

Harding survives the blast, but Capt. Shard dies. Bert has escaped from the mine and confronts Rulu. He is almost captured, but Harding rescues him.

Rulu and her Mercurians are defeated, but Rulu, escaping, sets an explosive device that will destroy the island. The castaways escape and are taken aboard a passing ship just as Mysterious Island disappears beneath the ocean waves.

Comments

Columbia's *Mysterious Island*, loosely based on Jules Verne's novel *L'Ile Mysterieuse*, is a real curiosity. Although serials regularly drew upon popular cultural sources like radio, pulp magazines and comic books, novel adaptation was relatively scarce. The Verne novel has been filmed with varying degrees of fidelity several times, by MGM in 1929, by the Russians in 1941, in 1961 as a feature by Columbia, and again in 1974. The best screen treatment to date (by far) has been the 1961 Columbia production *Mysterious Island*, which was filmed in color and benefited from impressive stop-motion special effects monsters created by Ray Harryhausen. The Harryhausen movie, although slow-paced, was competently directed by Cy Endfield and featured excellent characterizations from a versatile ensemble cast.

The 15-chapter serial examined here, though sporadically enjoyable in its own way, fails to attain the later Columbia feature's level of quality. To begin with, the scriptwriters tossed Verne's original novel out the window after the first chapter. After escaping from Confederate imprisonment in a hot air balloon and landing on the island, Capt. Harding and his men encounter a band of outer space aliens from the planet Mercury. Apparently catering to the contemporary science fiction boom, Columbia injected this completely unrelated element into the script, and

expanded the concept to dominate the balance of the serial. The aliens are led by Rulu, a sneering girl in a silver cape and mini-skirt, whose minions (befitting the serial's low budget, there are only two of them) wear discarded Buster Crabbe *Flash Gordon* costumes and masks left over from the 1938 Columbia serial *The Spider's Web*. They arrive on the island in a spacecraft that is actually a stock footage clip of the "time top" from Columbia's 1947 serial *Brick Bradford* (q.v.). The island tribesmen enslaved by the Mercurians (they are called "volcano people" in the serial) wear black tights, shorts, skullcaps and carry jagged metal spears bent into the shape of lightning bolts.

These irrelevant science fiction gimmicks are more of a nagging intrusion than a debilitating flaw (that is, if the viewer can ignore the source novel), but the serial is almost totally crippled by leaden direction (Spencer Bennet) and indifferent acting. Only Richard Crane as Harding, Karen Randle as Rulu and Gene Roth as the pirate Capt. Shard make any kind of an impression. The other castaways are interchangeable stock figures, and are easily confused by the viewer. Capt. Nemo himself, presented as a masked "mystery man" until the final episodes, should be the strongest character in the film, but he comes across as a frail, unimpressive figure. Predictably enough, it is eventually revealed that Nemo's futuristic submarine, the *Nautilus*, had been previously destroyed after his arrival on the island, thus saving Columbia's special effects department the expense of building a miniature.

Richard Crane, a journeyman actor of some charm and presence, imparts a degree of charisma to Harding, and

Karen Randle is a lot of fun as the alien girl Rulu in a performance similar to Patricia Laffan's in the '50s British feature *Devil Girl from Mars*. Their efforts, though, are not enough to salvage *Mysterious Island*. The serial was probably entertaining to juvenile audiences of the time, but today it falls short, even by Columbia's undemanding standards.

Although the serial version of *Mysterious Island* could never have matched the special effects of the Ray Harryhausen feature, produced only a decade later, the characterization in the serial's secondary roles could and should have been better realized; it is especially disappointing when compared to the slick playing of the Harryhausen cast.

Captain Video

(Columbia, 1951)

Producer: Sam Katzman. Directors: Spencer G. Bennet, Wallace A. Grissell. Screenplay: Royal K. Cole, Sherman L. Lowe, Joseph F. Poland. Original story: George H. Plympton, based on the television series *Captain Video and His Video Rangers*. Photography: Fayte Browne. Film editor: Earl Turner. Special effects: Jack Erickson. Music: Mischa Bakaleinikoff. Assistant director: Charles F. Gould.

Cast: Judd Holdren (Captain Video), Larry Stewart (Ranger), George Eldredge (Tobor), Gene Roth (Vultura), Don C. Harvey (Gallagher), William Fawcett (Alpha), Jack Ingram (Aker), I. Stanford Jolley (Zarol), Skelton Knaggs (Retner), Jimmy Stark (Rogers), Rusty Wescoatt (Beal), Zon Murray (Elko), George Robotham (Drock), Oliver Cross (Prof. Markham), Bill Bailey (Prof. Dean).

Chapter Titles

(1) *Journey Into Space*. (2) *Menace to Atoma*. (3) *Captain Video's Peril*. (4) *Entombed in Ice*. (5) *Flames of Atoma*. (6) *Astray in the Stratosphere*. (7) *Blasted by the Atomic Eye*. (8) *Invisible Menace*. (9) *Video Springs a Trap*. (10) *Menace of the Mystery Metal*. (11) *Weapon of Destruction*. (12) *Robot Rocket*. (13) *Mystery of Station X*. (14) *Vengeance of Vultura*. (15) *Video vs. Vultura*.

Story

A scientific genius who has invented numerous weapons and futuristic gadgets in the service of mankind, heroic Captain Video and his loyal group of "Video Rangers," along with his assistant Gallagher, are committed to the defense of Earth against terrestrial and extra-terrestrial dangers. In his secret mountain headquarters, the resourceful

Captain Video— Gene Roth as Vultura.

Captain Video has created scientific devices like the "opticon scillometer," the "cosmic vibrator," the "electronic wave detector," the "inertia light" and the "jetmobile."

After Captain Video and his chief Video Ranger apprehend a gang of thugs who mysteriously vanish into thin air, Captain Video's Agent 136 reports strange magnetic and electronic impulses affecting the weather. Captain Video and the Ranger visit the brilliant

Captain Video—Judd Holdren, Larry Stewart.

scientist Dr. Tobor in an effort to discover the cause of the disturbances, unaware that Tobor is secretly in league with Vultura, mad dictator of the planet Atoma, located in "the eighth time cycle."

Tobor attempts to prevent discovery of his dastardly alliance by leaving Earth and journeying to Atoma in a space projectile, but Captain Video and the Ranger learn of his flight and follow in their own spacecraft. On Atoma, Vultura and Dr. Tobor detect Captain Video's approach and try to destroy him by guiding two comets into a collision with Video's spacecraft. Video and the Ranger escape, ultimately discovering Dr. Tobor's perfidy.

Vultura attempts to freeze Captain Video, burn him alive and destroy him with an endless variety of powerful weapons, including an army of metallic "electronic men." The evil Dr. Tobor dies in a midair plane crash and Captain Video defeats Vultura, who is electrocuted by one of his own futuristic weapons.

Comments

Nothing illustrates the desperate nature of serial production in the early 1950s better than Columbia's *Captain Video*, which was the first and only serial to be based on a TV show. Many previous serials had been inspired by radio programs, but providing images for stories and characters from an audio medium had always made the serial seem more exciting (and perhaps more important) than their source. By the

Opposite: Captain Video poster (note the Robot, reused from The Phantom Empire).

early 1950s, though, television was providing real competition for movies, particularly for the juvenile audience that patronized matinee serials. It was a sad day when serial producers went begging to their most successful rival for new material.

The *Captain Video* serialized TV show premiered on June 27, 1949, on the Dumont network, and starred Richard Coogan in the title role. Coogan was replaced later in 1949 by Al Hodge, who would play the role for seven years. (Hodge had also played the Green Hornet on radio.) Don Hastings co-starred as The Ranger, with Hal Conklin as Captain Video's evil foe Dr. Pauli. Guest actors on the show over the course of its run included Ernest Borgnine, Jack Klugman and Tony Randall. Beginning as a half-hour show running four nights a week, *Captain Video* was soon on every weeknight, broadcast live from New York for its first six years. By the fall of 1953, the show was abridged to 15 minutes per episode, ending its run on April 1, 1955. In 1953, a second *Captain Video* TV series called *The Secret Files of Captain Video* appeared in a half-hour, non-continuing format, with each episode presenting a self-contained story. In 1956, Al Hodge hosted a syndicated cartoon series called *Captain Video's Cartoons*, after which the character finally vanished into television history. Guided by writer M.C. Brook, the television *Captain Video* was the first and most durable of the early 1950s science fiction TV shows, inspiring similar programs like *Atom Squad, Rocky Jones, Space Ranger, Rod Brown of the Rocket Rangers, Space Patrol* and *Tom Corbett, Space Cadet. Captain Video* regularly extolled high morality and other positive social qualities and, unlike a lot

of other children's entertainment in the 1950s, it was highly praised by educators and civic leaders.

By its very nature, the live TV show could not avoid a cheap appearance, and the 1951 Columbia serial, despite its own low-budget nature, could not help but look superior on a theater screen (especially with the inclusion of Cinecolor inserts, used as a gimmick). Still, the serial is hardly a classic, and suffered from the usual restrictive economies imposed by producer Sam Katzman. Judd Holdren, the competent but stolid actor who stars as Captain Video, seemed to have a virtual monopoly on the leading roles in 1950s science fiction serials, also starring in Republic's *Zombies of the Stratosphere* (q.v.) and Columbia's *The Lost Planet* (q.v.). Holdren is nearly defeated by the serial's tight budget, and spends a seemingly endless amount of time capering around the rock formations of Bronson Canyon with co-star Larry Stewart, cast as Captain Video's assistant the Ranger. The re-use of the ludicrous robot costumes originally made for Mascot's *The Phantom Empire* (q.v.) didn't help either. These robots had been unintentionally laughable in 1935, and certainly hadn't improved with age.

Any delights to be found in *Captain Video* (and they are meager at best) come in the portly form of character actor Gene Roth (also billed at various times in his career as Gene Stutenroth and Eugene Roth) as Vultura, a crazed interplanetary monarch out to conquer the universe and destroy Captain Video. Roth, a perennial at Columbia in Three Stooges comedies and serials, is an unwittingly comical sight in his ridiculous "futuristic" garb, complete with a chainmail headdress. After such relatively impressive villains as Ming the Merciless and the Crimson Ghost in previous serials, Vultura seems like a sadly tacky and run-down would-be conqueror; even his name is recycled, having been used before by the female antagonist of Republic's *Perils of Nyoka*

(1942). Nevertheless, Roth, clearly realizing that his chances of turning in a convincing performance are nil, hams it up in an entertaining manner. In the process, he injects a little honest entertainment value into one of Columbia's dullest serial efforts.

Radar Men from the Moon

(Republic, 1952)

Associate producer: Franklin Adreon. Director: Fred C. Brannon. Screenplay: Ronald Davidson. Photography: John MacBurnie. Film editor: Cliff Bell. Special effects: Howard Lydecker, Theodore Lydecker. Art director: Fred A. Ritter. Set decorators: John McCarthy, Jr., James Redd. Music: Stanley Wilson. Sound: Dick Tyler. RCA sound. Makeup: Bob Mark. Unit manager: Roy Wade. Optical effects: Consolidated Film Industries. Feature version: *Retik, the Moon Menace* (100 minutes), for television distribution.

Cast: George Wallace (Commando Cody), Aline Towne (Joan Gilbert), Roy Barcroft (Retik), William Bakewell (Ted Richards), Clayton Moore (Graber), Peter Brocco (Krog), Bob Stevenson (Daly), Don Walters (Henderson), Tom Steele (Zerg), Dale Van Sickel (Alon), Wilson Wood (Hank), Noel Cravat (Robal), Baynes Barron (Nasor), Paul McGuire (Bream), Ted

Thorpe (bartender), Dick Cogan (Jones).

Chapter Titles

(1) *Moon Rocket.* (2) *Molten Terror.* (3) *Bridge of Death.* (4) *Flight to Destruction.* (5) *Murder Car.* (6) *Hills of Death.* (7) *Camouflaged Destruction.* (8) *The Enemy Planet.* (9) *Battle in the Stratosphere.* (10) *Mass Execution.* (11) *Planned Pursuit.* (12) *Death of the Moon Man.*

Story

A mysterious series of atomic explosions devastates America's industrial centers and military installations. A brilliant research scientist known as Commando Cody, Sky Marshall of the Universe, investigates, assisted by his co-workers Joan Gilbert and Ted Richards. Using futuristic, advanced scientific devices such as his jet-powered flying suit and a rocketship capable of

Radar Men from the Moon—George Wallace as Commando Cody.

interplanetary travel, they attempt to track down those responsible for the attacks.

Determining that the explosions have been caused by a rare element called lunarium, found only on the Moon,

Cody, Joan and Ted fly there in the rocketship and discover a previously unknown lunar civilization. The Moon people are ruled by the evil Retik, who informs Cody that his people are dying because of the Moon's thin atmosphere, and that he intends to conquer Earth as a new home for his people. Retik tries to kill Cody with a ray gun, but after a tense battle in Retik's laboratory, Cody escapes and returns to Earth with Joan and Ted. Retik, however, has sent his aide Krog to Earth so that they can employ criminals in their struggle against Cody. Cody, Joan and Ted must contend with Krog's henchmen, Graber and Daly, in a hectic series of rocketship chases and gun battles as they defend humanity from the Moon men.

Frustrated because his plans have been continuously thwarted by Cody, Retik journeys to Earth himself in order to take personal command of the invasion. Krog and his thugs are finally defeated. Retik, attempting to escape back to the Moon in his rocketship, dies in a terrific explosion when Cody aims a ray gun at it.

Comments

Although completely unrelated to Republic's previous serial *King of the Rocket Men* (q.v.), *Radar Men from the Moon* used the same basic premise — a jet-propelled flying suit — and the same stock shots of Rocket Man in flight to evolve a "new" character named "Commando Cody, Sky Marshall of the Universe," as the audience is informed via a pre-credit title card. *King of the Rocket Men* had dealt with a traditional "mad scientist" threat, but *Radar Men from the Moon* follows in the footsteps of *The Purple Monster Strikes*, confronting its protagonist with an extra-terrestrial invasion. This type of plot was a natural in 1952, with the science fiction movie craze in full bloom, and there was enough action to keep the usual serial audience interested. But the material is presented with a noticeable lack of imagination, especially in comparison with features of the time like *The Thing from Another World* and *The Day the Earth Stood Still*.

Although pre-Sputnik, 1952 was still a little late in the day to postulate a dying civilization on the Moon, poorly represented here by a stock shot of a miniature Roman-style city lifted from Republic's 1936 serial *Darkest Africa*. There is plenty of space travel between Earth and the Moon by Commando Cody and the invading Moon men, led by Republic stalwart Roy Barcroft, but there is no sense of awe or mystery attached to the event of interplanetary travel, which the participants experience as a routine occurrence. Borrowing his strategy as well as his wardrobe from the Purple Monster, the evil Retik (Barcroft) soon resorts to hiring criminals on Earth through his minion Krog to assist in the invasion, with "Lone Ranger" Clayton Moore among the thugs; the serial degenerates into standard cops-and-robbers action with science fiction trimmings.

In the last episode, Republic falls back on its most irritating budget-saving technique — using entire scenes from previous films — when Retik finally travels to Earth to take command of his faltering invasion; Barcroft is dressed in his Martian costume from *The Purple Monster Strikes* so that the entire conclusion from that serial can be re-used. This still isn't as crass as the economy move used in the quasi-sequel *Zombies of the Stratosphere*, when the desperate alien invasion force gets involved in cattle rustling and footage from a color Roy Rogers Western is reprinted in black-and-white. In *Radar Men from the Moon*, Barcroft (unfortu-

Commando Cody, Sky Marshall of the Universe—Judd Holdren.

nately) has little to do but broadcast orders from the Moon to his minions on Earth; a few more scenes of this entertaining and likable actor would have improved the film. George Wallace as Cody, Aline Towne as Joan and William Bakewell as Cody's sidekick Ted are all competent actors, and Towne is attractive, but none of them are allowed a characterization and fail to register as real people. Only Clayton Moore as the villainous henchman Graber exhibits any real emotion in his zeal to destroy Cody. Commando Cody's helmet, incidentally, was re-designed slightly from its previous appearance in *King of the Rocket Men*, with a rubber neck extension added to make it air-tight for use on the Moon.

Radar Men from the Moon isn't a bad film, it simply isn't as good as it could have been, even on the undemanding level of an early '50s serial. Republic, however, clearly felt that their Commando Cody creation had value, and in 1953 released a series of 12 short subjects featuring the character. These were not cliffhanger serial chapters, but were self-contained episodes originally shown on television *and* released to theaters in an effort to exploit the changing marketplace for this type of fare. Judd Holdren starred as Cody, with Aline Towne as Joan and Gregory Gay (Republic's *Flying Disc Man from Mars*) as the Ruler. These shorts, presented under the series title *Commando Cody, Sky Marshall of the Universe*, were produced by Franklin Adreon, written by Ronald Davidson and Barry Shipman, and directed by Adreon, Fred Brannon and Harry Keller. The titles (in order) were *Enemies of the Universe, Atomic Peril, Cosmic Vengeance, Nightmare Typhoon, War of the Space Giants, Destroyers of the Sun, Robot Monster of Mars, Hydrogen Hurricane, Solar Sky Raiders, S.O.S. Ice Age, Lost in Outer Space, Captives of the Zero Hour.*

Video availability: Republic Home Video.

Zombies of the Stratosphere

(Republic, 1952)

Associate producer: Franklin Adreon. Director: Fred C. Brannon. Screenplay: Ronald Davidson. Photography: John MacBurnie. Film editor: Cliff Bell, A.C.E. Special effects: Howard Lydecker, Theodore Lydecker. Art director: Fred A. Ritter. Set decorators: John McCarthy, Jr., James Redd. Music: Stanley Wilson. Sound: Dick Tyler. Makeup: Bob Mark. Unit manager: Roy Wade. Optical effects: Consolidated Film Industries. Feature version: *Satan's*

Zombies of the Stratosphere newspaper ad.

Satellites (70 minutes), released theatrically in 1958.

Cast: Judd Holdren (Larry Martin), Aline Towne (Sue Davis), Wilson Wood (Bob Wilson), Lane Bradford (Marex), Stanley Waxman (Dr. Harding), John Crawford (Roth), Craig Kelly (Mr. Steele), Ray Boyle (Shane), Leonard Nimoy (Narab), Tom Steele (truck driver), Dale Van Sickel (telegraph operator), Roy Engel (Lawson), Jack Harden (Kerr), Paul Stader (fisherman), Gayle

Kellogg (Dick), Jack Shea (policeman), Robert Garabedian (Elah).

Chapter Titles

(1) *The Zombie Vanguard.* (2) *Battle of the Rockets.* (3) *Undersea Agents.* (4) *Contraband Cargo.* (5) *The Iron Executioner.* (6) *Murder Mine.* (7) *Death on the Waterfront.* (8) *Hostage for Murder.* (9) *The Human Torpedo.* (10) *Flying Gas Chamber.* (11) *Man vs. Monster.* (12) *Tomb of the Traitors.*

Story

Larry Martin, member of a government defense organization, detects a strange interplanetary rocketship as it lands on Earth. Donning his jet-propelled flying suit, he investigates the remote landing site and learns that two Martians, Marex and Narab, have arrived as the vanguard of an invasion force. With the assistance of Roth and Shane, two Earth criminals, the Martians plan to construct a hydrogen bomb that will blow Earth out of its orbit. This will make room for their own dying world, Mars, which will be moved into Earth's vacant orbital path, improving the Martian atmosphere and climate.

The Martians and their henchmen conspire to steal an array of instruments and scientific components vital to their plan, but they are stymied again and again by Larry and his assistants Bob Wilson and Sue Davis. The Martians operate from a base located in a cave accessible only through an underwater passage. While tracking uranium ore stolen by the Martians, Larry and Bob discover the Martians' lair and are almost killed in a struggle with the

aliens, who have the ability to remain underwater longer than humans.

The Martians set a timing mechanism on a detonator that will explode the H-bomb, hurling the Earth out of orbit and into space. They escape in their rocketship, but after a ray gun battle with Larry, the ship crashes and all of its occupants are killed except Narab, who reveals the location of the bomb to Larry just before he dies. Racing against time, Larry flies to the cave, entering the Martian headquarters through the underwater tunnel, and saves the Earth by disarming the bomb seconds before it was set to explode.

Comments

The third and last of Republic's "Rocket Man" serials, *Zombies of the Stratosphere* is also the third and last Republic serial to deal with an invasion from Mars. These three aborted Martian invasions are all seemingly unrelated; this time around, the ambitious Martians plan to blast Earth out of its orbit so that Mars can take its place. The amount of raw power needed to move entire planets around like billiard balls staggers the imagination, not to mention the complicated celestial mechanics involved. In this case, the feat is explained away as being accomplished by a single hydrogen bomb explosion.

The invading Martians, working on a tight budget as they must in a 1950s serial, are only three in number, and this ragtag force soon finds opposition in the person of "Rocket Man" Larry Martin, who represents a vaguely defined government agency with an interplanetary patrol division. As in Republic's two previous "Martian invasion"

serials, *The Purple Monster Strikes* (q.v.) and *Flying Disc Man from Mars* (q.v.), the desperate Martians recruit Earth criminals for use in their dubious scheme, with the expected cycle of mundane bank robberies and jewel thefts taking place.

Larry Martin zooms back and forth in his jet-propelled flying suit, giving Republic's film editors an excuse to again use the flying scenes from *King of the Rocket Men.* The familiar Republic robot puts in another appearance here, used by the Martians in their planned invasion. As Larry, Judd Holdren is competent but unimpressive, and Aline Towne is an attractive heroine. The rest of the cast fails to register. The Martians themselves, with dark (presumably green) facial makeup, exaggerated eyebrows and skin-tight hooded costumes improbably decorated with sequins, are not very intimidating figures, nor do their meager resources pose much of a threat.

Zombies of the Stratosphere has gained some latter-day notoriety due to the presence of *Star Trek*'s "Mr. Spock," Leonard Nimoy, in the cast as one of the Martians. Nimoy, then 21 years old, does not have much dialogue, and turns in a run-of-the-mill supporting performance, which is about all he could have done, considering the material. In a recent television interview, Nimoy recalled that he did not think much of the serial at the time, and only took the role for the money ($500), which he needed badly at that point in his career.

As threadbare as *Zombies of the Stratosphere* looks today, it boasts the customary production gloss that Republic was known for; compared to the lousy science fiction serials produced by Columbia at the same time, the serial at least looks slick and professional. One negative factor that no degree of technical expertise can excuse, though, is a dearth of imagination, and *Zombies of the Stratosphere* is badly crippled by this flaw. As previously mentioned, 1950s science fiction features like *The Thing* and *The Day the Earth Stood Still* offered plenty of mood and imagination, and the wide conceptual and artistic disparity between those films and serials like *Zombies of the Stratosphere* is alarming in retrospect. Granted, the serials were intended for a largely juvenile audience, but a little more effort in the scriptwriting would have improved them considerably and might even have prolonged their commercial viability.

Zombies of the Stratosphere, however is a product of the serials' dying days, and the bland, unimaginative script, full of two-bit B-movie crooks rubbing elbows with interplanetary would-be conquerors, illustrates why the fast-approaching demise of the cliffhangers was unavoidable. Even children in 1952 realized that they shouldn't by paying for kiddie fare like this when it was available for free on television.

Video availability: Republic Home Video.

Opposite: Zombies of the Stratosphere— Aline Towne, Judd Holdren, Wilson Wood and robot.

The Lost Planet

(Columbia, 1953)

Producer: Sam Katzman. Director: Spencer G. Bennet. Screenplay: George H. Plympton, Arthur Hoerl. Photography: William Whitley. Film editor: Earl Turner. Special photography: Jack Erickson. Music: Ross DiMaggio. Set decorator: Sidney Clifford. Set continuity: Moree Herring. Sound: Josh Westmoreland. Assistant director: Charles S. Gould. Production manager: Herbert Leonard.

Cast: Judd Holdren (Rex Barrow), Vivian Mason (Ella Dorn), Ted Thorpe (Tim Johnson), Forrest Taylor (Prof. Dorn), Michael Fox (Dr. Grood), Gene Roth (Reckov), Karl Davis (Karlo), Leonard Penn (Ken Wolper), Jack Cason (Hopper), Nick Stuart (Darl), Joseph Mell (Lah), Jack George (Jarva), Frederic Berest (Alden), Lee Roberts (Robot #9/Wesley Bren), Pierre Watkin (Ned Hilton).

Chapter Titles

(1) *The Mystery of the Guided Missile.* (2) *Trapped by the Axial Propeller.* (3) *Blasted by the Thermic Disintegrator.* (4) *The Mind Control Machine.* (5) *The Atomic Plane.* (6) *Disaster in the Stratosphere.* (7) *Snared by the Pyramic Catapult.* (8) *Astray in Space.* (9) *The Hypnotic Ray Machine.* (10) *To Free the Planet People.* (11) *Dr. Grood Defies Gravity.* (12) *Trapped in a Cosmic Jet.* (13) *The Invisible Enemy.* (14) *In the Grip of the De-Thermo Ray.* (15) *Sentenced to Space.*

Story

Within a dormant volcano, electronics genius Dr. Ernst Grood and his lackey Jarva have established a super-scientific laboratory from which Grood is able to control the planet Ergro. Prof. Edmund Dorn, exploited by Grood for his vast scientific knowledge, is held prisoner on Ergro. Reporter Rex Barrow and his photographer Tim Johnson are sent to investigate when Dr. Grood's cosmojet crashed on Mt. Vulcan, but Dr. Grood observes their approach on his radarscope and captures them. Grood forces Rex and Tim, along with Ella, Prof. Dorn's daughter, into the cosmojet and launches them toward Ergro. On Ergro, Dorn, unaware that his daughter is in the cosmojet, sends it off course, plunging it toward the crater of an active volcano. Dorn is warned that the cosmojet is occupied just in time to rectify its course and land it safely.

Rex, Tim and Ella are captured by Reckov, Grood's assistant, who hypnotizes them with mind-controlling headsets. They are ordered to mine cosmonium, a rare metal, but Rex resists the hypnosis and escapes, meeting Prof. Dorn in his laboratory. Back on Earth, Grood sees the meeting of Rex and

The Lost Planet—Ted Thorpe, Judd Holdren.

Dorn through a viewing device and blasts off for Ergro, planning to kill Ella in order to punish Dorn for plotting against him. Learning this, Rex takes Ella to a cave for protection. The rays of Grood's axial propeller detect them, and they are violently spun around, vanishing in a burst of light.

Rex and Ella return to visibility when Dorn saves them by blasting the axial propeller with a cosmic ray gun; Dorn is then disarmed. Rex and Ella leave the cave and find Tim in the mine, but they are captured by robot men. Dorn then reveals a new device to Rex, a small box of powerful dornite. Dornite is a secret metal which, in combination with cosmonium, produces an invisibility ray. They decide to make Rex invisible so that he can journey back to Earth unseen aboard Grood's cosmojet. Rex, now invisible, hides in the cosmojet, but after landing on Earth Grood discovers him when Rex accidentally loses the dornite box and returns to visibility. Grood orders Rex blasted with the thermic disintegrator, but Rex finds the dornite box just in time and again becomes invisible.

Back at the newspaper office, editor Ned Hilton is understandably skeptical when Rex tells him about his interplanetary flight. Since government authorities will not help him, Rex finally realizes that he must return to the planet Ergro alone. He is again captured by Grood, who uses a subconscious mind-control machine on him. Rex is then confined in a sonic tunnel, which Grood explodes, but Rex saves himself by dropping into a lower branch of the tunnel.

Instead of killing Rex, Grood decides to use him in order to learn Dorn's secrets, and sends Rex back to Dorn on Ergro. Dorn shows Rex a hidden atomic plane, and they try to win robot #9 over to their cause. Ella and Tim, under hypnosis and instructed to kill Rex and Dorn, blast them with neutron detonators, but Grood neutralizes the detonators by remote control in order to save Dorn's life.

Rex and robot #9 take off in the atomic plane after it has been fueled, but Grood, having arrived on Ergro, finds Dorn monitoring the plane's flight on a fluoroscope transparency. Dorn is ordered by Grood to focus a weapon on the atomic plane, but the controls malfunction and the plane spins out of control. Rex and robot #9 are saved when a fragment of cosmic waste intercepts the beam. Rex and robot #9, whose true name is Wesley Bren, land safely on Earth. Bren tells his employer, Ken Wolper, a novelty manufacturer, of the many scientific gadgets he has seen, and Wolper instructs Hopper, one of his employees, to assist Bren. Bren and Hopper meet Rex on Mt. Vulcan, and they attempt to capture Grood. A pyramic catapult suddenly ensnares Rex and hurls him through space, but he is saved when his fall is cushioned by a sand bank.

Communicating with Dorn on Ergro over a cosmic radio, Rex is told that Grood has captured Bren and Hopper. Using his scientific machinery, Dorn is able to stop the atomic plane and the cosmojet containing Bren and Hopper, stalling them in outer space until Rex is able to give them a dornite box that will render them invisible when they reach Ergro. But Rex's plane vanishes when it is blasted with a cosmic cannon; he is saved when Dorn blacks out the plane with an infrangible ray machine before the cosmic cannon blast hits it. Rex lands safely with Bren and Hopper.

Back on Earth, Wolper has sent Darl and another man to find Bren and Hopper, but Grood captures them and decides to form an alliance with Wolper. Grood and Darl fly to Ergro in the cosmojet; Bren deserts Rex, joining up with Grood. Rex and Dorn are then placed in a hypnotic ray cabinet and seem to vanish, but they have actually been made invisible by Alden, Dorn's assistant.

Darl, Bren, Hopper and Ella are imprisoned with Ted by Grood, but Rex, now invisible, frees Ella and Tim. While they try to dismantle the cosmic cannon, Ella and Tim are recaptured. Using Ella as a hostage, Grood forces Alden into restoring Rex and Dorn to visibility. Grood then uses a solar thermo-furnace to melt the rocks of Forbidden Crest, and a deadly lava flow rushes toward Rex, Ella, Tim and Alden. Dorn, however, reverses the charge of the solar thermo-furnace into a de-thermo flame, and the fires that engulf them become cold and harmless.

Dorn is then captured and used to lure Rex and his friends into the degravitizer, a machine that nullifies the force of gravity. Rex and Tim are hurled upward, but manage to stop their ascent by grabbing a ledge. Ella apparently vanishes in a puff of smoke. Now out of control, the degravitizer begins to affect Grood and his assistant, Reckov, and Grood tells Dorn to shut off the ray, which saves Rex, Tim and Ella. The inhabitants of Ergro then rise up in rebellion and order the Earth people to leave. Rex, Tim, Grood and Reckov are ordered into the cosmojet and are launched into outer space.

Dr. Grood gains control of the cosmojet and returns to Ergro. Grood and Reckov are then taken prisoner. Rex and Darl blast off for Earth, and are attacked by cosmic cannon blasts fired by Grood's assistant Jarva. Rex evades the blasts and lands safely. On Ergro, Grood and Reckov escape from their captors by becoming invisible. On Earth, Rex and Darl approach Grood's underground laboratory, and are horrified when a speeding train appears out of thin air and rushes toward them. Unharmed, they realize that it had only been an

illusion created by one of Grood's machines.

Jarva, ambushing Rex and Darl, freezes their brains with the de-thermo ray, but Wolper suddenly appears, overpowers Jarva and frees Rex and Darl. Back on Ergro, Grood, still invisible, orders all of the Earth people imprisoned. Grood watches what has transpired on Earth through a fluororay-stellarscope. When he sees Rex and Darl take off for Ergro, Grood launches a cosmojet toward their plane, but Rex saves himself and Darl with evasive action. After landing on Ergro, Rex discovers that Alden is the only Earthman still free. Believing that Rex is dead, the power-mad Grood now intends to rule the universe and aims his cosmic cannon at Earth, but Rex diverts the cannon just before Grood fires. Grood and Reckov, defeated, try to escape in the cosmojet but are hurled into infinity instead, doomed to journey through space forever. Ergro is liberated. On Earth, Jarva decides to join Grood in space, but first destroys Grood's mountain laboratory and all of its secrets.

Comments

Similar in style and content to Columbia's earlier *Captain Video* (q.v.), even to the extent of casting the same actor, Judd Holdren, in the lead, *The Lost Planet* is one of the most science fiction-crazed serials ever made, and one of the worst serials ever made as well. The sheer number of fantastic, super-scientific weapons and gadgets, most of them mentioned in the individual chapter titles, is amazing, and because of its lofty ambitions the low-budget cliffhanger soon outstrips its meager budget and falls flat.

Opening with an impressive main

title shot of the planet Ergro illuminated by crashing lightning bolts, *The Lost Planet* slides progressively downhill from that point. The main title shot is, in fact, the most impressive thing in the film; oddly enough, it appears nowhere in the serial itself. The bulk of the special effects are unforgivably tacky, even by serial standards, employing unconvincing miniatures and more of producer Sam Katzman's sketchy cartoon animation, even lifting a cartoon shot of a flying saucer from *Atom Man vs. Superman* (q.v.) at one point. Conceptually, *The Lost Planet* is embarrassing even on its intended juvenile level, with the scientific low point occurring in a scene where two spaceships glide to a halt side-by-side in airless space and the occupants throw their hatches open and engage in affable conversation. Even kids in 1953 must have groaned in exasperation. The best thing that can be said for the serial is that it at least surpasses the even cheaper science fiction TV shows of the same era, like *Space Patrol*.

Spencer Bennet's direction, as in most of his work for Columbia, is mechanical and uninspired. The cast, from lead Judd Holdren on down, is pretty disappointing. Leading lady Vivian Mason, although very attractive, is kept mostly in the background and plays a conventional "damsel in distress" role. Character actor Michael Fox, cast as the evil Dr. Grood, brings an odd interpretation to the role; he plays the ostensibly ruthless Grood as sort of a tweedy, bespectacled eccentric dressed in an outdated suit, his appearance completely at odds with his ambitious goal of world domination. Columbia stalwart Gene Roth takes time out from his appearances in Three Stooges shorts to play

Reckov, Grood's lieutenant. Dressed in a pseudo-military uniform, Roth looks more like a member of the Salvation Army than the chief assistant to an interplanetary conqueror. In fact, Reckov is such a bumbling assistant, and Grood himself is such a befuddled, unintentionally comical figure, their stated plans of conquest never seem real. The serial's most demented plot twist deals with a novelty manufacturer from Earth attempting to muscle in on Grood's plans for his own personal gain. A story so lacking in believability to begin with isn't helped by even more outrageous subplots like this.

The technicians in Columbia's serial unit were simply unable to meet the technical requirements of this demanding script, and even the wardrobe department was stymied. The rebellious "planet people" on Ergro wear a bizarre mixture of Arab headdresses and discarded *Flash Gordon* shirts, as though someone tossed an armful of leftover costumes into the air and chose whatever they could grab first. The most infuriating scene in the film has Rex Barrow (Holdren) and a supporting character stealthily approaching Grood's hideout on Earth, only to be suddenly menaced by an onrushing locomotive at the cliffhanger conclusion of the chapter; the threat is casually explained away as a harmless immaterial vision in the next episode's resolution. *The Lost Planet* was an obvious attempt to capitalize on the popularity of contemporary juvenile science fiction TV shows. As cheap as it is, the serial is better than those shows simply by virtue of its studio production. *The Lost Planet* failed to make much of an impression though, and stands as a low point in movie serial history.

Panther Girl of the Kongo

(Republic, 1955)

Associate producer/director: Franklin Adreon. Screenplay: Ronald Davidson. Photography: Bud Thackery. Special effects: Howard Lydecker, Theodore Lydecker. Film editor: Cliff Bell, A.C.E. Art director: Frank Hotaling. Set decorators: John McCarthy, Jr., Edward G. Boyle. Sound: Roy Meadows. RCA Sound. Music: R. Dale Butts. Makeup: Bob Mark. Unit manager: Roy Wade. Assistant director: Leonard Kunody. Optical effects: Consolidated Film Industries. Feature version: *The Claw Monsters* (100 minutes), for television distribution.

Cast: Phyllis Coates (Jean Evans, "The Panther Girl"), Myron Healey (Larry Sanders), Arthur Space (Dr. Morgan), John Day (Cass), Mike Ragan (Rand), Morris Buchanan (Tembo), Roy Glenn, Sr. (Chief Danka), Archie Savage (Ituri), Ramsay Hill (Commissioner Stanton), Naaman Brown (Orto), Dan Ferniel. James Logan.

Chapter Titles

(1) *The Claw Monster.* (2) *Jungle Ambush.* (3) *The Killer Beast.* (4) *Sands of Doom.* (5) *Test of Terror.* (6) *High Peril.* (7) *Double Trap.* (8) *Crater of Flame.* (9) *River of Death.* (10) *Blasted Evidence.* (11) *Double Danger.* (12) *House of Doom.*

Story

Dr. Morgan, a brilliant research chemist working in Africa, has discovered chemicals that will mutate ordinary crawfish into gigantic monsters. With his ruthless henchmen Cass and Rand, Morgan uses his artificially created monsters to frighten away the local villagers so that he can gain control of a diamond mine he has discovered. Morgan's henchmen are opposed by the heroic Jean Evans, also known as the Panther Girl, and her friend, big-game hunter Larry Sanders, both of whom are unaware that Morgan is behind the plot. Photographing movies of jungle animals for research purposes, Jean accidentally films one of Morgan's enlarged beasts. Morgan attempts to seize the film, aware that there will be an investigation if the authorities should see it. With the help of renegade tribesmen, Cass and Rand attack Larry and steal the film, destroying the evidence of Morgan's activities.

Morgan controls a number of the local tribesmen by addicting them to a habit-forming drug. Aware that Jean and Larry are now on the alert after the theft of their film, Morgan orders Cass and Rand to release the giant monster now being grown in Morgan's compound, and to have the tribesmen drive it into the jungle to prevent discovery of the monster. One of the tribesmen is injured by the monster as it is being released. Cass and Rand send the tribesman to Jean for medical treatment, intending to lure her out into an ambush. Examining the injured tribesman, Larry

gathers a hunting party and Jean sets out atop her pet elephant to search for the monster.

Cass, Rand, and two tribesmen under their control spot Jean and attack her. Jean leaves her elephant and flees, running into the jungle and diving off a cliff into a lake. The tribesmen, followed by Cass and Rand, pursue her, but she eludes them by swimming underwater. As she wades ashore, Jean is captured by more tribesmen working with Cass and Rand. The tribesmen tie Jean to a tree and, signaling with their drums, attract a gorilla which attacks Jean. Larry arrives and shoots the ape, but is knocked unconscious in a violent struggle with the savage beast. The gorilla continues to attack Jean and nearly kills her, but Larry then regains consciousness and fires more bullets into the already-wounded ape, finally killing it. He then unties Jean.

Believing that a tribal uprising may occur due to fear of the giant monsters, Larry goes to Dr. Morgan's isolated research compound to warn Morgan about a possible revolt. Morgan bluffs Larry, concealing his real intentions, but Cass and Rand arrive and Larry draws his gun, ordering them to disarm. Morgan denies knowing Cass and Rand. Larry announces that he is taking Cass and Rand to the authorities for questioning, and Morgan pretends to help Larry tie them up. The two henchmen break free and, in the fight that erupts, Morgan falls to the floor and feigns unconsciousness. After Larry is knocked out by Cass and Rand, Dr. Morgan "revives," sending the two hoods away. When Larry comes to, Morgan lies that he drove Cass and Rand away with a

gun. After Larry departs, Morgan signals Cass and Rand to return.

When Jean and Larry summon Constable Harris to investigate what is going on in the jungle, Cass and Rand lure them into a riverbed filled with quicksand. Larry is trapped, sinking, as Jean and Constable Harris are held off by tribesmen who shoot arrows at them. Jean, standing on firm ground, tosses a vine to Larry and is able to pull him to safety as Constable Harris wounds one of the tribesmen and drives the other away with riflefire. Constable Harris takes the wounded tribesman in for questioning, and Larry rides with him.

Cass and Rand drive Morgan's giant monsters through the jungle and toward the village in an effort to provoke a tribal uprising, and one of the monsters kills a villager. The tribesmen start to believe that Jean is somehow responsible for the monsters, since she has previously failed to kill the beasts, and they begin to lose faith in her. To regain their loyalty and obedience, Jean agrees to enter a cage and face a lion in combat, armed only with a knife. After a violent struggle, she slays the beast as the tribesmen watch.

Larry returns and tracks down one of Morgan's giant monsters with Jean. As they follow the monster, they spot Cass and Rand and a fight erupts, during which Jean is knocked out. Jean revives and a gunfight begins. A lighted stick of dynamite is thrown at Jean and Larry, but they escape by climbing through a cave opening leading to the surface.

Mistakenly believing that Jean and Larry died in the explosion, Dr. Morgan sends Cass and Rand to panic the tribesmen by telling them that Jean and

Opposite: Panther Girl of the Kongo poster.

Larry were killed by one of the giant monsters. Meanwhile, Jean riding her pet elephant, and Larry, accompanied by a guide, set out separately to track down Cass and Rand. Two tribesmen see Jean and ambush her, leaving her tied up and unconscious in the jungle as they hurry to tell Cass and Rand. Surprised that Jean wasn't killed in the mine explosion, Cass and Rand find her first, though, and seeing one of Morgan's giant monsters in the jungle nearby, drive it toward the unconscious Jean, hoping that it will do their job for them and kill her.

Larry arrives before the monster can attack Jean, and unties her just as she comes to. Larry drives Cass and Rand away with riflefire. Jean and Larry then trail them from atop her elephant. Cass and Rand escape in their Jeep, but Larry soon finds them hiding out in a village bar. A fight breaks out, and Larry is knocked unconscious. Cass and Rand flee, climbing from the street to the second floor of a nearby building, but Larry comes to and follows them. The fight continues on a balcony and Larry is knocked through a wooden railing, falling toward sharp spikes on a fence below. Larry misses the spikes and lands safely on the soft dirt street. After Cass and Rand escape, Larry returns to the bar, where the saloonkeeper tends his wounds. A murderous thug hired by Cass and Rand enters the bar and attacks Larry with a knife. They fight, but the man is killed when he falls on his own knife during the struggle.

Realizing that the authorities do not believe the stories about the giant monsters, Jean and Larry intend to shoot more films of the beasts as proof. Jean and Larry discover one of the monsters in the jungle; while Jean leaves to retrieve her camera equipment, Larry stays behind and attempts to keep the monster within camera range by controlling the beast with riflefire. Ambushed by Cass and Rand, Larry retreats to cover. Jean arrives on the scene and comes to Larry's aid with her own rifle. A case of dynamite that Cass and Rand had intended to hurl at Larry explodes, toppling a huge tree toward Larry. Larry rolls away from the falling tree. Cass and Rand escape.

Dr. Morgan, aware that Jean and Larry know about Cass and Rand's activities, instructs the hoods to lay low for awhile and spend their time excavating the diamond mine. Attempting to track down Cass and Rand, Jean and Larry decide to begin their search at the mine, but they are soon spotted by Cass and Rand. They shoot at Jean and Larry, but Larry avoids the riflefire, paddling his canoe to shore. Jean and Larry separate; one of the hoods shoots at Larry, overturning the canoe. Jean is driven off by riflefire as she stealthily approaches the pair, but she escapes by swinging through the jungle on vines. She sees Larry floundering in the river, being attacked by a ravenous crocodile. Diving into the water, she saves him by killing the beast with her knife.

Swimming to shore, they are again attacked by Cass and Rand. Outgunned, Jean and Larry retreat to the nearby diamond mine. Cass and Rand set nearby bushes afire and throw the burning foliage into the mine to smoke out Jean and Larry. They then rush through the mine entrance to attack Jean and Larry. As they fight, the burning foliage tumbles down an elevator shaft; Larry falls after it into the flames. He is saved when he lands on a rock ledge in the shaft away from the fire.

Panther Girl of the Kongo —Phyllis Coates.

Panther Girl of the Kongo— Myron Healey, Phyllis Coates.

Jean continues shooting at Cass and Rand, driving them away, then she helps Larry out of the elevator shaft.

Jean and Larry plan to capture one of the giant monsters by trapping it in a camouflaged pit, but Cass and Rand learn about this and arrive at the pit early the next morning to find one of the monsters already caught in it. Before they can free the monster, Jean and Larry appear and drive Cass and Rand away with gunfire. The trapped monster reaches out of the pit and catches Jean's ankle in its claw, but Larry frees her from its grip and they retreat. As the monster emerges from the pit, Jean films it with her movie camera.

While Larry goes by canoe to get some chemical supplies so that Jean can develop the film, Cass and Rand ambush her, trying to steal the film. Knocking Jean out in a struggle, they tie her up and take her to the waterfront just as Larry returns with the supplies. They hide as Larry spots the unconscious Jean lying on the dock and rushes to her aid. As Larry tries to revive her, he is attacked by Cass and Rand. As they fight, Jean, still bound, is thrown off the dock into the river. Larry, after driving Cass and Rand away, dives into the water and saves her.

Jean develops the movie film of the giant monster and screens the startling footage for District Commissioner Stanton. Learning of this, Dr. Morgan tries to destroy the incriminating film, and gives Cass and Rand a powerful bomb to throw into Jean's cabin. Cass and Rand toss the bomb in and it explodes, but Jean, Larry and Commissioner Stanton are all shielded from the blast by a heavy wooden table.

Commissioner Stanton leaves to bring back reinforcements. Cass and Rand report this to Dr. Morgan, and Morgan instructs them to return to the mine and excavate as many diamonds as possible before Stanton returns. Larry returns to the diamond mine, but he is attacked by tribesmen left on guard by Cass and Rand. He drives the tribesmen away with gunfire, but they race ahead and surprise him when he follows them; Larry falls off a cliff and into the river after they attack him. Jean arrives and, leaping into the river, saves Larry. Jean and Larry then confront another one of Morgan's giant monsters in the jungle and kill it with gunfire.

The renegade tribesmen are rounded up when Commissioner Stanton returns with his reinforcements. Cass and Rand are both killed in a dynamite explosion when Jean and Larry track them to Morgan's diamond mine.

Examining the mine, Jean and Larry find a bottle of acid that could only have come from Morgan's laboratory, and they realize that he has been responsible for the creation of the monsters. When Jean and Larry confront Morgan with his misdeeds, he resists. As they struggle desperately, a bottle of deadly gas shatters. Jean and Larry escape from the room just as Morgan dies from inhaling his own poisonous gas.

Comments

Considering that it is Republic's next-to-last serial (the last one was *King of*

the Carnival, made the same year), *Panther Girl of the Kongo* is surprisingly good. For once, the two leads turn in convincing performances. Phyllis Coats and Myron Healey, both B-Western stalwarts, actually seem like real people, a rarity in Republic serials, and even John Day and Mike Ragan as secondary villains Cass and Rand lend a dimension of believability to their stock roles. Blonde Coates, who played Lois Lane in the 1951 feature *Superman and the Mole-Men* as well as the first season of the *Adventures of Superman* TV series, actually looks younger here than she did a few years earlier on the *Superman* show. For that TV series, she had successfully impersonated a professional career girl, Katharine Hepburn-type newspaper reporter, and the somewhat conservative wardrobe and brunette hairstyle she wore reflected her character. As the title heroine in *Panther Girl of the Kongo*, Coates essays more of a "pin up" sort of role and, despite being in her early thirties at the time, cuts a cute figure in a miniskirt. Nevertheless, the Panther Girl is no helpless damsel in distress; she acquits herself admirably, even when caught in the grip of a giant crawfish talon. For this serial, Coates wore an exact duplicate of Francis Gifford's costume from the 1941 Republic serial *Jungle Girl*, and long shots of Gifford from the earlier film were used as an economy move.

Footage of Ray "Crash" Corrigan as a gorilla from Republic's first serial *Darkest Africa* (1936) is also used, intercut (none too convincingly) with a new gorilla scene in *Panther Girl of the Kongo*. One aspect of the serial that Coates definitely did not enjoy were the water scenes, shot on Republic's back lot in a small pond that the studio maintained in less than sanitary condition. As Coates recalled in an interview with the author, a dip in the pond for a scene was usually followed by a trip to the studio infirmary and an appointment with a hypodermic needle.

The serial's monsters are less than satisfactory; for once, Republic's usually dependable technical staff failed to deliver. The "giant" crayfish look exactly like what they are — normal crustaceans either filmed in miniature sets or blown-up by enlargement on a rear-projection screen. The results were so disappointing that Republic felt it was necessary to jazz up their advertising posters with lurid cartoons of the monsters; they even cheated by including a shot of a horned dinosaur from a completely different film, the 1951 Lippert adventure *Lost Continent*. Needless to say, those expecting to see Phyllis Coates grapple with a dinosaur were disappointed.

The film's racial attitudes are worth comment. While many earlier serials such as *The Lost City* (q.v.) treated their black characters in a condescending, exploitative and all-around insulting manner, there is no such racism in *Panther Girl of the Kongo*. While the African tribesmen in the story are still stock "natives," they are at least allowed a modicum of dignity and are allowed to behave as mature human beings.

This relatively progressive attitude and the solid performances suggest that the movie serial could have grown and matured in ways that it was never allowed to. In most discussions of Republic's serials, *Panther Girl of the Kongo* is usually dismissed and casually tossed aside, coming as it does at the end of the studio's cliffhanger run. True, the serial's plot is basic "mad scientist" fodder, and giant monsters (whether they were convincing or not) had become a tiresome movie cliché by 1955. But there are enough good qualities in the film to make it likable, and the nearing demise of movie serials all the more regrettable.

Video availability: Republic Home Video.

Appendix:
37 Serials with Incidental
Science Fiction Elements

This filmography lists 37 additional motion picture serials containing incidental elements that might be called science fiction but were not integral to the story. These serials are listed in the order of their original release. Each entry contains the following information: releasing company, year of release, director(s), principal cast, feature version and/or re-release titles (where applicable), pertinent notes and science fiction plot elements.

The Voice from the Sky (Ben Wilson Prods./G.Y.B. Prods., 1930). 10 chapters.
Director: Ben Wilson.
Cast: Wally Wales (a.k.a. Hal Taliaferro), Jean Delores.
Note: The first optical (soundtrack-on-film) serial.
A mad scientist projects his voice through the air.

The Jade Box (Universal, 1930). 10 chapters.
Director: Ray Taylor.
Cast: Jack Perrin, Louis Lorraine, Monroe Salisbury, Francis Ford, Leo White, Wilber S. Mack, Eileen Sedgwick.
Note: Silent/part sound.
Invisibility.

Detective Lloyd (Universal, 1932). 12 chapters.
Director: Henry MacRae.

Cast: Jack Lloyd, Wallace Geoffrey, Muriel Angelus, Lewis Dayton, Janice Adair, Tracy Holmes, Emily Fitzroy, Humberstone Wright, John Turnbull, Shale Gardner, Clifford Buckton, Vic Kaley, Fewlass Llewillyn, Ethel Ramsey.
Death ray.

The Airmail Mystery (Universal, 1932). 12 chapters.
Director: Ray Taylor.
Cast: James Flavin, Lucille Browne, Wheeler Oakman, Frank S. Hagney, Sidney Bracey, Nelson McDowell, Walter Brennan, Al Wilson, Bruce Mitchell, Jack Holley, Cecil Kellogg, Bob Reeves.
"Aerial catapult" device.

The Phantom of the Air (Universal, 1933). 12 chapters.
Director: Ray Taylor.
Cast: Tom Tyler, Gloria Shea, LeRoy Mason, Hugh Enfield, William Desmond, Sidney Bracey, Walter Brennan, Jennie Cramer, Cecil Kellogg.
Anti-gravity device.

The Wolf Dog (Mascot, 1933). 12 chapters.
Directors: Harry Fraser, Colbert Clark.
Cast: Rin-Tin-Tin, Jr., Frankie Darro, George J. Lewis, Boots Mallory, Henry B. Walthall, Hale Hamilton, Fred Kohler, Niles Welch, Stanley G. Blystone, Tom London, Sarah Padden, Max Wagner, Carroll Nye, Cornelius Keefe, Harry Northrup, Lane Chandler, Dickie Moore, Donald Reed, Gordon DeMain, George Magrill, Lionel Backus, Lew Meehan, Yakima Canutt, Leon Holmes, Jack Kenny, Wes Wagner.
Electrical ray.

The Whispering Shadow (Mascot, 1933). 12 chapters.
Directors: Albert Herman, Colbert Clark.
Cast: Bela Lugosi, Viva Tattersall, Malcolm MacGregor, Henry B. Walthall, Robert Warwick, Ethel Clayton, Roy D'Arcy, Karl Dane, Lloyd Whitlock, Bob Kortman, Lafe McKee, George J. Lewis, Jack Perrin, Max Wagner, Kernan Cripps, Eddie Parker, Gordon DeMain, George Magrill, Tom London, Lionel Backus, Norman Fusier.
Note: Bela Lugosi's first serial.
Death ray.

The Perils of Pauline (Universal, 1934). 12 chapters.
Director: Ray Taylor.
Cast: Evalyn Knapp, Robert Allen, James Durkin, John Davidson, Sonny Ray, Frank Lackteen, Pat O'Malley, William Desmond, Adolph Muller, Josef Swickard, William Worthington, Hugh Enfield.

Note: A quasi-remake (in title only) of the famous Pearl White silent serial. Secret gas formula.

Mystery Mountain (Mascot, 1934). 12 chapters.
Directors: Otto Brower, B. Reeves Eason.
Cast: Ken Maynard, Tarzan the Wonder Horse, Verna Hillie, Edward Earle, Edmund Cobb, Lynton Brent, Syd Saylor, Carmencita Johnson, Lafe McKee, Al Bridge, Edward Hearn, Bob Kortman, Wally Wales (a.k.a. Hal Taliaferro), George Chesebro, Hooper Atchley, Gene Autry, Smiley Burnette, Jack Kirk, Lew Meehan, Jack Rockwell, William Gould, Tom London, Philo McCullough, Frank Ellis, James Mason, Steve Clark, Cliff Lyons, Art Mix, Curley Dresden.
Note: Future cowboy star Gene Autry appears in a supporting role. Futuristic electrical devices.

The Miracle Rider (Mascot, 1935). 15 chapters.
Directors: Armand Schaefer, B. Reeves Eason.
Cast: Tom Mix, Jean Gale, Charles Middleton, Jason Robards, Edward Hearn, Pat O'Malley, Robert Frazer, Ernie Adams, Wally Wales (a.k.a. Hal Taliaferro), Bob Kortman, Blackhawk, Chief Standing Bear, Tony, Jr., Smiley Burnette, Jack Rockwell.
Note: The first serial appearance of Charles ("Ming the Merciless") Middleton. "X-94" explosive.

Fighting Marines (Mascot, 1935). 12 chapters.
Directors: B. Reeves Eason, Joseph Kane.
Cast: Grant Withers, Adrian Morris, Ann Rutherford, Robert Warwick, George J. Lewis, Jason Robards, Warner Richmond, Frank Reicher, Robert Frazer, Frank J. Lewis, Jason Robards, Warner Richmond, Frank Reicher, Robert Frazer, Frank Glendon, Richard Alexander, Donald Reed, Tom London, Stanley G. Blystone, Milburn Stone, Franklin Adreon, Billy Arnold, Lee Shumway, Grace Durkin.
"Radio gravity gun."

Ace Drummond (Universal, 1936). 13 chapters.
Directors: Ford Beebe, Cliff Smith.
Cast: John King, Jean Rogers, Noah Beery, Jr., Guy Bates Post, Arthur Loft, Chester Gan, Jackie Morrow, James B. Leong, James Eagle, Selmer Jackson, Robert Warwick, C. Montague Shaw, Frederick Vogeding, Al Bridge, Lon Chaney, Jr., Stanley G. Blystone, Edmund Cobb, Richard Wessel, Louis Vincenot, Sam Ash, Hooper Atchley.
Feature version (theatrical): *Squadron of Doom.*
Note: Based on the King Features Syndicate newspaper comic strip. Remote-controlled airplane destruction.

Robinson Crusoe of Clipper Island (Republic, 1936). 14 chapters.
Directors: Mack V. Wright, Ray Taylor.
Cast: Mala, Rex, Buck, Mamo Clark, Herbert Rawlinson, William Newell, John Ward, Selmer Jackson, John Dilson, John Picorri, George Chesebro, Bob Kortman, George Cleveland, Lloyd Whitlock, Tiny Roebuck, Tracy Layne.
Feature version (television): *Robinson Crusoe of Mystery Island.*
Electronically controlled volcano eruption.

Radio Patrol (Universal, 1937). 12 chapters.
Directors: Ford Beebe, Cliff Smith.
Cast: Grant Withers, Catherine Hughes, Mickey Rentschler, Adrian Morris, Max Hoffman, Jr., Frank Lackteen, Leonard Lord, Monte Montague, Dick Botiller, Silver Wolf, Jack Mulhall, Tom London, Wheeler Oakman.
Note: Based on the King Features Syndicate newspaper comic strip.
Secret formula for bullet-proof steel.

S.O.S. Coast Guard (Republic, 1937). 12 chapters.
Directors: William Witney, Alan James.
Cast: Ralph Byrd, Bela Lugosi, Maxine Doyle [Mrs. William Witney], Herbert Rawlinson, Richard Alexander, Lee Ford, John Picorri, Lawrence Grant, Thomas Carr, Carleton Young, Allen Conner, George Chesebro, Ranny Weeks.
Feature version (theatrical): *SOS Coast Guard.*
Disintegrating gas.

Blake of Scotland Yard (Victory, 1937). 15 chapters.
Director: Robert F. Hill.
Cast: Ralph Byrd, Joan Barclay, Dickie Jones, Herbert Rawlinson, Lloyd Hughes, Nick Stuart.
Note: This was the last independently produced serial.
Death ray.

The Secret of Treasure Island (Columbia, 1938). 15 chapters.
Director: Elmer Clifton.
Cast: Don Terry, Gwen Gaze, Grant Withers, Hobart Bosworth, William Farnum, Walter Miller, George Rosener, Dave O'Brien, Yakima Canutt, Warner Richmond, Bill Boyle, Sandra Karina, Joe Caits, Colin Campbell, Patrick J. Kelly.
Death bombs.

The Green Hornet (Universal, 1940). 13 chapters.
Directors: Ford Beebe, Ray Taylor.
Cast: Gordon Jones, Wade Boteler, Keye Luke, Anne Nagel, Philip Trent, Walter

McGrail, John Kelly, Gene Rizzi, Douglas Evans, Ralph Dunn, Arthur Loft, Edward Earle, Cy Kendall.

Feature version (video): *The Green Hornet.*

Note: Based on the popular radio drama.

Futuristic weapons.

The Shadow (Columbia, 1940), 15 chapters.

Director: James W. Horne.

Cast: Victor Jory, Veda Ann Borg, Roger Moore, Robert Fiske, J. Paul Jones, Jack Ingram, Charles Hamilton, Edward Piel, Sr., Frank LaRue.

Note: Based on the popular radio drama starring Orson Welles.

Death ray.

Drums of Fu Manchu (Republic, 1940). 15 chapters.

Directors: William Witney, John English.

Cast: Henry Brandon, William Royle, Robert Kellard, Gloria Franklin, Olaf Hytten, Tom Chatterton, Luana Walters, Lal Chand Mehra, George Cleveland, John Dilson, John Merton, Dwight Frye, Wheaton Chambers.

Note: Based on the character created by Sax Rohmer.

"Dacoits" (human robots).

King of the Royal Mounted (Republic, 1940). 12 chapters.

Directors: William Witney, John English.

Cast: Allan Lane, Robert Strange, Robert Kellard, Lita Conway, Herbert Rawlinson, Harry Cording, Bryant Washburn, Budd Buster, Stanley Andrews, John Davidson, John Dilson, Paul McVey, Lucien Prival.

Feature version (theatrical): *The Yukon Patrol* (7 reels, released in 1942).

Note: Based on the newspaper comic strip.

"Compound X" medical cure.

The Green Hornet Strikes Again (Universal, 1940). 15 chapters.

Directors: Ford Beebe, John Rawlins.

Cast: Warren Hull, Keye Luke, Wade Boteler, Anne Nagel, Eddie Acuff, Pierre Watkin, Joe A. Devlin, William Hall, Dorothy Lovett, Jay Michael, C. Montague Shaw, Bob Kortman, Jack Perrin.

Note: Based on the radio drama. This was a sequel to *The Green Hornet* (q.v.), released earlier the same year.

Futuristic weapons.

Gang Busters (Universal, 1942). 13 chapters.

Directors: Ray Taylor, Noel Smith.

Cast: Kent Taylor, Irene Hervey, Ralph Morgan, Robert Armstrong, Richard

Davies, Joseph Crehan, George Watts, Victor Zimmerman, George Lewis, William Haade, Grace Cunard.
Note: Based on the popular radio drama.
Death simulation drug.

Spy Smasher (Republic, 1942). 12 chapters.
Director: William Witney.
Cast: Kane Richmond, Sam Flint, Marguerite Chapman, Hans Schumm, Tristram Coffin, Franco Corsaro, Hans Von Morhart, George Renavent, Robert O. Davis [Rudolph Anders], Henry Zynda, Paul Bryar, Tom London, Richard Bond, Crane Whitley, John James.
Feature version (television): *Spy Smasher Returns.*
Futuristic aircraft.

King of the Mounties (Republic, 1942). 12 chapters.
Director: William Witney.
Cast: Allan Lane, Gilbert Emery, Russell Hicks, Peggy Drake, George Irving, Abner Biberman, William Bakewell, Duncan Renaldo, Francis Ford, Jay Novello, Anthony Warde.
Note: A sequel to Republic's serial *King of the Royal Mounted* (q.v.).
Synthetic rubber formula.

G-Men vs. the Black Dragon (Republic, 1943). 15 chapters.
Director: William Witney.
Cast: Rod Cameron, Roland Got, Constance Worth, Nino Pipitone, Noel Cravat, George J. Lewis, Maxine Doyle, Donald Kirke, Ivan Miller, Walter Fenner, C. Montague Shaw, Harry Burns, Forbes Murray, Hooper Atchley.
Feature version (television): *Black Dragon of Manzanar.*
Suspended animation drug.

Captain America (Republic, 1944). 15 chapters.
Directors: John English, Elmer Clifton.
Cast: Dick Purcell, Lorna Gray, Lionel Atwill, Charles Trowbridge, Russell Hicks, John Davidson, George J. Lewis, Tom Chatterton, John Hamilton, Crane Whitley, Norman Nesbitt, Frank Reicher.
Re-release title: *The Return of Captain America.*
Note: Loosely based on the popular Marvel (then Timely) Comics character.
"Purple death" gas, sonic vibrator.

The Great Alaskan Mystery (Universal, 1944). 13 chapters.
Directors: Ray Taylor, Lewis D. Collins.
Cast: Milburn Stone, Marjorie Weaver, Edgar Kennedy, Samuel S. Hinds, Martin

Kosleck, Ralph Morgan, Joseph Crehan, Fuzzy Knight, Harry Cording, Anthony Warde, Edward Gargan.
"Peratron" (advanced weapon).

The Master Key (Universal, 1945). 13 chapters.
Directors: Ray Taylor, Lewis D. Collins.
Cast: Milburn Stone, Jan Wiley, Dennis Moore, Addison Richards, Byron Foulger, Maris Wrixon, Sarah Padden, Russell Hicks, Alfred LaRue, George Lynn.
"Orotron" gold extraction machine.

Hop Harrigan (Columbia, 1940). 15 chapters.
Director: Derwin Abrahams.
Cast: William Bakewell, Jennifer Holt, Robert "Buzz" Henry, Sumner Getchall, Emmett Vogan, Claire James, John Merton, Wheeler Oakman, Ernie Adams, Peter Michael, Terry Frost, Anthony Warde, Jackie Moran, Bobby Stone, Jack Buchanan, Jim Diehl.
Note: Based on the radio show.
Futuristic power unit, death ray.

Lost City of the Jungle (Universal, 1946). 13 chapters.
Directors: Ray Taylor, Lewis D. Collins.
Cast: Russell Hayden, Jane Adams, Lionel Atwill, Keye Luke, Helen Bennett, Ted Hecht, John Eldredge, John Miljan, John Gallaudet, Ralph Lewis.
Note: This was character actor Lionel Atwill's last film. He died during production, and the serial had to be finished using a double.
"Meteorium 245" atomic bomb defense.

Jack Armstrong (Columbia, 1947). 15 chapters.
Director: Wallace Fox.
Cast: John Hart, Rosemary LaPlanche, Claire James, Joe Brown, Pierre Watkin, Charles Middleton, Wheeler Oakman, Jack Ingram, Eddie Parker, Hugh Prosser, John Merton, Gene Stutenroth (a.k.a. Gene Roth).
Note: Based on the radio series.
Cosmic radioactivity, atomic airplane engine.

The Black Widow (Republic, 1947). 13 chapters.
Directors: Spencer Bennet, Fred C. Brannon.
Cast: Bruce Edwards, Virginia Lindley, Carol Forman, Anthony Warde, Ramsay Ames, I. Stanford Jolley, Theodore Gottlieb [Brother Theodore], Virginia Carroll, Sam Flint, Gene Stutenroth [Roth], Tom Steele, Dale Van Sickel, LeRoy Mason, Forrest Taylor, Ernie Adams, Keith Richards.
Feature version (television): *Sombra the Spider Woman.*
Futuristic weapons.

Tex Granger (Columbia, 1948). 15 chapters.

Director: Derwin Abrahams.

Cast: Robert Kellard, Peggy Stewart, Buzz Henry, Smith Ballew, Jack Ingram, I. Stanford Jolley, Terry Frost, Jim Diehl, Britt Wood, Duke, the Wonder Dog.

Note: Based on the comic book.

Electronically controlled flying disc.

Bruce Gentry (Columbia, 1949). 15 chapters.

Directors: Spencer Bennet, Thomas Carr.

Cast: Tom Neal, Judy Clark, Ralph Hodges, Forrest Taylor, Hugh Prosser, Tristram Coffin, Jack Ingram, Terry Frost, Eddie Parker, Charles King, Stephen Carr, Dale Van Sickel.

Note: Based on the newspaper comic strip distributed by the Hall Syndicate.

Futuristic weapons and gadgets.

Blackhawk (Columbia, 1952). 15 chapters.

Director: Spencer Bennet.

Cast: Kirk Alyn, Carol Forman, John Crawford, Michael Fox, Don Harvey, Rick Vallin, Larry Stewart, Weaver Levy, Zon Murray, Nick Stuart, Marshall Reed, Pierce Lyden, William Fawcett, Rory Mallinson, Frank Ellis.

Note: Based on the comic book published by National Periodical Publications (now DC Comics).

Electronic ray, futuristic weapons.

Canadian Mounties vs. Atomic Invaders (Republic, 1953). 12 chapters.

Director: Franklin Adreon.

Cast: Bill Henry, Susan Morrow, Arthur Space, Dale Van Sickel, Pierre Watkin, Mike Ragan, Stanley Andrews, Harry Lauter, Hank Patterson, Edmund Cobb, Gayle Kellogg, Tom Steele, Jean Wright.

Feature version (television): *Missile Base at Taniak.*

Atomic-powered guided missiles.

Bibliography

Barbour, Alan G. *Cliffhanger*. A&W, 1977.
_____. *Days of Thrills and Adventure*. New York: Macmillan, 1970.
Cline, William C. *In the Nick of Time: Motion Picture Sound Serials*. Jefferson, N.C.: McFarland, 1984.
_____. *Serials-ly Speaking: Essays on Cliffhangers*. McFarland, 1994.
Collura, J. "A Dynamic Duo: William Witney and John English." *Classic Images* #101, November 1983.
DeMarco, Mario. "Sam McKim: Working with the Long Ranger." *Classic Images* #129, March 1986.
Doherty, J. "Music from the Serials." *Soundtrack*, June 1982.
_____. "The Music of Republic, the Early Years, 1937–1941." *Soundtrack*, March 1986.
Dolven, F. "The Western Serials and Their Stars: The Great! The Good! The Forgettable!" *Classic Images* #207, September 1992.
Edelman, R. "Vintage 40s and 50s Film Serials Were Smashes Before TV Did 'Em." *Variety*, July 8, 1987.
Everett, E.K. "Ford Beebe Recalls Helen Holmes and J.P. McGowan." *Classic Images* #85, August 1982.
Hagedorn, R. "Technology and Economic Exploitation: The Serial as a Form of Narrative Presentation." *Wide Angle* #4, 1988.
Harmon, Jim, and Donald F. Glut. *The Great Movie Serials*. Garden City, N.Y.: Doubleday, 1972.
Hayes, R.M. *The Republic Chapterplays: A Complete Filmography of the Serials Released by Republic Pictures Corporation, 1934–1955*. Jefferson, N.C.: McFarland, 1992.
Jackson, C.L. "Flying Disc Man from Mars." *Filmfax* #8, October-November 1987.

Kinnard, Roy. *Fifty Years of Serial Thrills*. Metuchen, N.J.: Scarecrow, 1983.
_____. "The Flash Gordon Serials." *Films in Review*, April 1988.
_____. "Jean Rogers." *Films in Review*, September-October 1995.
_____. "Kay Aldridge." *Films in Review*, September-October 1994.
_____. "The Lost City." *Filmfax* #10, April-May 1988.
Lahue, Kalton C. *Continued Next Week: A History of the Moving Picture Serial*. Norman: University of Oklahoma Press, 1964.
_____. *Bound and Gagged*. Cranbury, N.J.: A.S. Barnes, 1968.
Laube, C. "The Serial with Feature-Length Chapters." *Classic Images* #106, April 1984.
Lucas, W. D. "The Dick Tracy Serials." *Classic Images* #96, June 1983.
_____. "The Serials of Bela Lugosi." *Classic Images* #87, September 1982.
Mathis, Jack. *Valley of the Cliffhangers*. Jack Mathis Advertising, 1975.
Newton, M. "Barry Shipman, a Memorial Tribute to a Friend." *Classic Images* #207, September 1992.
Rainey, Buck. *Those Fabulous Serial Heroines: Their Lives and Films*. Waynesville, N.C.: World of Yesterday, 1990.
Schutz, Wayne. *The Motion Picture Serial: An Annotated Bibliography*. Metuchen, N.J.: Scarecrow, 1992.
Singer, B. "Female Power in the Serial-Queen Melodrama: The Etiology of an Anomaly." *Camera Obscura*, January 1990.
Smith, J. "The Adventures of Captain Marvel." *Filmfax* #9, February-March 1988.
Stedman, Raymond William. *The Serials*. Norman: University of Oklahoma Press, 1971.
Turner, George. "Making the Flash Gordon Serials." *American Cinematographer*, June 1983.
Weiss, Ken, and Ed Goodgold. *To Be Continued....* New York: Crown, 1972.
Witney, William. *In a Door, Into a Fight, Out a Door, Into a Chase: Moviemaking Remembered by the Guy at the Door*. Jefferson, N.C.: McFarland, 1995.

Index

Numbers in **boldface** refer to pages with photographs.

ABC Films, Inc. 40
Abrahams, Derwin 156, 203, 204
Ace Drummond (comic strip) 36
Ace Drummond (serial) 7, 199
Action Comics 139
Acuff, Eddie 77, 201
Adair, Janice 198
Adams, Ernie 84, 199, 203
Adams, Jane 141, 147, 148, 203
Adams, Ted 149
Adreon, Franklin 61, 91, 148, 160, 152, 175, 179, 189, 199, 204
The Adventures of Captain Marvel (serial) 152, 159
The Adventures of Superman (TV series) 156, 159, 195
Ahn, Philson 69, **71**
Ainslie, Ann 48
The Airmail Mystery (serial) 198
Aldridge, Kay 162
Alexander, Richard 30, 53, **57**, 199, 200
Allan, Edgar 48
Allen, Robert 198
Alten, Frank 109
Altweiss, James 14

Alyn, Kirk 137, **138**, 140, 156, **158**, 159, 204
American Movie Classics (AMC cable TV network) 40, 109, 148
Ames, Ramsay 203
Anders, Robert *see* Davis, Robert O.
Anderson, Gene 103
Anderson, Murphy 74
Andrews, R.M. 132, 137, 141, 156, 164
Andrews, Stanley 201, 204
Angelus, Muriel 198
Armageddon 2419 A.D. (novel) 74
Armstrong, Robert 201
Arnold, Billy 199
Arnold, Dorothy 77, 83
Ash, Jerry 30, 38, 69, 77, 84
Ash, Sam 199
Askam, Earl 30
Atchley, Hooper 53, 99, 199, 202
Atom Man vs. Superman (serial) 120, 156–159, **158**, 188
Atom Squad (TV series) 174
Atomic Peril (theatrical short) 179
Atwill, Lionel 202, 203
Aubran, Jacques 30, 41
Austin, William 103

Autry, Gene **25**, **28**, 29, 199
Averill, Anthony 77

Backus, Lionel 198
Bailey, Bill 170
Bailey, Richard 109, 115
Bakaleinikoff, Mischa 132, 136, 141, 156, 164, 170
Baker, Loren 48
Baker, Sam **18**
Bakewell, William 175, 179, 202, 203
Ballew, Smith 204
Barclay, Joan 200
Barcroft, Roy 48, 84, 109, **113**, 115, 121, 122, **125**, 162, 175, 177
Barish, Mildred 77
Barron, Baynes 175
Barron, Robert 132, 137
Barry, Dan 36
Bassett, Rex 47
Batman (comic strip) 105
Batman (serial) 6, 103–109, **104**, **105**, **106**, **107**, 147
Batman (TV series) 105, 106, 107, 109
Batman and Robin (serial) 107, 141–148, **142**, **144**, **145**, 155, 157
Beach, Richard 48
Beatty, Warren 51

Beche, Robert 61
Beebe, Ford 53, 69, 77, 84, 199, 200, 201
Beery, Noah, Jr. 199
Beghon, Jean 51
Bell, Cliff 109, 121, 126, 148, 152, 160, 175, 179, 189
Benedict, Brooks 48
Bennet, Bruce *see* Brix, Herman
Bennet, Spencer 109, 121, 132, 136, 139, 141, 156, 164, 169, 170, 184, 188, 203, 204
Bennett, Helen 203
Berest, Frederic 184
Berger, Ralph 14, 21, 30
Best, Willie 116
Biberman, Abner 202
Big Jim McLain (feature) 162
The Big Reel (publication) 7
Birnbaum, Irving 77
The Black Cat (1934 feature) 37
The Black Widow (serial) 203
Blackhawk (serial) 204
Blaine, James C. 53
Blair, Robert 84
Blake of Scotland Yard (serial) 200
Blazing the Overland Trail (serial) 6, 120
Bletcher, William **16**, 21
Blue, Monte 41
Blystone, Stanley G. 25, 27, 156, 198, 199
Bond, James (character) 53, 107
Bond, Richard 202
Bond, Tommy 137, 140, 156
Booth, Adrian *see* Gray, Lorna
Borg, Veda Ann 201
Borgnine, Ernest 174
Boring, Wayne 139
Borland, Carroll 30
Borschell, Ed 109, 121
Bosworth, Hobart 200
Boteler, Wade 200–201
Botiller, Dick 200
Boyd, William 21
Boyd, William (Stage) 16, **17**, 21
Boyle, Bill 200
Boyle, Edward G. 189
Boyle, Ray 180
Bracy, Sidney 11, 198
Bradford, John 41, 48

Bradford, Lane 152, 180
Bradford, Marshall 141
Bradley, Harry C. 84
Brandon, Henry 69, 75, 201
Brannon, Fred C. 121, 126, 148, 152, 160, 175, 179, 203
Breil, Joseph Carl 47
Brennan, Walter 198
Brent, Lynton 30, 92, 199
Bretherton, Howard 116, 120
Brick Bradford (comic strip) 133
Brick Bradford (serial) 132–136, **134**, **135**, 169
Brick Bradford Comics 136
Bride of Frankenstein (feature) 36, 60, 74, 90
Bridge, Al 194, 199
Briggs, Austin 36
Brix, Herman (a.k.a. Bruce Bennet) 61, **66**, 67, 68
Brocco, Peter 175
Brodie, Don 11, 30
Brook, M.C. 174
Brooks, Jean *see* Kelly, Jeanne
Brother Theodore *see* Gottlieb, Theodore
Brower, Otto 22, 199
Brown, Bernard B. 69
Brown, Everett 16
Brown, Hiram S., Jr. 91
Brown, James S. 103, 108
Brown, Joe 203
Brown, Naaman 189
Browne, Fayte 164, 170
Browne, Lucille 198
Bruce Gentry (serial) 204
Bryar, Paul 202
Buchanan, Jack 203
Buchanan, Morris 189
Buck (horse) 200
Buck Rogers (comic strip) 36, 74
Buck Rogers (1970s TV series) 76
Buck Rogers (radio series) 74
Buck Rogers (serial) 14, 40, 69–75, **71**, **72**, **73**, **75**, 89
Buck Rogers Conquers the Universe (serial) 76
Buck Rogers in the 25th Century (1950s TV series) 76
Buckton, Clifford 198
Burnette, Lester (Smiley) 25, 41, 48, 199
Burnley, Jack 105, 139
Burns, Forrest 152

Bushman, Francis X. 48
Burns, Fred 27
Burns, Harry 202
Burns, Iris 22
Burns, R. Dale 189
Buster, Budd 201
Butler, John 48
Byrd, Ralph 48, **50**, 98, **100**, **101**, 102, 200

Cagney, James 108
Cain, Dean 159
Caits, Joe 200
Caldwell, Dwight 103, 116, 141
Calkins, Dick 74
Cameron, Rod 202
Campbell, Colin 200
Canadian Mounties vs. Atomic Invaders (serial) 204
Canutt, Yakima 109, 198, 200
Captain America (serial) 202
Captain Marvel (character) 159
Captain Mephisto and the Transformation Machine (serial featurization) 109
Captain Video (serial) 170–175, **171**, **172**, **173**, 187
Captain Video and His Video Rangers (TV series) 170, 174
Captain Video's Cartoons (TV series) 174
Captives of the Zero Hour (theatrical short) 179
Carlton, George 121
Carlyle, Jack 27
Carr, Michael 160
Carr, Stephen 137–204
Carr, Thomas 132, 136, 137, 140, 200, 204
Carroll, Virginia 137, 203
Carroll, Zelma 14
Carter, Ellis W. 148
Caruth, Burr 48
Cason, Jack 184
Cassidy, Edward 109, 137
Cassidy, Hopalong (character) 21
Cavan, Allan 84
Central Press Association 133
Chambers, Wheaton 53, 121, 126, 201
Chandler, Lane 30, 41, 53, 109, 198
Chaney, Lon, Jr. 41, **46**, 47, 199

Chapman, Marguerite 202
Chatterton, Tom 84, 201, 202
Cheatham, Jack 48
Cheron, Andre 48
Cherwin, Richard 109, 121
Chesebro, George 199–200
Chicago Tribune–New York Times Syndicate 51
Chief Standing Bear 199
Christie, Dorothy 25, **28**, 29
Christie, Howard 30
Cianelli, Edward (Eduardo) **92**, 97, 98
City of Lost Men (serial featurization) 14
Clark, Colbert 198
Clark, Judy 204
Clark, Mamo 200
Clark, Steve 199
Clark, William E. 126
Clarke, Mae **148, 150**
The Claw Monsters (serial featurization) 189
Claxton, David 30
Clay, Lewis 132, 136, 164
Clayton, Ethel 198
Clement, Dora 77
Cleveland, George 30, 200, 201
Clifford, Sidney 136, 164, 184
Clifton, Elmer 200, 202
Cline, Jasper 121
Clooney, George 109
Coates, Phyllis 189, **193, 194**, 195, 196
Cobb, Eddie 12, 62, 199, 204
Cobb, Lee J. 77, 83
Coffin, Tris 148, **150, 151**, 202, 204
Cogan, Dick 160, 175
Cohen, Ben 20
Cole, Jack 22
Cole, Royal K. 116, 121, 141, 148, 164, 170
Collier, Lewis D. 202, 203
Collyer, Bud 139
Columbia Pictures 5, 6, 105, 106, 108, 120, 121, 133, 136, 147, 158, 159, 169, 170, 173, 174, 175, 183, 187, 188
Columbo, Alberto 48, 51, 61, 68
Commando Cody (character) 177, 179
Commando Cody, Sky Marshall of the Universe

(theatrical shorts) 152, **178**, 179
Conkolin, Hal 174
Connor, Allen 200
Consolidated Film Industries 148, 152, 160, 175, 179, 189
Conway, Lita 201
Coogan, Richard 174
Cooper, Willis 77
Cording, Harry 201, 203
Corey, Jim 27, 30
Corrado, Gino 16, 22
Corrigan, Ray "Crash" 30, 41, **46**, 47, 116, 120
Corsaro, Franco 202
Cosmic Vengeance (theatrical short) 179
Cox, Morgan 48
Crabbe, Larry "Buster" **ii**, 5, 30, **35**, 38, **39, 54**, 55, **56**, 69, **71, 72**, 84, **87, 89**, 90, 169
Crain, Earl, Sr. 148, 152, 160
Cramer, Jennie 198
Cramer, Richard 11
Crane, Richard 164, **168**, 169
Cravat, Noel 175, 202
Craven, James 121, 122, 148, 160, 162
Crawford, John 152, 180, 204
The Crimson Ghost (character) 175
The Crimson Ghost (serial) 126–132, **130**
Cripps, Kernan 48, 198
Croft, Douglas 103, **105**, **107**, 108, 147
Cross, Oliver 170
Crystal Pictures 76
Cunard, Grace 202
Curtis, Alan 41
Curtis, Donald 84
Cyclotrode "X" (serial featurization) 126

D-Day on Mars (serial featurization) 121
D'Agostino, Mack 22, 61, 91, 98
Dalmus, Herbert 53
Dane, Karl 198
Daniels, Harold 84
D'Antonio, Carmen 84
D'Arcy, Roy 198
Darkest Africa (serial) 177
Darro, Frankie 25, 29, 198
Davidson, John 61, 98, **99**, 101, 121, 198, 201, 202

Davidson, Ronald 61, 91, 98, 109, 121, 126, 152, 160, 175, 179, 189
Davies, Richard 201, 202
Davis, Karl 184
Davis, Robert O. (a.k.a. Robert Anders) 202
Dawn, Norman 14
Day, John 189, 195
The Day the Earth Stood Still (feature) 159, 164, 177, 183
Dayton, Lewis 198
DC Comics *see* National Periodical Publications
The Deadly Ray from Mars (serial featurization) 55
Deane, Shirley 84, **91**
de Cordova, Leander 48
DeGarro, Harold 48
DeLacy, Ralph 22, 53, 69, 74, 77
Dell, Claudia **16, 17, 18, 19, 20**, 21
Delores, Jean 197
Deluge (feature) 102
DeMain, George 198
DeMille, Cecil B. 20
DeMond, Albert 109, 121, 126
DeNormand, George 41, 48, 132
DeSimone, John 160
Desmond, William 11, 198
Deste, Luli 84
Destination Moon (feature) 1
Destination Saturn (serial featurization) 69, 76
Destroyers of the Sun (theatrical short) 179
Detective Comics 104
Detective Lloyd (serial) 197–198
The Devil Girl from Mars (feature) 169
Devlin, Joe 201
Dewes, Norman 30
Dick Tracy (serial) 48–53, **49, 50, 52**, 67, 101
Dick Tracy (serial featurization) 48
Dick Tracy Returns (serial) 53
Dick Tracy vs. Crime, Inc. (serial) 53, 98–103, **99, 100, 101**, 150, 155
Dick Tracy vs. Crime, Inc. (serial featurization) 98
Dick Tracy vs. the Phantom Empire (rerelease title of

Dick Tracy vs. Crime, Inc.) 98

Dick Tracy's G-Men (serial) 53

Dickey, Basil 11, 30, 77, 84, 109, 121, 126

Diehl, Jim 141, 203, 204

Dillon, Robert 14, 20

Dilson, John 48, 99, 200, 201

DiMaggio, Joe 83

DiMaggio, Ross 184

Dinehart, Alan III 137

Disney, Walt 21, 152

Dr. Satan's Robot (serial featurization) 91

Dorr, Lester 160

Douglas, Earl 53

Douglas, Paul 84

Doyle, Maxine 200–202

Dracula (1931 feature) 3, 82

Dracula's Daughter (feature) 36–37, 106

Drake, Oliver 41

Drake, Peggy 202

Dresden, Curley 16, 199

Drew, Roland 84

Drums of Fu Manchu (serial) 75, 201

Duffy, Jesse 109, 126

Duke, the Wonder Horse 204

Dumont TV Network 174

Duncan, John 141, **145**, 147

Duncan, Kenne 53, 69, 109, 121, 126, 132

Dunn, Ralph 201

Dunworth, Charles 47

Durkin, Grace 199

Durkin, James 11, 14, 198

D'Use, Margot 16, 22

D'Usseau, Leon 14

Dwire, Earl 84

Eden, Barbara 60

Edwards, Bruce 203

Edwards, Edgar 84

Eldredge, George 170

Eldredge, John 203

Elliott, Frank 84

Ellis, Frank 27, 137, 199, 204

Emery, Gilbert 202

Endfield, Cy 169

Enemies of the Universe (theatrical short) 179

Enfield, Hugh 198

Engel, Roy 180

English, John 61, 68, 91, 98, 201, 202

Erickson, Jack 170, 184

Estrada, Ric 36

Evans, Douglas 149, 201

An Evening with Batman and Robin (serial) 103, 106, 109

Famous Funnies 74

Fantl, Dick 41

Farley, James 77

Farnum, William 41, 200

Faulkner, Phil 137

Fawcett, William 141, 156–157, 170, 204

The FBI (organization) 51

Fenner, Walter 202

Ferguson, Al 11, 48

Ferniel, Dan 189

Ferro, Michael 149

Fetherstone, Eddie 16

Feuer, Cy 91, 98

The Fighting Devil Dogs (serial) 61–68, **63**, **64**, **66**

Fighting Marines (serial) 199

Filcraft 19, 76

Finger, Bill 105

Fiske, Robert 99, 103, 201

Fitzroy, Emily 198

The Five Star Library 22

Flash Gordon (a.k.a. *Rocketship*— serial featurization) 40

Flash Gordon (comic strip) 133

Flash Gordon (serial) **ii**, 3, 4, 5, 21, 28, 30–40, **31**, **34**, **35**, **39**, 42, 47, 60, 74, 76, 83, 89, 90, 133, 134, 155, 169, 188

Flash Gordon (TV series) 90

Flash Gordon Conquers the Universe (serial) 84–91, **85**, **87**, **89**, **91**, 121, 122

Flash Gordon's Trip to Mars (serial) 6, 14, 29, 40, 53–61, **54**, **56**, **57**, **58**, **59**, 74, 89, 90

Flavin, James 198

Fleming, Alice 48

Flint, Sam 48, 61, 202, 203

Flothow, Rudolph C. 103, 116, 120

The Fly (1958 feature) 114

The Flying Disc Man from Mars (serial) 126, 160–164, **161**, **163**, 183

Ford, Francis 197, 202

Ford, Lee 200

Forman, Carol 132, 137, 140, 203, 204

Forte, Joe 126

Foster, Preston 38

Foulger, Byron K. 48, 84, 203

Fox, Michael 184, 188, 204

Fox, Wallace 203

Fox Studios 37, 74

Frank, Jerry 16, 53

Frankenstein (1931 feature) 3, 14, 29, 82, 83

Franklin, Gloria 201

Fraser, Harry 103, 198

Frazer, Robert 99, 199

French, Charles K. 25

Friedlander, Louis (a.k.a. Lew Landers) 11

Friedman, Harry 22

Frost, Terry 137, 156, 164, 203, 204

Frye, Dwight 201

Fryer, Richard 11, 30

Fulton, John 38

Fulton, Lou 48

Fusier, Norman 198

G-Men vs. the Black Dragon (serial) 202

Gale, Jean 199

Gallaudet, John 203

Gan, Chester 199

Gang Busters (serial) 201–202

Garabedian, Robert 181

Gardner, Jack 48, 84

Gardner, Jerry 53

Gardner, Shale 198

Gargan, Edward 203

Gay, Gregory 160, 162, **163**, 179

Gaze, Gwen 200

Geary, Bud 92, 121, 126

Geoffrey, Wallace 198

George, Jack 184

Geraghty, Maurice 41

Gerahty, Gerald 22

Gerall, Roscoe 48

Gerard, Gil 76

Getchall, Sumner 203

Gibbons, Everett 41

Gifford, Frances 162, 195

Gilbert, Billy 22

Gittens, Wyndham 53

Glassmire, Gus 103

Gleason, Pat 84

Glendon, Frank 25, 199

Glenn, Roy, Sr. 189

Gluck, Joe 53, 69, 77, 84

Goodkind, Saul A. 30, 53, 69, 77, 84

Goodrich, Jack 103
Goodspeed, Muriel 30
Goodtimes Home Video 108, 148
Goodwill (film distributor) 19, 76
Gordon, Roy 153
Got, Ronald 202
Gottlieb, Theodore 203
Gould, Charles 84, 170, 184
Gould, Chester 51, 53, 75
Gould, William 69, 199
Graham, Fred 126, 132
Graneman, Eddy 14
Grant, Lawrence 200
Graves, Ralph 141
Gray, Erin 76
The Great Alaskan Mystery (serial) 202–203
Green, Duke 109
Green Hell (feature) 89
The Green Hornet (character) 174
The Green Hornet (serial) 200–201
The Green Hornet (serial featurization) 201
The Green Hornet Strikes Again (serial) 201
Greene, Harrison 48
Gregg, Alan 62, 93
Grey, Clarence 133
Grey, Harry 41, 48
Grissell, Wallace A. 48
Gunga Din (feature) 97
Gwynne, Anne 84

Haade, William 202
Hackett, Karl 69
Hadley, Henry 29
Haggerty, Don 148
Hagney, Frank 84, 198
Hajos, Karl 51
Hale, Monte 121
Hall, Harry 48
Hall, Henry 16, 27
Hall, Jon 38
Hall, Norman S. 53, 69, 91, 98
Hall, William 201
Hamilton, Bernard 164
Hamilton, Charles 201
Hamilton, Fred 48
Hamilton, Hale 198
Hamilton, John 84, 152, 156, 202
Haney, Sarah C. 53

Harden, Jack 180
Harlan, Kenneth 99
Harling, W. Franke 37
Harron, Raymond 41
Harryhausen, Ray 169, 170
Hart, John 132, 203
Harvey, Don 141, 156, 170, 204
Hastings, Don 174
Hayden, Russell 203
Hayes, George F. (Gabby) 16, **20**, 21
Healy, Myron 189, **194**, 195
Hearn, Edward 199
Hearst Entertainment 40
Hecht, Ted 203
Henry, Bill 204
Henry, Robert "Buzz" 203, 204
Herbert, Dorothy 92, 98
Herman, Albert 198
Herring, Moree 184
Hervey, Irene 201
Hickman, Howard 99
Hicks, Russell 202, 203
Hill, Ramsay 189
Hill, Robert F. 53, 200
Hillie, Verna 199
Hillyer, Lambert 103, 105, 106, 108
Hinds, Samuel S. 202
Hodge, Al 174
Hodges, Ralph 137, 164, 204
Hoerl, Arthur 132, 136, 184
Hoffman, Max, Jr. 200
Holcombe, Herb 53
Holden, William 108
Holdren, Judd 170, **173**, 174, **178**, 180, **182**, 183, 184, **185**, 187, 188
Holland, John 48
Holland, Steve 90
Holley, Jack 198
Holmes, Leon 198
Holmes, Ralph 41
Holmes, Sherlock (character) 105, 115, 139
Holmes, Tracy 198
Holt, Jennifer 203
Hop Harrigan (serial) 203
Horne, James W. 120, 201
Horsley, David 41
Hotaling, Frank 189
House of Dracula (feature) 13, 148
House of Horrors (feature) 148
Howard, Boothe 41

Howard, Frederick 121
Howes, Reed 53, 62, 69, 77, 84
Hughes, Carol 84, **87**, **89**, 90, **91**
Hughes, Catherine 200
Hughes, Kay 48
Hughes, Lloyd 200
Hull, Warren 201
Humphrey, William 48
Hunter, Bill 84
Huntley, Hugh 77
The Hydrogen Hurricane (theatrical short) 179
Hytten, Olaf 201

I Dream of Jeannie (TV series) 60
L'Île Mysterieuse (novel) 164, 169
I'm Oscar (song) 25
In My Vine Covered Cottage (song) 22
In Old Santa Fe (feature) 28
Ince, Ada 11, **12**, 13
Indiana Jones (character) 7
The Indians Are Coming (serial) 4
Ingram, Jack 41, 48, 109, 116, 132, 137, 156, 170, 201, 203, 204
International Sound Recording Co. 22
The Invisible Agent (feature) 155
The Invisible Man (1933 feature) 14, 37, 155
The Invisible Man (novel) 155
The Invisible Man Returns (feature) 155
The Invisible Man's Revenge (feature) 155
The Invisible Monster (serial) 152–156, **153**, **154**
The Invisible Ray (feature) 106
The Invisible Thief (silent film) 155
The Invisible Woman (feature) 155
Irving, George 202
Irving, Richard 160
It! The Terror from Beyond Space (feature) 108
It Conquered the World (feature) 3
Ivins, Perry 61

Jaccard, Jacques 84
Jack Armstrong (serial) 203
Jackson, Selmer 199
The Jade Box (serial) 197
James, Alan 48, 109, 200
James, Claire 203
James, John 202
James, Rosamonde 121
January, Lois 14
John F. Dille Syndicate 74
Johnson, Carmencita 199
Johnson, Elmer A. 11, 30, 38
Johnson, Linda 132, **134**, 136
Jolley, I. Stanford 48, 126, 148, 170, 203, 204
Jones, Dickie 200
Jones, Gordon 200
Jones, J. Paul 201
Jory, Victor 201
Jungle Girl (serial) 162, 195
Just Come on In (song) 22
Just Imagine (feature) 37, 38, **73**, 74

Kaley, Vic 198
Kane, Bob 104, 105
Kane, Joseph 41, 42, 199
Karina, Sandra 200
Karloff, Boris 82, 83
Katzman, Sam 6, 107, 120, 132, 133, 136, 139, 140, 141, 147, 156, 164, 170, 174, 184, 188
Kay, Arthur 41, 47, 51
Keaton, Michael 109
Keaton, Russell 74
Keckley, Jane 48
Keefe, Cornelius 198
Kellard, Robert 201, 204
Keller, Harry 179
Kellogg, Cecil 198
Kellogg, Gayle 180–181, 204
Kellogg's Corn Flakes 74
Kellum, Terry 22, 41, 48
Kelly, Craig 180
Kelly, Jeanne (a.k.a. Jean Brooks) 84
Kelly, John 201
Kelly, Mary 48
Kelly, Patrick J. 200
Kelsey, Fred 156
Kendall, Cy 201
Kennedy, Edgar 202
Kenny, Jack 198
Kent, Robert 77, 83
Kerr, Donald 48, **54**, 55, **56**, **57**, 60
Keys, Eddie 53

Kilmer, Val 109
King, Charles 132, 137, 204
King, John 199
King Comics 136
King Features Syndicate 36, 133, 199, 200
King Kong (1933 feature) 21, 38
King of the Carnival (serial) 6, 195
King of the Mounties (serial) 202
King of the Rocket Men (serial) **2**, **3**, 102, 148–152, **150**, **151**, 177, 179
King of the Royal Mounted (serial) 201
Kirk, Jack 199
Kirke, Donald 202
Klugman, Jack 174
Knaggs, Skelton 170
Knapp, Evelyn 198
Knight, Fuzzy 203
Knight, Tracy 41
Kohler, Fred, Jr. 30, 198
Korda, Alexander 1, 102
Kortman, Bob 198, 199, 200, 201
Kosleck, Martin 202–203
Krellberg, Sherman S. 14, 19, 28, 76
Kunody, Leonard 189

Lackteen, Frank 198, 200
Laemmle, Carl 4
Laffan, Patricia 170
The Land Unknown (feature) 108
Landers, Lew *see* Louis Friedlander
Lane, Allan 201, 202
Lane, Tracy 41, 200
Lang, Fritz 1
Lanning, Reggie 98
LaPlanche, Rosemary 203
LaRue, Alfred 203
LaRue, Frank 201
The Last Frontier (serial) 5
Laurel and Hardy 39
Lauter, Harry 160, 204
Lawson, Priscilla 30, 38, 39
Lawton, Kenneth 41
Lease, Rex 126
LeBarron, Bert 152
Leigh, Nelson 132, 137
Leighton, Helen 76
Leonard, Herbert 141, 164, 184

Leong, James B. 199
LeSaint, Edward 48
L'Estrange, Richard 14
Levine, Nat 22, 28, 41, 48, 136, 204
Levy, Weaver 204
Lewis, Ben 53
Lewis, George J. 198, 199, 202
Lewis, Joseph H. 41
Lewis, Ralph 16, 203
Linden, Edward 14
Lindley, Virginia 203
Lindsay, Raymond A. 11, 30
Lippert, Pictures 196
Lipson, John 30, **35**
Liszt, Franz 90
Lively, William 98, 148
The Little Rascals 140
Llewellyn, Fewlass 198
Lloyd, Jack 198
Loft, Arthur 199, 201
Logan, James 189
Lois and Clark: The New Adventures of Superman (TV series) 159
London, Tom 11, 62, 137, 198, 199, 200, 202
The Lone Ranger (character) 177
The Lone Ranger (TV series) 132
Long, Walter 48
Lorch, Theodore 30, 48
Lord, Leonard 200
Lorraine, Louis 197
The Lost City (serial) 14–22, **15**, **16**, **17**, **18**, **19**, **20**, 28, 37, 196
The Lost City (serial featurization) 14, 22
Lost City of the Jungle (serial) 203
The Lost Continent (1951 feature) 196
Lost in Outer Space (theatrical short) 179
The Lost Planet (serial) 155, 184–188, **185**
Lost Planet Airmen (serial featurization) 148
Lovett, Dorothy 201
Lowe, Sherman L. 116, 170
Lowery, Robert 116, **117**, 120, 141, **145**, 147, 148
Lucas, George 7, 48, 74
Lugosi, Bela 21, 77, **81**, 82, 83, 198, 200
Luke, Keye 200, 201, 203

Lydecker, Howard 22, 41, 48, **52**, 53, 98, 109, 121, 126, 148, 152, 160, 175, 179, 189
Lydecker, Theodore 22, 41, **52**, 53, 98, 109, 121, 126, 148, 152, 160, 175, 179, 189
Lyden, Pierce 204
Lynn, George 203
Lyons, Cliff 199
Lyons, Edgar 41, 48

MacArthur, Harold 84
MacBurnie, John 175, 179
McCarthy, John, Jr. 121, 126, 148, 152, 160, 175, 179, 189
McClure, Greg 141
McClure Syndicate 105, 139
McClure's Ladies' World 3
McCullough, Philo 11, 13, 199
McDonald, Wallace 22
McDowell, Nelson 198
McGowan, Millard 41
McGrail, Walter 92, 200–201
McGregor, Malcolm 41, 198
McGuire, Paul 175
Mack, Wilbur S. 197
McKee, Lafe 198, 199
McKenzie, Eva 48
McLeod, Victor 103
MacRae, Henry **4**, 11, 30, 36, 77, 84, 197
MacReady, George 116, 120
McVey, Paul 201
Madonna 51
Magnetic Video 76
Magrill, George 153, 198
Mala, Ray 84, 200
Mallinson, Rory 204
Mallory, Boots 198
Manhunt of Mystery Island (serial) 109–115, **113**, 148
Mann, Ned 102
Mannheim, Het 11
Mapes, Ted 116, **118**
Margolies, Lyonel 77
Marion, Paul 92
Mark, Bob 121, 126, 148, 152, 160, 175, 179, 189
Mark, Michael 84
Mars Attacks the World (serial featurization) 40, 54
Martinelli, Tony 98
Marvin, Frankie 27, 41
Mascot Pictures 14, 19, 20, 136
Mason, James 199

Mason, LeRoy 198, 203
Mason, Philip 48
Mason, Vivian 184, 188
The Master Key (serial) 203
Mathews, Allan 62
Mathews, Carole 116, **118**
Mathews, David 156
Maynard, Ken 28, 199
Mayo, Frank 77
Meadows, Roy 189
Meehan, Lew 198, 199
Meeker, George 137, 152
Mehra, Lal Chand 201
Mell, Joseph 184
Men with Steel Faces (serial featurization) see *Radio Ranch*
Merrick, George M. 14
Merrill, Lon 53
Merton, John 41, 132, 201, 203
Metropolis (feature) 1
MGM 5, 38, 169
Michael, Jay 201
Michael, Peter 203
Middleton, Charles 30, **35**, 38, 55, **58**, 60, 84, **91**, 103, 108, 199, 203
The Midnight Sun (feature) 37
Mildred Pierce (feature) 68
Miljan, John 203
Miller, Ernest 22
Miller, Ivan 202
Miller, Walter 11, 200
Miller, Winston 48
Millman, William 16
Mills, John 48
Ming the Merciless (character) 175
Minter, Harold R. 109, 121, 126
The Miracle Rider (serial) 199
Missile Base at Taniak (serial featurization) 204
Missile Monsters (serial featurization) 160
Mitchell, Bruce 48, 198
Mitchell, Howard 152
Mix, Art 199
Mix, Tom 199
Monogram Pictures 82
The Monster and the Ape (serial) 116–121, **117**, **118**
Montague, Monte 11, 30, 48, 200
Montana, Bull 30
Moon-Eyed View of the World (song) 25

Moore, Clayton 125, 126, **130**, 132, 175, 177, 179
Moore, Constance 69, **75**
Moore, Dennis 121, **123**, 203
Moore, Dickie 198
Moore, Don 36
Moore, Mary 121, 125
Moore, Roger 201
Moore, William 25
Moran, Jackie 69, 71, **72**, **75**
Moranti, Milburn 16, **19**, **20**, 203
Morgan, George 11, 48
Morgan, Ira H. 132, 136, 156
Morgan, Ralph 98, 116, 201, 203
Morrell, Louis 48
Morris, Adrian 199, 200
Morrison, Chuck 99
Morrow, Jackie 199
Morrow, Susan 204
Mortimer, Edward 84
Movie Collector's World (publication) 7
Mulhall, Jack 41, 53, 69, 92, 99, 200
Muller, Adolph 198
The Mummy (1932 feature) 37
The Mummy's Ghost (feature) 148
Murray, Forbes 48, 109, 202
Murray, Zon 170, 204
The Mysterious Dr. Satan (serial) 90–98, **92**, **94**, 139
Mysterious Island (1961 feature) 169
Mysterious Island (serial) 164–170, **165**, **168**
Mystery Mountain (serial) 28, 199
The Mystery Squadron (serial) 136

Nagel, Anne 200, 201
Naish, J. Carrol 103, 105, **106**
National Periodical Publications (DC Comics) 98, 104, 139, 204
Neal, Ella 92, **94**, 98
Neal, Tom 204
Neill, Noel 132, 137, **139**, 140, 156
Nelson, Grant 109
Nesbitt, Norman 202
The New Adventures of Tarzan (serial) 68

Newell, William 92, 200
Newfield, Violet 164
Nightmare Typhoon (theatrical short) 179
Nilsen, Sigurd 84
Nimoy, Leonard 180, 183
No Need to Worry (song) 25
Nobles, William 22, 41, 48, 61, 68, 91
Nolte, William 14
North, Jack 137
Northrup, Harry 198
Novello, Jay 202
Nowell, Wedgewood 48
Nowlan, Philip 74
NPS Video 40
Nye, Carroll 195

Oakman, Wheeler 25, **28**, 29, 53, 69, 132, 198, 200, 203
O'Brien, Dave 200
O'Connell, L.W. 116
O'Connor, Frank 149, 152
O'Donnell, Joseph 149, 152
Of Mice and Men (feature) 47
O'Gatty, Jimmy 160
O'Malley, Pat 198, 199
O'Neill, Ella 11, 30
O'Neill, Thomas F. 11
O'Sullivan, William J. 98
Otho, Henry 62
Otterson, Jack 69
Owen, Michael 98

Padden, Sarah 198, 203
The Painted Stallion (serial) 68
Pal, George 1
Palmentola, Paul 136, 141
The Panther Girl (character) 195
Panther Girl of the Kongo (serial) 189–196, **190, 193, 194**
Pardo, Don 109
Paris, Charlie 105
Parker, Eddie 41, 53, 116, 149, 152, 198, 203, 204
Parsifal (opera) 37
Pastene, Robert 76
Patterson, Hank 204
Patterson, Shirley (a.k.a. Shawn Smith) 103, **104, 107**, 108
Payson, Edward 84
Penn, Leonard 132, 137, 141, 164, 184

Perils from the Planet Mongo (serial featurization) 84
Perils of Nyoka (a.k.a. *Nyoka and the Tigermen*) 162, 175
The Perils of Pauline (1914 serial) 3, **5**
The Perils of Pauline (1934 serial) 198–199
Perkins, Lynn 121
Perrin, Jack 197, 198, 201
Peters, House, Jr. 30, 141, 148
Peters, William Frederick 51
The Phantom Creeps (serial) 13, 77–83, **78, 79, 81**, 121, 156
The Phantom Creeps (serial featurization) 77
The Phantom Empire (serial) 3, 14, 19, 22–28, **23, 24, 25, 26, 28**, 47, 121, 174
The Phantom of the Air (serial) 198
Phillips, Charlie 48
Piccori, John 48, 61, 67, 200
Piel, Edward, Sr. 27, 201
Pierce, James 30
Pipitone, Nino 202
Plan 9 from Outer Space (feature) 148
Planet Outlaws (serial featurization) 69, 76
Plastino, Al 139
Platt, Ed 48
Plympton, George 30, 77, 84, 132, 136, 141, 156, 156, 164, 170, 184
Poff, Lon 30
Poland, Joseph 91, 98, 109, 121, 136, 141, 156, 170
Post, Guy Bates 199
Powell, Lee 61, **66**, 67, 68, 84, **89**
Les Preludes 90
Prentis, Lou 76
Previn, Charles 69
Price, Hal 48
Price, Roland 14
Price, Stanley 53, 69, 116, 126, **130**, 137, 149, 152, **153**, 155
Prival, Lucien 201
Prosser, Hugh 164, 203, 204
Purcell, Dick 202
The Purple Death from Outer Space (serial featurization) 84
The Purple Monster Strikes

(serial) 121–126, **123, 125**, 162, 177, 183
Purvis, Melvin 51

Quigley, Charles 126, 131, 132, 137

Raboy, Mac 36
Radar Men from the Moon (serial) 126, 152, 156, 175–179, **176**
Radio Patrol (serial) 200
Radio Ranch (serial featurization — *Men with Steel Faces*) 25, 29
Ragan, Mike 189, 195, 204
Ramsey, Ethel 198
Randall, Tony 174
Randle, Karen 164, 169, 170
Rathmell, John 22, 41
Rawlins, John 201
Rawlinson, Herbert 84, 137, 200, 201
Ray, Joey 84
Ray, Sonny 198
Raya, Sana 30
Raymond, Alex 36, 37, 90, 133
RCA Sound System 30, 41, 61, 91, 98, 103, 109, 121, 126, 141, 148, 152, 160, 175, 189
Redd, James 148, 152, 160, 175, 179
Reed, Donald 198, 199
Reed, Marshall 152, 164, 204
Reed, Paul 84
Reed, Walter 160
Reeve, Christopher 159
Reeves, Bob 48, 198
Reeves, George 140, 159
Regal Pictures 19
Regan, Charles 152
Reicher, Frank 199, 202
Reisenfeld, Hugo 51
Renaldo, Duncan 202
Renavent, George 202
Rentschler, Mickey 200
Republic Home Video 47, 68, 98, 115, 126, 132, 152, 156, 164, 179, 183, 196
Republic Pictures 5, 6, 7, 42, 47, 51, 67, 68, 75, 97, 98, 107, 115, 120, 126, 131, 132, 139, 140, 149, 150, 152, 155, 156, 159, 162, 164, 175, 177, 179, 181, 183, 195, 196

Retik, the Moon Menace (serial featurization) 175
The Return of Captain America (serial) see *Captain America*
Revier, Dorothy 20
Revier, Harry 14, 20, 21, 76
Rex 200
Reynolds, William **20**
Richards, Addison 203
Richards, Keith 152, 203
Richmond, Kane 16, **18**, 21, 53, 132, 133, **134**, 202
Richmond, Warner 53, 199, 200
Riebe, Loren 48
Riefenstahl, Leni 90
Rin-Tin-Tin, Jr. 198
Ritt, William 133
Ritter, Fred A. 121, 126, 148, 152, 160, 175, 179
Rizzi, Gene 201
RKO 5, 97, 102
Roach, Hal 47
Robards, Jason 199
Roberts, Beatrice 55, **57**, 60
Roberts, Lee 184
Robot Monster of Mars (theatrical short) 179
Robotham, George 156, 170
Robinson Crusoe of Clipper Island (serial) 200
Robinson Crusoe of Mystery Island (serial featurization) 200
Rocket Ship (serial featurization) 30, 40
The Rocketeer (comic book) 152
The Rocketeer (feature) 152
Rockwell, Jack 199
Rocky Jones, Space Ranger (TV series) 174
Rod Brown of the Rocket Rangers (TV series) 174
Roebuck, Tiny 200
Rogers, Buck (character) 76
Rogers, Jean **ii**, 30, **34**, **35**, 37, 38, 39, **54**, 55, **56**, **57**, 61, 90, 199
Rogers, Roy 21, 177
Rohmer, Sax 201
Romanoff, Constantine 30
Roosevelt, Buddy 48, 149
Roper, Jack 84
Rosebrook, Leon 47
Rosener, George 200
Ross, Betsy King 25, 29

Roth, Gene 137, 164, 169, **171**, 174, 175, 184, 188, 203
Rowan, Don 41, 84
Royle, William 84, 201
Ruberg, Cliff 14
Rutherford, Ann 199

Sackin, Louis 30, 53, 69, 84
Salisbury, Monroe 197
Sanders, Sandy 160
Sarecky, Barney 41, 53, 69, 121
Satan's Satellites (serial featurization) 179–180
Savage, Archie 189
Saylor, Syd 199
Schaeffer, Armand 22, 199
Schaeffer, Rube 41
Schumm, Hans 202
Schuster, Joe 139
Sears-Roebuck 147
Secret Agent X-9 (comic strip) 26
The Secret Files of Captain Video (TV series) 174
The Secret of Treasure Island (serial) 200
Secret Service in Darkest Africa (serial) 140
Sedgwick, Eileen 197
Seldeen, Murray 48
Seymour, Al 41
The Shadow (serial) 201
Shannon, Frank 30, 38, **54**, 55, **56**, **57**, 84, **89**
Shapiro, Leonard J. 116
Sharad of Atlantis (serial featurization) 41
Sharpe, David 69, 149, 152
Shaw, C. Montague 41, **46**, 53, **54**, **57**, 69, 75, 92, 102, 199, 201, 202
Shea, Gloria 198
Shea, Jack 181
Sheehan, Poorley Poore 14
Sherlock, Charles 84
Sherry, Clarice 84
Sherwood, George 160
Shipman, Barry 48, 61, 84, 179
Shor, Sol 61, 91, 126, 148
Shumway, Lee 199
Sickner, William 77, 84
Siegel, Jerry 139
Silver Wolf 200
Sinister Cinema 22
Slaves of the Invisible Monster (serial featurization) 152

Smith, Cliff 199, 200
Smith, Ernie 41
Smith, Jack C. 77
Smith, Noel 201
Smith, Shawn see Patterson, Shirley
Solar Sky Raiders (theatrical short) 179
Sombra, the Spider Woman (serial featurization) 203
Sommers, Fred 30
Son of Frankenstein (feature) 30
S.O.S. Coast Guard (serial) 200
S.O.S. Coast Guard (serial featurization) 200
S.O.S. Ice Age (theatrical short) 179
S.O.S. Tidal Wave (feature) 102
Sothern, Hugh 61, 68
The Soul of a Monster (feature) 120
Space, Arthur 189, 204
Space Patrol (TV series) 174, 188
Space Soldiers see *Flash Gordon*
Space Soldiers Conquer the Universe see *Flash Gordon Conquers the Universe*
Space Soldiers' Trip to Mars see *Flash Gordon's Trip to Mars*
Spaceship to the Unknown (serial featurization) 30
Speed Limited (feature) 21
The Spider's Web (serial) 6, 169
Sprang, Dick 105
Springsteen, R.G. 109
Spy Smasher (serial) 21, 162, 202
Spy Smasher Returns (serial featurization) 202
Squadron of Doom (serial featurization) 199
The Squaw Man (1914 feature) 20
Stader, Paul 137, 156, 180
Standing Bear, Chief 199
Stahl, William 41
Stanley, Edwin 48, 53, 77, 92
Stanley, Helene 132
Star Trek (TV series) 183
Star Wars (feature) 7, 74, 76

Stark, Jimmy 170

Starr, Sam 148, 152, 160

Steele, Tom 41, 53, 109, 126, 149, 152, 160, 175, 180, 203, 204

Steel, William 11

Stephani, Frederick 30, 38

Stevens, Dave 152

Stevens, Onslow 11, **12**, 13

Stevenson, Bob 175

Stewart, Eleanor 61

Stewart, Jack 48

Stewart, Larry 170, **173**, 174, 204

Stewart, Peggy 204

Stirling, Linda 109, 115, 121, 126, 131, 162

Stone, Bobby 203

Stone, Milburn 199, 202, 203

Strang, Harry 48, 109

Strange, Glenn 30

Strange, Robert 201

Strenge, Walter 160

Strickfaden, Kenneth 11, 14, 21, 30, 53, 84

Strong, Mark 152

Stuart, Nick 184, 200, 204

Stutenroth, Gene *see* Roth, Gene

Sullivan, Charles 152

Super-Serial Productions 19

Superboy (character) 159

Supergirl (character) 159

Superman (comic book) 98

Superman (Broadway musical) 159

Superman (radio series) 139

Superman (serial) 5, 6, 120, 136–141, **138, 139,** 157, 159

Superman (theatrical cartoon series) 139

Superman and the Mole-Men (feature) 159, 195

Swabacker, Leslie 103

Swan, Curt 139

Swickard, Joseph **16**, 198

Sylvester, Henry 48

Taggart, Benjamin 84

Talbot, Lyle 141, 147, 148, 156, 157

Taliaferro, Hal *see* Wales, Wally

Talmadge, Richard 27

Tarzan (character) 139, 159

Tarzan the Wonder Horse 199

Tarzan's New York Adventure (feature) 38

Tattersall, Viva 198

Taylor, Al 48, 93

Taylor, Elizabeth 115

Taylor, Forrest 61, 109, 126, 137, 184, 203, 204

Taylor, Kent 201

Taylor, Mimi 84

Taylor, Ray 30, 38, 48, 84, 197, 198, 200, 201, 202, 203

Teague, Guy 153

Temple, Shirley 131

Terrell, Kenneth 93, 121

Terry, Don 200

Tex Granger (serial) 204

Thackery, Ellis "Bud" 22, 41, 109, 121, 126, 189

The Thing from Another World (feature) 38, 53

Things to Come (1936 feature) 38, 53

Thompson, Charles 109

Thompson, Walter 22

Thompson, William 91

Thorpe, Ted 175, 184, **185**

The Three Little Pigs (theatrical cartoon) 21

Three Smart Girls (feature) 40

The Three Stooges 174, 188

The Tiger Woman (serial) 115, 162

Tillie the Toiler (comic strip) 36

Tim Tyler's Luck (newspaper strip) 36

Time magazine 107

Todd, Alvin 11, 30, 53, 69, 77, 84

Todd, Edward 11, 30, 48, 61, 91, 98

Todd, Holbrook 14

Tom Corbett, Space Cadet (TV series) 174

Tony, Jr. (horse) 199

Toomey, Regis 77, 83

Torpedo of Doom (serial featurization) 61

Tower of London (1939 feature) 89

Towne, Aline 152, **154**, 156, 175, 179, 180, **182**, 183

The Treasure of the Sierra Madre (feature) 68

Trent, Philip 200

Trowbridge, Charles 92, 97, 202

Tucker, Richard 30

Turnbull, John 198

Turner, Earl 22, 116, 132, 136, 141, 156, 164, 170, 184

Turner, Helene 41, 48, 61

Tuska, George 74

20th Century–Fox 5

Twitchell, Archie 92

Tyler, Dick 175, 179

Tyler, Edward 84

Tyler, Tom 198

Uncle Noah's Ark (song) 25

Undersea Kingdom (serial) 14, 41–47, **43, 44, 45, 46,** 98

Universal Pictures 1, 5, 6, 7, 13, 36, 37, 40, 42, 61, 74, 82, 83, 89, 90, 105, 120

Usher, Guy 69

Vallin, Rick 141, 204

Vallon, Michael 103

Van Atta, Lee 41, 48

Vandergrift, Monte 77

The Vanishing Shadow (serial) 1, 7, 11–14, **12,** 121, 155

Van Sickel, Dale 109, 126, 149, 152, 160, 175, 180, 203, 204

Van Sloan, Edward 77, 83

Vaughan, Clifford 30, 37

VCI Video 29, 53, 76, 83, 90, 103

Verne, Jules 164

Vincenot, Louis 199

Vincent, Russ 109

Vogan, Emmett 121, 126, 137, 203

Vogeding, Frederick 199

The Voice from the Sky (serial) 197

Volk, George 152

Von Morhart, Hans 202

Wade, Roy 121, 148, 152, 160, 175, 179, 189

Wagner, Max 198

Wagner, Richard 37

Wagner, Wes 198

Waldron, Charles, Jr. 84

Wales, Wally 27, 197, 199

Wallace, George 175, **176**, 179

Walters, Don 175

Walters, Luana 137, 201

Walthall, Henry B. 198

War of the Space Giants (theatrical short) 179
War of the Worlds (radio drama) 40
Ward, John 48, 200
Warde, Anthony 53, 69, 72, 74–75, 99, 116, 121, 202, 203
Warner, Wes 41
Warner Bros. 5, 21
Warner Home Video 141, 159
Warwick, Robert 198, 199
Washburn, Bryant 201
Waterfront (TV series) 38
Waters, Bunny 30
Watkin, Pierre 132, 140, 156, 184, 201, 203, 204
Watts, George 202
Waxman, Franz 83
Waxman, Stanley 180
Wayne, John 82
Weaver, Marjorie 202
Webb, Richard 152, 154, 156
Weber, Herbert 48
Weeks, Ranny 200
Welch, Niles 198
Welles, Orson 201
Wells, H.G. 53, 155
Werewolf of London (feature) 37
Wescoatt, Rusty 137, 141, 156, 164, 170
Wessel, Richard 199
West, Adam 105, 106, 109
West, Wally 48, 156

Western Electric Sound System 69, 77, 84, 136
Westmoreland, Josh 156, 184
Whale, James 155
Whalen, Michael 141
What Happened to Mary? (serial) 3
The Whispering Shadow (serial) 198
Whitaker, Charles 30
White, Leo 197
White Hell of Pitz Palu (feature) 90
White Zombie 21, 37
Whitley, Crane 202
Whitley, William 184
Whitlock, Lloyd 41, 198, 200
Wickland, J. Laurence 48
Wilcox, Robert 92, 94, 97, 98
Wilde, Lois 41
Wiley, Jan 98, 203
Williams, Buddy 48
Willson, Meredith 47
Wilson, Al 61, 98, 198
Wilson, Ben 197
Wilson, Charles C. 103
Wilson, Eric 141
Wilson, Lewis 103, 104, 105, 106, 107, 108, 147
Wilson, Stanley 148, 152, 160, 175, 179
Withers, Grant 199, 200
Witney, William 6, 48, 61, 68, 91, 98, 126, 200, 201, 202

The Wolf Dog (serial) 198
Wolfe, Charles "Bud" 53, 126, 152
Wood, Britt 204
Wood, Ed 148
Wood, Wilson 175, 180, 182
Wooden, Earl 126
Worth, Constance 202
Worthington, William 198
Wright, Humberstone 198
Wright, Jean 204
Wright, Mack V. 200
Wrixon, Maris 203
Wynn, Peggy 137

Yager, Ric 74
Yankee Doodle Dandy (feature) 108
York, Duke, Jr. 30
Young, Carleton 48, 61, 69, 200
Yowlatchie, Chief 84
Yrigoyen, Bill 41
Yukon Patrol (serial featurization) 201

Zahler, Lee 14, 103, 108, 116
Zimmerman, Victor 84, 202
Zombies of the Stratosphere (serial) 98, 126, 152, 156, 174, 177, 180, 182
Zorro (character) 105
Zorro Rides Again (serial) 68
Zorro's Fighting Legion (serial) 21
Zynda, Henry 202